Septuagint:

Maccabees

Septuagint, Volume 14

SCRIPTURAL RESEARCH INSTITUTE
Published by Digital Ink Productions, 2024

Copyright

Septuagint: Maccabees

Second edition. March 10, 2024

ISBN: 978-1-998288-64-9

The Septuagint was translated into Greek and complied at the Library of Alexandria between 250 and 132 BC. 1st Maccabees was likely composed in Aramaic in the late 2nd century BC, and was translated into Greek by 132 BC. The fourth version of the Septuagint which included the first 3 books of Maccabees, was published circa 132 BC. 4th Maccabees appears to have been composed in Greek, and added as an appendix to the Septuagint in the 1st century AD.

This English translation was created by the Scriptural Research Institute in 2019 through 2024, primarily from the Codex Sinaiticus, although the Codex Alexandrinus was also used for reference.

The image used for the cover is 'The Expulsion of Heliodorus from the Temple' by Raphael, painted between 1511 and 1512. The original painting is in the Apostolic Palace, in Vatican City.

Table of Contents

TABLE OF CONTENTS

TABLE OF CONTENTS

TABLE OF CONTENTS

Table of Contents

TABLE OF CONTENTS

Forward

In the mid 3rd century BC, King Ptolemy II Philadelphus of Egypt ordered a translation of the ancient Israelite scriptures for the Library of Alexandria, which resulted in the creation of the Septuagint. The original version, published circa 250 BC, only included the Torah, or in Greek terms, the Pentateuch. The Torah is the five books traditionally credited to Moses, circa 1500 BC: Cosmic Genesis, Exodus, Leviticus, Numbers, and Deuteronomy. According to Jewish tradition, the original Torah was lost when the Babylonians destroyed the Temple of Solomon and was later rewritten by Ezra the Scribe from memory during the Second Temple period.

It is generally accepted that there were several versions of the ancient Judahite and Samaritan scriptures before the translation of the Septuagint, mostly written in Canaanite dialects and Aramaic, although the older sections of the Torah appear to have originated in Akkadian Cuneiform.

Four books of Maccabees were ultimately added to the Septuagint, three in the 1st century BC, and the 4th as an appendix in the 1st century AD. No trace of these books has been found among the Dead Sea Scrolls, and they are generally thought to have been written in Greek. 1st and 2nd Maccabees do include several Aramaic loanwords that support an Aramaic source text. The Syriac Bibles also include a 5th Maccabees, which is a translation of book 6 of Josephus' The Judean War. The Judean War is considered extended canon in the Ethiopic Bibles, however, the Ethiopic Bibles also include three books of Maccabees, which are not based on the Greek books, or Josephus. An Arabic book of Maccabees also exists, which is often mislabeled as 5th Maccabees in English language literature, because it was initially misidentified as being the same book as Syriac 5th Maccabees. The Arabic book is a translation of a Palestinian Aramaic book from circa 525 AD, which itself appears to be based on the Hebrew book of Maccabees, which surfaced much later.

The Hebrew version of Maccabees was collected with other Hebrew language manuscripts from various eras in a Yiddish compilation in the 1300s. The Hebrew translation of Maccabees was likely composed in Iberia earlier than 500 AD and was probably based on an Aramaic text, along with an Iberian tale about Hannibal. The Aramaic text that was used is closely related to the text found in the Josippon, which is believed to have been composed in southern Italy in the 900s. The Josippon claims to be a copy of the book of Joseph ben Gurion (יוסף בן גוריון), one of the leaders of the Judean Revolt of 66 AD. Joseph died in 68 AD, and Josephus, who survived the war, did not report that Joseph was a writer, however, it stands to reason his faction must have had some form of propaganda, likely based on the Maccabean Revolt. These Josippon-related versions of Maccabees are of very little historic value, as they are replete with historical errors. Their original function appears to have been to serve as inspiration rather than to educate.

1st Maccabees tells the story of the Maccabean Revolt against the rule of the Seleucid Empire in the 2nd century BC. The content of 1st Maccabees appears to be a Sadducee text, as it clearly gives all credit to the self-declared high-priests that led the rebellion against the Greeks, and barely mentioned the sky-god Shamayim, or the earth-goddess Eretz. It also omits the names of the other gods that 2nd Maccabees and 3rd Maccabees mentions the Judeans worshiping, such as Dionysus, which supports its authorship in the Hasmonean Dynasty, when the other gods were no longer tolerated.

2nd Maccabees claims to be an abridged version of Jason of Cyrene's now lost five-volume version of Maccabees. Jason's books of the Maccabees were likely composed earlier than 1st Maccabees, as the story ends decades earlier, and contains many references to Sabaoth, translated into Greek as Dionysus, which are missing from the 1st Maccabees. While 1st Maccabees is a very secular version of the events that led to the creation of the Hasmonean kingdom, and was, therefore, almost certainly composed by a Sadducee, 2nd Maccabees claims that Judas the Hammer, the protagonist of both 1st and 2nd Maccabees was a Hasidean, suggesting that either Jason of Cyrene, or whoever abridged his work, was a Hasidean. 1st Maccabees mentioned the Hasideans joining Judas' forces, but did not claim he was one. The Hasideans (Ασιδαῖοι) were one of two Judahite sects that were mentioned in the various books of the Maccabees whose relationship to other sects is unclear. Some scholars have theorized that they may be the precursors to the Pharisees.

The other sect mentioned was the Nasoreans (Ναζιραίους), whose name has been interpreted various ways. The Nasoreans were only mentioned in 1st Maccabees, and not 2nd Maccabees, which means they were either added to the story by the author of 1st Maccabees or removed by the author of 2nd Maccabees. The meaning of this name is debatable. The Jewish interpretation, as defined in the Talmud, was a Jew that took vows to abstain from wine, not cut their hair, and not touch corpses, however, the Talmud was compiled centuries after the books of the Maccabees were written, and they are referred to as a sect in the books, not as devout Jews. They are sometimes theorized to be an earlier reference to the Essenes.

The term Nazarene was used in the Christian gospels as a title of Jesus, and therefore became the Arabic and

Hebrew term for 'Christian,' however, the Mandaeans claimed the term referred to their priesthood, which had once been led by John the Baptist, who had baptized Jesus. In the early centuries of the Christian era, the Mandaeans were called the Nasoreans (Ναζωραῖοι) by the Greeks, however, this changed once Christianity spread through the Middle East, and the name Nazarene was applied to Christians. The Mandeans do not appear to have been a Judahite sect, although did include many Judahites and other Israelites. The sacred texts of the Mandeans were focused on the prophets Adam, Abel, Seth, Enoch, Noah, Shem, and Aram, indicating an Aramean origin for the religion, not a Samaritan or Judahite origin. The mention of the Nasoreans in 1st Maccabees, but not 2nd Maccabees, suggests that the author of 2nd Maccabees was not a Nasorean, whatever the term meant at the time.

2nd Maccabees appears to be an anti-Phrygian work, although it is not clear if this was added by the author, or found in Jason's earlier work. 3rd Maccabees also seems anti-Phrygian, or at least anti-Sabaoth/Dionysus, suggesting it is another relic of Jason's work, and Jason's work was anti-Sabaoth in nature. In 3rd Maccabees, the worship of Sabaoth at the Temple in Jerusalem is mentioned, under his Greek name Dionysus, while Philip the Phrygian in 2nd Maccabees is sent to govern

Jerusalem decades later, he does appear to have been in charge of the Temple in Jerusalem.

References to the Judean god Sabaoth appear at this point in the Greek language literature, either transliterated directly in the form of Sabaoth (Σαβαώθ) or translated into Greek as Dionysus (Διόνυσος). While there is a similar word in the ancient Israelite scriptures, it as translated as ṣbåwt (צבאות), meaning 'armies,' when the Hebrew translations were made under the Hasmoneans, which is likely a direct translation of the Aramaic term. This god Sabaoth was considered at the time, to be the same god as the Phrygian god Sabazdiôs (ΣΑΒΑΤΧΟΣ), who the Greeks also considered a local variant of Dionysus. The fact that Dionysus was the Greek name of Sabaoth and Sabazios was recorded by the many Classical Era scholars, including Strabo, Diodorus Siculus, Tacitus, Lydus, Cornelius Labeo, and Plutarch.

1st Maccabees does not mention Sabaoth or Dionysus, which supports its later authorship, after the Hasmonean Dynasty had been established, and Sabaoth was no longer consider the god of the Judeans. While 1st Maccabees does not mention the name of the god in question, it does mention the events of the year 148 (164 BC), when Judas the Hammer was granted autonomous rule of Jerusalem by King Antiochus, that he pulled down the altar that had been profaned, and built a new one.

Clearly, the author of 1st Maccabees did not consider the god's name worth mentioning, however, a foreign god had been worshiped in the temple immediately before the year 148 (164 BC), which is when Philip was the governor of Jerusalem according to 2nd Maccabees.

The author of 2nd Maccabees wrote a long preface to his abridged version of Jason's work, which spans the first two chapters. This preface addresses the book to the Judahites in Egypt, from the Judahites in Jerusalem, and asked that they observe the feast of tabernacles in the year 188 (124 BC). There are a number of Aramaic loan-words throughout the book that point to the original being written in Aramaic, most notably the nicknames of Judas and his brothers, all of which appear to be Aramaic words. Judas' nickname Maccabaeon (Μακκαβαῖον) is derived from the Aramaic word for 'hammer,' mkkbå (𐡌𐡊𐡊𐡁𐡀), which makes sense, as the language of Judea at the time was Aramaic, like the rest of the Middle East north of the Arabian Peninsula. 2nd Maccabees also contains a scribal note which refers to the name of the twelfth month being Adar 'in the Syrian language.' The Greeks referred to Aramaic as the Syrian language, meaning that the Greek translator was working from an Aramaic text.

The introduction, however, also contains a number of references to Moses, Solomon, Jeremiah, and Nehemiah that are not found in the surviving versions of the various books about them. The author of 2nd Maccabees clearly viewed Nehemiah's religion as being a continuation of the ancient religion of Moses, and bridged the two by telling a story about Jeremiah, who found a secret temple of Moses in the caves of Mount Nebo (جَبَل نِيبُو), in modern Jordan. The tabernacle, box, and the altar of incense were hidden there, however, the Greek text does not make it clear if they were hidden there by Jeremiah, or if he found them hidden there. It is generally assumed the story was written as a claim that he hid them there, after saving them, somehow, from the Babylonians who had destroyed King Solomon's Temple, and most of the city of Jerusalem. As Jeremiah was imprisoned in Jerusalem throughout the siege, and considered a heretic, it is difficult to imagine how he would have got his hands on the most sacred relics of the temple, and as the story is not found in the other books attributed to Jeremiah, or Baruch, his scribe, it is generally dismissed as a late addition, likely in the era of the Maccabees, with no historical merit.

Nevertheless, the quote in 2nd Maccabees contains a curious term which is neither Greek, nor Aramaic, but Canaanite, suggesting that the text the author was quoting was either something written in the era of Jeremiah, when Canaanite (Judahite) was the script of the Kingdom of Judah, or, something written by a Samaritan, as the Samaritans continued using the Canaanite script throughout the Assyrian, Babylonian, and Persian occupations of Samaria. The term in question is in the middle of the phrase 'topos cathagiasthê megalôs' (τόπος καθαγιασθῆι μεγάλως), which in Greek means, 'place cathagiasthe greatness.' The word in the middle of the sentence is not Greek or Aramaic, but a transliteration of the Canaanite term htgyysty (𐤄𐤕𐤂𐤉𐤉𐤎𐤕𐤉), meaning 'he chose.' This means the sentence originally read 'place he chose for greatness,' in a Canaanite source text.

The term is in a quote of Jeremiah's meaning the quote was taken from a Judahite or Samaritan copy of a book or letter attributed to Jeremiah. There were many books attributed to Jeremiah and/or his scribe Baruch in the Second Temple era, including the Septuagint's Book of Jeremiah, Peshitta's Book of Jeremiah, Masoretic Book of Jeremiah, Book of Baruch, Lamentations, Letter of Jeremiah, 2nd Baruch, Syriac Apocalypse of Baruch, Letter of Baruch to the Nine and a Half Tribes, Greek Apocalypse of Baruch (3rd Baruch), Paralipomenon of Jeremiah, and Meneo 4th Baruch. Some of these books are attributed to Jeremiah in one language, and Baruch in another language. Translations of the various books have survived in Armenian, Greek, Hebrew, Syriac, Old

Slavonic, Ge‘ez, and Romanian, but not in Canaanite. Nevertheless, Jeremiah was in Jerusalem before the Babylonians conquered the Kingdom of Judah, and so would have been writing in Canaanite. This story does not appear in any of the surviving books of Jeremiah or Baruch, which means there was at least one other book or letter attributed to Jeremiah in Judea during the Greek Era.

The purpose of the author's retelling of the story of Jeremiah finding Moses secret temple in the caves of Mount Nebo, was to support the claim the Nehemiah was a great prophet, which, he is generally not interpreted as by either Jews or Christians. The author of 2nd Maccabees quotes Jeremiah as stating:

> "The place will be unknown until the time that God gathers his people together again and show them mercy. Then the Lord will reveal these things, and the glory of the Lord will be seen, and the cloud as Moses saw it, and like when Solomon was worthy to see the place he chose for greatness."

The author of 2nd Maccabees is clearly trying to link the temple cave of Moses, to the place where the sacred fire was hidden when the Persians took the Judahites away to Persia. This is itself a contradiction, as the Persians are generally seen as the liberators of the Judahites and Samaritans that had been held in the Babylonian and Median Empires. Nevertheless, a number of Judahites were reported to have been working for the Persians, which suggests that not all of them were allowed to return in the time of Cyrus II. However, prior to the Persian Era, there was no evidence of an eternal fire being used in Jerusalem. Eternal fires were used in Zoroastrian fire temples, and, like the eternal fire the author describes, used naphtha and asbestos.

1st Ezra, the older of the two books attributed to Ezra, and the only one probably dating to the Persian Era, refers to 'eternal fire' (πυρὸς ενδελεχοῦσ) in relation to the temple, when Darius II found the orders of Cyrus to rebuild the temple in 539 BC, meaning that eternal fire was already being used at the temple before the time of Nehemiah. To some degree, this supports the claims of the author that Nehemiah found the 'thick water' which he called naphtha, already in the temple. Nehemiah does appear to have been more of a Zoroastrian than an Israelite and may have tried to re-establish a Zoroastrian fire temple in Jerusalem. If so, he is likely the origin of the story that the author is referring to, in which the sacred fire was hidden when the Judahites were taken to Persia.

The author of 2nd Maccabees appears to be trying to justify Nehemiah, by linking Moses encounter with the fire-god of Mount Horeb in Exodus, Solomon's encounter with the genies from folklore, and Jeremiah's finding of Moses' secret cave temple, where, he implies, the sacred fire had been stored with the rest of the relics from Solomon's Temple, although, he does not come out and state the sacred fire was with the rest of the relics. Only the encounter between Moses and the fire god of Horeb is considered canon to Judaism and Christianity, although Solomon's encounters with the genies, a group of fire-beings, did end up in the Quran. The Testament of Solomon, likely an early Christian era work, retold the story from Jewish folklore, however, made the genies into demons. In Jewish folklore, Solomon had commanded genies to build his palace in the Anti-Lebanon mountains, which is similar to, and likely based on, the much older Ba'al Cycle story from the late bronze-age, in which 'fires' worked for six days to build the Temple of Ba'al on Mount Zephon. The author's promotion of Nehemiah as a great prophet, and the sacredness of fire, suggests a surviving Judean sect that was influenced by Zoroastrianism.

3rd Maccabees happens earlier than 1st and 2nd Maccabees, set between 217 and 205 BC, and does not include Judas the Hammer (the Maccabee), or his brothers, which implies it is part of a larger collection of Maccabean texts, possibly Jason of Cyrene's now lost five-volume version of Maccabees. If it was part of Jason's version of Maccabees, then it was likely the second or third volume, as it is before Jason and his brothers enter the story, but its abrupt beginning indicates it was not the first volume. Unlike 1st Maccabees, 3rd Maccabees does have a supernatural element, as messengers descend from the sky to save the Judahites, although the Judahites were apparently unable to see them. As the story told within 3rd Maccabees cannot be historically proven, it is generally considered to be a work of historical fiction, however, this cannot be proven either.

4th Maccabees is a philosophical interpretation of 2nd Maccabees. It was added to the Septuagint in the 1st century AD, however, it could have been written anywhere between 140 BC and 100 AD. This text includes more details regarding the torture of the Israelite youths from 2nd Maccabees, which may have come from Jason of Cyrene's original five-volume version of Maccabees.

The author of 4th Maccabees accepts the flying horsemen of 2nd Maccabees as sky messengers, which implies the Phrygian imagery was widely accepted by Jews at the time and supports the Greek and Roman records that indicate the Phrygians and Judeans worshiped the same god. Unlike 2nd and 3rd Maccabees, 4th Maccabees does not mention the god Dionysus/ Sabaoth, indicating that the book was written during the

Hasmonean Dynasty or later. 4th Maccabees also does not have any Aramaic loanwords, indicating it was almost certainly written in Greek. There is one word that appears to have been incorrectly transliterated from a Samaritan source, however, the transliteration error was probably in an earlier Greek translation that the author was referencing.

In 200 BC, the Greek Kingdom of Syria under the Seleucid Dynasty took Judea from Egypt, and began an effort to Hellenize the Judeans, which included erecting a statue of Zeus in the Second Temple in Jerusalem, and effectively banning traditional Judaism. This Hellenizing activity was partially successful, creating the Sadducee faction of Judaism, however, it also led to the Maccabean Revolt in 165 BC, which itself created the independent Kingdom of Judea. This Kingdom had a tenuous alliance with the Roman Republic until General Pompey conquered Syria into the Roman Republic in 69 BC. Pompey's goal was to liberate Greek-speaking communities in the Middle East that had fallen under the rule of non-Greeks when the Seleucid Syrian Empire had collapsed, and he carved up Judea, and Edom to the east, placing Greek-speaking cities under the protection of the Roman province of Syria. He also liberated several smaller communities that had been occupied by Judea, granting them self-government, including Ashdod, Yavne, Jaffa, Dora, Marissa, and Samaria.

A series of wars including both Julius Caesar's campaigns, and a Parthian invasion led to the weakening of the Hasmonean dynasty, and in 37 AD, the Roman Senate appointed Herod the Great as King of the Jews. Herod's rule wasn't particularly popular, as he allowed the Romans to establish themselves within Judea, however, he did expand Judea, reintegrating the Greek and Samaritan cities, and annexing Galilee and Edom. When he died, his kingdom was divided between four successors, a situation that ended in 66 AD when the Romans conquered the region. An uprising in 120 AD led to the Jews being exiled from Judea, and the region became a Greco-Roman colony. In the wake of the Jews, the Samaritans rose in numbers, along with the Christians once Christianity was legalized. Between 529 and 555 AD, the Samaritans revolted and were effectively annihilated, by the Byzantine Empire.

Outside of Judea, the Septuagint was the dominant form of Jewish scriptures across the Greek-speaking world, which by the beginning of the Christian era, extended from the Roman Empire in the west, to the Indo-Greek Kingdom in the east. Jewish traders had established small colonies along the trade routes of the Red Sea and the Indian Ocean, reaching as far south as

Yemen, and as far east as southern India, and these Jews spoke Greek and Aramaic, and used the Septuagint.

The earliest Christian Bibles, all used the Septuagint, however, by the 4th century some Christian scholars were debating whether they should retranslate the Old Testament from the version the Jews were using, and some even suggested using the Samaritan version. Both suggestions were generally dismissed as heretical, as Jesus and the Apostles had quoted from the Septuagint, even though they had access to the Hebrew version then in use. This argument held in the west until the Middle Ages, when Catholic Bibles switched to the Masoretic Texts.

In the east, Orthodox Bibles continued to use the Septuagint, as they do today. To the south, the Ethiopian Tewahedo Church continued to use the Septuagint, and across Asia, the Thomas Christians and Nestorians continued to use the Septuagint. Only in Western Europe were the later Masoretic Text adopted, abandoning the more ancient Septuagint, on the assumption that the Jews had transcribed their texts more faithfully than the Greeks had translated them. This assumption was carried forward into the Protestant Churches that broke off from the Catholic Church, and therefore almost all Protestant Bibles use the Masoretic Texts for the basis of the Old Testament.

Unfortunately, this means that the earliest Christian writing is generally confusing and ignored by Protestants and Catholics. The earliest Christians of the first and second centuries quoted books that are no longer in the Bible, and as such, their writings are not always understood. Septuagint: Maccabees is a 21st century translation aimed at correcting this problem.

One of the problems with academic translations of the Septuagint, is the use of unfamiliar names or terms, as the Septuagint was in Greek, and therefore many names are unrecognizable to modern readers. This project uses the more commonly understood Hebrew-derived names instead of their Greek translations, such as Canaan instead of Chanaan, and Melchizedek instead of Melchisedec. Common modern names are also used instead of either Greek or Hebrew terms when geographical locations are known, such as the archaeological name Uruk instead of the Greek Orech, or the Hebrew Erech, and the archaeological term Sumer instead of Shinar or Senar. While this could be argued as not being a correct academic procedure, it does fulfill the goal of making the translation easy to read.

1st Maccabees: Chapter 1

After the invasion of Alexander the son of Philip[1] the Macedonian,[2] who came from the land of the Greeks,[3] had killed King Darius[4] of the Persians and Medes,[5] and replace him as ruler, (previously he ruled Greece),[6] he launched many wars, and conquered many strongholds, and killed the kings of the earth. He went to the ends of the earth and plundered many nations, so much that the earth was peaceful after him, and he was exalted and he was happy. He gathered a mighty strong army and ruled over countries, and nations, and kings, who became tributaries to him.

After these things he fell sick and knew that he would die, so he called his servants that were honorable, and had been raised with him from his youth, and divided his kingdom among them, while he was still alive. Alexander ruled twelve years, and then he died, and his officers ruled over everyone in his own region. After his death, they all crowned themselves, and so did their sons after them for many years, and evils were multiplied on the earth. There came from them an evil root, Antiochus Epiphanes,[7] the son of King Antiochus,[8] who had been a hostage in Rome,[9] and he ruled in the year 137[10] of the kingdom of the Greeks.

In those days, there were wicked men in Israel who persuaded many, saying, "Let's go and make a treaty with the nations[11] that are around us, as since we departed from them we've had much sadness."

This decision made them happy, and some of the people were so liberal, that they went to the king, who permitted them to follow the laws of the nations. They built a temple of worship in Jerusalem following the customs of the nations, and made themselves uncircumcised, and forgot the holy covenant, and married themselves to nations, and were sold as mercenaries.

Now, when the kingdom was established under Antiochus, he intended to rule over Egypt and have the dominion of both nations, so he invaded Egypt with a great army, with chariots, elephants, cavalry, and a great navy, and made war against King Ptolemy[12] of Egypt. Ptolemy was afraid of him, and fled and many were wounded and killed. They captured the fortified cities in the land of Egypt and he plundered them. After Antiochus had attacked Egypt, he returned in the year 143,[13] and attacked Israel and Jerusalem with a great army, and proudly entered the sanctuary, and plundered the golden altar, candlesticks, vessels, table for the showbread, pouring vessels, vials, censers of gold, the veil, the crown, and the golden ornaments that were outside the temple which he pulled down. He also took the silver and gold, and precious vessels, and hidden treasures which he found.

When he had taken everything away, he returned to his own land, having massacred many, and proudly bragged about it. There was great mourning in Israel. In every place where they were, the princes and elders mourned, the virgins and young men were made weak, and the women were no longer beautiful. Every bridegroom lamented, and she that sat in the marriage chamber was sad, and all the house of Jacob was filled with confusion. After two years, the king sent his chief tribute-collector to the cities of Judah, who came to Jerusalem with a great army and spoke peaceful words to them, but all was deceit. When they had paid him respect, suddenly he attacked the city and slaughtered many people of Israel.

When he had taken plunder from the city, he lit it on fire and pulled down the houses and walls on every side. They took the women and children captive and took the livestock. Then they built the city of David with a great and strong wall, and with mighty towers, and made it a fortified hold for them. They set up a sinful nation of wicked men and fortified themselves. They stored within it also armor and food, and when they had gathered together the plunder of Jerusalem, they stored them up there, and so they became a terrible trap, as it was a place to lie in wait against the sanctuary, and an evil enemy for Israel. They shed innocent blood on every side of the sanctuary and defiled it so much that the inhabitants of Jerusalem fled because of them, and the city became the home of foreigners and became foreign to those that were born in it, and her own people left her. Her sanctuary was laid waste like a wilderness, her feasts turned into mourning, her sabbaths into an insult, and her honor into contempt. Her glory became her dishonor, and her excellency was turned into sadness.

King Antiochus wrote to his whole kingdom that all should be one people, and everyone should follow the same laws. The nations agreed to follow the commandments of the king, and many of the Israelites agreed to his religion, and sacrificed to idols, and profaned the sabbath. The king had sent letters by messengers to Jerusalem and the cities of Judah that they should follow the foreign laws of the land, and forbid burnt offerings, sacrifice, and drink offerings in the temple, and that they should profane the sabbaths and festival days, and pollute the sanctuary and holy people, and set up altars, and groves, and chapels of idols, and sacrificed swine's flesh, and unclean beasts, and that they should also leave their children uncircumcised, and make their souls abominable with all manner of uncleanness and profanation.

He ordered that whoever did not do according to his commandments he should die. In the same manner, wrote he to his whole kingdom, and appointed overseers over all the people, commanding the cities of Judah to sacrifice, city by city. Then many of the people were gathered around them, all that forgot the law, and they committed evils in the land, and drove the Israelites into secret places, wherever they could flee for safety. On the fifteenth day of Kislev,[14] in the year 145,[15] they erected the disgraceful abomination on the altar and built idol altars throughout the cities of Judah on every side. They burned incense at the doors of their houses, and in the streets. They ripped copies of the books of the law and burned them in the fire.

Whoever was found with any book of the testament, or if any committed to the law, the king's commandment was that they should put him to death. They did so by their authority over the Israelites every month, to as many as were found in the cities. On day 25 of the month, they sacrificed to the idol altar, which was on the altar of burnt offerings. According to the commandment they put to death the women who had circumcised their children, and the families who had circumcised them. They hanged the infants around their mother's necks. Many in Israel decided not to eat any unclean things. They decided they would rather die, than that they might be defiled with meats, and that they might not profane the holy covenant, and so they died, and very great anger was in Israel.

1st Maccabees: Chapter 1 Notes

1 Codex Vaticanus: Alexandron ton Philippou (ΑΛΕΞΑΝΔΡΟΝΤΟΝΦΙΛΙΠΠΟΥ). Translation: Alexander of Phillip

Alexander the son of Phillip, had conquered the Persian empire in the late 4th century BC.

2 Codex Vaticanus: Macedona (ΜΑΚΕΔΟΝΑ). Translation: Macedonia

Alexander and his father Phillip were kings of Macedonia.

3 Codex Vaticanus: gês Chettiim (ΓΗΣΧΕΤΤΙΙΜ). Translation: land of Chettiim

Kittim was a kingdom in eastern Cyprus, founded in the 13th century BC, and used by the Arameans and Canaanites as the name of the island of Cyprus. The name was recorded during the Egyptian New Kingdom as Kåtjåy ([hieroglyphs]), Phoenician as Kty (𐤊𐤕𐤉), and ancient Greek as Cition (Κίτιον). It was also applied to the Aegean islands and Greece in later periods. Similar terms are found in earlier Israelite works: Chettaeos (Χετταῖος / חִתִּי) in the Torah, and Chettaeon (Χετταῖον / חִתִּי) in Joshua, Chettiin (Χεττιιν /חִתִּים) in Judges, all of which appear to refer to the bronze age and early iron age kingdom in Cyprus.

The presence of the transliterated word 'Chettiim' in 1st Maccabees supports it being translated from either an Aramaic or Canaanite source text, as a Greek writer would not have referred to the Greeks as 'Chittiim.' The probable source of the word Chittiim is Jason of Cyrene's five-volume History of the Maccabbean Revolt, however, it is not clear if it was written in Aramaic or Punic.

4 Codex Vaticanus: Darion (ΔΑΡΕΙΟΝ). Translation: Darius

Darius III was the last king of the Persian Empire, who was defeated by Alexander in 331 BC.

5 Codex Vaticanus: Persôn cae Mêdôn (ΠΕΡϹΩΝΚΑΙ ΜΗΔΩΝ). Translation: Persians and Medians

6 Codex Vaticanus: Ellada (ΕΛΛΑΔΑ). Translation: Greece

7 Codex Vaticanus: Antiochos Hepiphanês (ΑΝΤΙΟΧΟϹ ΕΠΙΦΑΝΗϹ). Translation: Antiochus Epiphanes

This is accepted as King Antiochus IV Epiphanes, ruler of the Seleucid Dynasty between 175 and 164 BC.

8 Codex Vaticanus: Antiochou (ΑΝΤΙΟΧΟΥ). Translation: Antiochus

- LXX 19: Seleucou (Σελευκου)

This is accepted as the Antiochus III the Great, ruler of the Seleucid Dynasty between 222 and 187 BC.

9 Codex Vaticanus: Rômê (ρωμη). Translation: Rome

This is a reference to Antiochus IV Epiphanes being held hostage in Rome between 188 and 175 BC, prior to his ascension to the throne.

10 Year 137 of the Seleucid era was 175 BC.

11 Codex Vaticanus: ethnôn (εθνων). Translation: nations

12 Codex Vaticanus: Ptolemaeon (πτολεμαιον). Translation: Ptolemy

In 175 BC, the king of Egypt was Ptolemy VI Philometor, who ruled between 180 and 164 BC, and again between 163 and 145 BC. His reign was dominated by the wars against the Seleucid Dynasty's Syrian Empire. He briefly lost control of Egypt to a coup lead by Ptolemy VIII, and fled to Cyprus, which was part of Egypt at the time. He appealed to Rome for assistance restoring his government, however, they decided to not get involved. The people of Alexandria rebelled against Ptolemy VIII the following year, and Ptolemy VI was able to take back control of Egypt.

13 Year 143 of the Seleucid era was 169 BC.

14 Codex Vaticanus: Chaseleu (ΧΑϹΕΛΕΥ)

- Codex Sinaiticus: Chasaleu (ΧΑϹΑΛΕΥ)
- Codex Alexandrinus: Chaseleou (ΧΑϹΕΛΕΟΥ)
- LXX 19: Chasleu (χασλευ)
- LXX 728: Chasêleu (χασηλευ)

Kislev is the eighth Jewish calendar corresponding to late November and early through mid-December.

15 Year 145 of the Seleucid era was 167 BC.

1st Maccabees: Chapter 2

In those days Mattathias the son of John the son of Simeon,[1] a priest of the sons of Joarib[2] from Jerusalem, lived in Modi'in.[3] He had five sons: John, the one called lucky,[4] Simon, the one called zealot,[5] Judas, the one called the hammer,[6] Eleazar, the one called watcher,[7] and Jonathan, the one called the translator.[8]

When he saw the blasphemies that were committed in Judah and Jerusalem, he said, "I am cursed to have been born to see this misery of my people, and the ruin of the holy city, and to live there when it was given into the hands of the enemy, and the sanctuary is in the hand of foreigners! Her temple has become like a man without honor. Her glorious vessels are carried away into captivity. Her infants are killed in the streets, and her youths by the sword of the enemy. Which nation has not taken from her kingdom and not taken plunder from her? All her ornaments have been taken away, and a free woman has become a slave-woman. I saw our sanctuary, even our beauty, and our glory laid waste, and the nations had profaned it. Why do we still live?"

Mattathias and his sons ripped their clothes, and put on sackcloth, and mourned in a great depression.

The king's officers came to compel the apostates in the city of Modi'in to make them sacrifice.

When many of Israel came to meet them, Mattathias and his sons also came with them. They spoke for the king, and said to Mattathias, "Archon,[9] glorious and great one in this city, strengthened by his sons and brothers. Now, therefore, come first to fulfill the king's commandment, like all the nations and the Judeans[10] who remain in Jerusalem. You and your sons will be honored with silver and gold, and many rewards."

Mattathias answered in a loud voice, "Though all the nations that are in the king's dominion obey him, and follow his commandments, each leaving the religion of their fathers, yet I and my sons and brothers will follow the covenant of our forefathers. We would never abandon the law and the ordinances. We will not listen to the king's words, and turn from our religion, either to the right hand, or the left."

When he had finished stating these words, a Judean came forward in the sight of all to sacrifice following to the king's commandment on the altar in Modi'in. When Mattathias saw it, he was irate with hatred in his heart. He could not hold back his fury and judgment, so he ran to him and murdered him on the altar. Then he murdered the king's officer, who was compelling them to sacrifice, and he tore down the altar.

He zealously murdered according to the law, like Phinehas[11] had done to Zimri the son of Salu,[12] and Mattathias shouted throughout the village with a loud voice, "Whoever is zealous of the law, and follows the covenant, follow me!"

He and his sons fled into the mountains and left all that they had in the city. Many that wanted justice and judgment went out into the wilderness to live there, with their children, wives, and livestock, because problems increased against them.

When the king's officers were told, and the army that was in Jerusalem, in the city of David, that men had broken the king's commandment and had gone out to hidden places in the wilderness, they chased after them and found them. They camped near them, and attacked them on the sabbath.

They said to them, "End this. Come back and follow the laws of the king, and you will live."

But they answered, "We will not go back, and we will not follow the king's laws to profane the sabbath."

Then they quickly attacked them, but they did not counterattack, or sling a stone at them, or block up the places where they were hiding, but said, "Let us all die innocently. Shamayim[13] and Eretz[14] will testify for us, that you are unjustified in killing us."

They attacked them on the sabbath, and they died, with their wives, children, and livestock, numbering 1000. When Mattathias and his friends heard it, they mourned for them, and each said to each other, "If we all do as our brothers have done, and don't fight against the nations for our lives and laws, they will quickly destroy us out of the earth."

At that time, therefore they decided, "Whoever will come to battle against us on the sabbath, we will fight against him, and we will not die as our brothers that were slaughtered in the hidden places."

Then a company of Hasideans[15] came to them, who were mighty men of Israel, including all that were voluntarily devoted to the law. Also all those who fled for persecution joined with them. They joined their forces and murdered sinful men in their anger and wicked men in their anger, but the rest fled to the nations for punishment. Then Mattathias and his friends went around and pulled down the altars, and any children they found within the borders of Israel that were uncircumcised, those they forcibly circumcised. They hunted the proud men, and the work prospered in their hands. They recovered the law out of the hand of the nations and the kings, and did not allow the sinner to triumph.

When the time drew close for Mattathias to die, he said to his sons, "Pride and rebuke have been strengthened, and the time of destruction and the anger of indignation. Now, therefore, my sons, be zealous for the law and give your lives for the covenant of your fathers. Remember what our fathers did in their time, and you will receive great honor and an eternal name. Was Abraham[16] not found faithful during temptation, and was viewed as righteousness? Joseph in the time of his distress kept the commandment and was made lord of Egypt. Phinehas our forefather in being zealous, obtained the covenant of an eternal priesthood. Joshua for fulfilling the command was made a judge in Israel. Caleb, because he testified before the congregation, received a heritage in the land. David, because he was merciful, inherited the eternal throne of the kingdom. Eliou, because of his zeal for the law was taken up into the sky. Hananiah, Azariah, and Mishael, through belief, were saved out of the flame. Daniel for his innocence was saved from the mouths of lions."

"Consider throughout all ages that none that put their trust in him will be undone. Don't be afraid then of the words of a sinful man, for his glory will be dung and worms. Today he will be glorified and tomorrow he will not be found, because he has returned into the dust, and his thought has come to nothing. Therefore, my sons, be valiant and show yourselves men of the law, for by it will you obtain honor. Look, I know that your brother Simon is a man of counsel, listen to him always. He will be a father to you. Judas the hammer has been a mighty warrior since he was a youth, so let him be your captain and fight the battles against the peoples. Take in also all those that observe the law, and avenge the wrong of your people. Repay fully the nations, and follow the commandments of the law."

He blessed them and was gathered to his fathers. He died in the year 146,[17] and his sons buried him in the tomb of his forefathers in Modi'in, and all Israel lamented for him.

1st Maccabees: Chapter 2 Note

1 Codex Vaticanus: Mattathias huios Iôannou tou Symeôn (ΜΑΤΤΑΘΙΑϹ ΥΙΟϹ ΙΩΑΝΝΟΥ ΤΟΥ ϹΥΜΕΩΝ). Translation: Mattathias son of John the Simeon

2 Codex Vaticanus: Iôarib (ΙΩΑΡΙΒ)

- Codex Sinaiticus: Iôarim (ΙΩΑΡΕΙΜ)
- LXX 19: Iôarêm (Ιωαρημ)
- LXX 46: Iôarhim (Ιωαρειμ)
- LXX 542: Iôrib (Ιωρειβ)
- LXX 93: Iôiaraêb (Ιωιαραηβ)

3 Codex Vaticanus: Môdin (ΜΩΔΕΙΝ)

- Codex Sinaiticus: Môdaen (ΜΩΔΑΕΙΝ)
- Codex Venetus: Môdiô (Μωδιω)
- LXX 19: Môdaem (Μωδαειμ)
- LXX 93: Môlaeim (Μωλαιειμ)
- LXX 542: Môdeim (Μωδεειμ)

The village of Mwdyôyn (מודיעין) was also recorded in the Talmud, although its location is unclear.

4 Codex Vaticanus: Iôannês o epicaloumenos Gaddi (ΙΩΑΝΝΗϹ Ο ΕΠΙΚΑΛΟΥΜΕΝΟϹ ΓΑΔΔΙ). Translation: John the nicknamed Gaddi

• Codex Sinaiticus: Iôannês o epicaloumenos Gae (ΙΩΑΝΝΗϹΟΕΠΙΚΑΛΟΥΜΕΝΟϹΓΑΕΙ). Translation: John the nicknamed Gae

• Codex Alexandrinus: Iôannês o epicaloumenos Gaes (ΙΩΑΝΝΗϹ Ο ΕΠΙΚΑΛΟΥΜΕΝΟϹ ΓΑΕΙϹ). Translation: John the nicknamed Gaes

• LXX 74: Iôannês o epicaloumenos Gaddês (ιωαννης ο επικαλουμενος γαδδης). Translation: John the nicknamed Gaddes

The nickname gaddi, appears to have been Aramaic word for 'lucky,' gaḏyā (גדיא).

5 Codex Vaticanus: Simôn o caloumenos Thassi (ϹΙΜΩΝΟ ΚΑΛΟΥΜΕΝΟϹΘΑϹϹΙ). Translation: Simon the called Thassi

The nickname thassi is translated as the Aramaic term tśy (תשי), meaning 'the wise,' or 'the zealot.'

6 Codex Vaticanus: Ioudas o caloumenos Maccabaeos (ΙΟΥΔΑϹ Ο ΚΑΛΟΥΜΕΝΟϹ ΜΑΚΚΑΒΑΙΟϹ). Translation: Judas the called Maccabeus

The nickname Maccabeus is derived from the Aramaic word for Hammer, mkkbå (מככבא).

7 Codex Vaticanus: Eleazar o caloumenos Ayaran (ΕΛΕΑΖΑΡ Ο ΚΑΛΟΥΜΕΝΟC ΑΥΑΡΑΝ). Translation: Eleazar the called Ayaran

• Codex Sinaiticus: Eleazar o caloumenos Ayaran o (ΕΛΕΑΖΑΡ Ο ΚΑΛΟΥΜΕΝΟC Ο ΑΥΡΑΝ). Translation: Eleazar the called the Auran

• Codex Venetus: Eleazar o caloumenos o Ayaran (ΕΛΕΑΖΑΡ Ο ΚΑΛΟΥΜΕΝΟC Ο ΑΥΑΡΑΝ)· Translation: Eleazar the called the Auaran

• LXX 64: Eleazar o caloumenos Ayran (ελεαζαρ ο καλουμενος αυραν). Translation: Eleazar the called Ayran

The nickname Ayaran is derived from the Aramaic term ḥwr (חור), meaning 'the watcher.'

8 Codex Vaticanus: Iônathês o caloumenos Apphous (ΙΩΝΑΘΗC Ο ΚΑΛΟΥΜΕΝΟC ΑΠΦΟΥC). Translation: Jonathan the called Apphous

• Codex Alexandrinus: Iônathas o caloumenos Sapphous (ΙΩΝΑΘΑC Ο ΚΑΛΟΥΜΕΝΟC CΑΠΦΟΥC). Translation: Jonathan the called Sapphous

• Codex Alexandrinus: Iônathas o caloumenos Saphphous (ΙΩΝΑΘΑC Ο ΚΑΛΟΥΜΕΝΟC CΑΦΦΟΥC). Translation: Jonathan the called Saphphous

• Codex Venetus: Iônathan o epicaloumenos Apphous (ΙΩΝΑΘΑΝ Ο ΕΠΙΚΑΛΟΥΜΕΝΟϹ ΑΠΦΟΥϹ). Translation: Jonathan the accused Apphous

• LXX 46: Iônathês -- Apphous (ιωναθης -- Απφουσ). Translation: Johnathan – Apphous

• LXX 106: Iônathan o epicaloumenos Samphous (ιωναθαν ο επικαλουμενοc cαμφουc). Translation: Johnathan the called Samphous

The nickname Apphous is believed to be devised from the Aramaic word for 'translator,' indicating that Jonathan was probably the source of the 'Hebrew' translations of the Judahite, Samaritan, and Aramaic texts.

9 Codex Vaticanus: Archôn (ΑΡΧΩΝ). Translation: ruler

10 Codex Vaticanus: andres Iouda (ΑΝΔΡΕϹΙΟΥΔΑ). Translation: men of Judea (or Judah)

11 Codex Vaticanus: Phinees (ΦΙΝΕΕϹ). Translation: Phinehas

The Phinehas (פִּינְחָס) who killed in Zimrî ben-Sālûå in Numbers chapter 25 was the grandson of Aaron. The name is Egyptian ([illegible]), and means 'the Nubian.

12 Codex Vaticanus: Zambri huiô Salôm (ΖΑΜΒΡΙΥΙΩΙ ϹΑΛΩΜ). Translation: Zambri son of Salôm

This is accepted as a reference to Zimri ben-Salu (זִמְרִי בֶּן־סָלוּא), who was killed by Phinehas in Numbers chapter 25.

13 Codex Vaticanus: ouranos (ΟΥΡΑΝΟϹ). Translations: Uranus (or the vaulted sky)

Uranus was used as a translation of the ancient Canaanite and Israelite sky-god name, Shamayim (שמיים) in the Septuagint and other Greek translations of Israelite texts. He was often called on, along with Eretz, to witness the actions of man and God. As the Judean rebels would not have been worshiping the Greek version of the sky-god, the Hebrew term is used in this translation.

14 Codex Vaticanus: Gê (ΓΗ). Translation: Ge (or land, dirt)

Ge was the was used as a translation of the ancient Canaanite and Israelite sky-god name, Eretz (אֶרֶץ) in the Septuagint and other Greek translations of Israelite texts. She was often called on, along with Shamayim, to witness the actions of man and God. As the Judean rebels would not have been worshiping the Greek version of the earth-goddess, the Hebrew term is used in this translation.

15 Codex Vaticanus: Asidaeôn (ΑCΙΔΑΙΩΝ). Translation: Hasideans

- Codex Sinaiticus: Ioudaeôn (ΙΟΥΔΑΙΩΝ). Translation: Judean

- LXX 542: basileôn (υλσιλσοον). Translation: kings

The Hasideans were an Israelite sect mentioned in the various books of the Maccabees. The Vetus Latina version of the book of Esther claims to be a Hasidean version of the book, suggesting the Hasideans were closer theologically to the Egyptian and Kushite Israelites than the Judean sects.

16 Codex Vaticanus: Abraam (ΑΒΡΑΑΜ). Translation: Abraham

17 Year 146 of the Seleucid era was 166 BC.

1st Maccabees: Chapter 3

His son Judas who was called the hammer took his place, and his brothers and all who had joined his father helped him, and they cheerfully fought for Israel. He brought his people great honor and wore the breastplate of a giant. He wore his war armor and battled, protecting the army with his sword.

His acts were like a lion, and like a lion's cub roaring for his prey. He chased the wicked and incinerated those who troubled his people. Therefore, the lawless shrunk in fear from him, and all the lawbreakers were confused, as salvation was in his hand. He also attacked many kings, and made Jacob rejoice through his acts. He and his memory will be blessed forever. He went through the cities of Judah slaughtering the unlawful from across the land, and angrily defended Israel. He was renowned to the farthest regions of the earth, and he received many of those that were ready to die.

Then Apollonius gathered the nations together, and a great army out of Samaria, to fight against Israel. When Judas found out, he went out to meet him, and attacked him and killed him, and also many were slaughtered, but the rest fled. When they counted their spoils, Judas took Apollonius' sword, and with it, he fought for the rest of his life.

When Seron, a commander in the Syrian army, heard that Judas had gathered around him a great army of loyal men who went out with him to war, he said, "I will earn a name and honor in the kingdom by fighting Judas and his companions, who despised the king's laws."

He prepared a great army of unlawful men to go with him, to take vengeance on the Israelites. When he approached the ascent of Beth Horon,[1] Judas went out to meet him with a small force. When they saw the army coming to meet them, they asked Judas, "How will we being so few, be able to fight against such a great multitude? We are already so weak from fasting all day!"

Judas answered, "It is early for many to be trapped by the hands of a few. Within the sight of Shamayim it is all the same to save a great army or a small company. Victory in battle comes not from the number in an army, but strength comes from Shamayim. They come to attack us with great pride and iniquity to destroy us, and our wives and children, and to plunder us, but we will fight for our lives and our laws. He himself will overthrow them before us, and as for you, don't be afraid of them!"

As soon as he had finished speaking, he rushed suddenly at Seron and his army, and they were crushed before him. They chased them from the ascent of Beth Horon to the plain, where they slaughtered eight hundred of them, while the rest fled to the land of the Pelesets.[2] Then the fear of Judas and his brothers fell on the nations around them. His fame was heard by the king, and all nations talked of the battles of Judas. When King Antiochus heard these things, he was enraged, he sent and gathered together all the forces of his kingdom, a very strong army. He opened his treasury, and paid his soldiers for a year, ordering them to be ready whenever he should need them. However, when he saw that the silver of his treasury had run out, and the taxes from across the country were small, because of dissension and troubles which he had caused across the land by abolishing the laws that had existed from the ancient days.

He was afraid that he would not be able to carry the cost any longer, or to have gifts to give as liberally as he did before, as he had given more lavishly than the kings that were before him. He was greatly confused, he decided to go to Persia to collect the taxes of the countries, and to gather great wealth. He left Lysias, a nobleman and one of the royal blood, to oversee the affairs of the king between the River Euphrates to the border of Egypt, and he was to raise Antiochus' son until he returned.

He provided him with half of his forces, and the elephants, and gave him orders for all things that he would like done. Concerning those that lived in Judah and Jerusalem, he ordered an army to be sent against them, to destroy the strength of Israel, and the remnant in Jerusalem, to wipe out all records of them from that place. He should settle foreigners in all their territory and divide their lands. The king took half of the forces that remained, and departed from Antioch, his capital city, the year 147,[3] and having crossed the Euphrates River, he traveled through the highlands.

Lysias chose Ptolemy the son of Dorymenes, and Nicanor, and Gorgias, mighty men from among the king's friends, and sent with them 40,000 infantry and 7000 cavalry to go into the land of Judah and destroy it, as the king had commanded. So they went out with all their forces and camped near Emmaus[4] in the plain country. The merchants of the country, hearing their fame, took a great deal of silver and gold, with chains, and went into the camp to buy the Israelites as slaves. Also, the forces from Syria and the lands of the nations joined them there.

When Judas and his brothers saw their problems were multiplying, and the army camped within their territory, they also learned the king had given the order to destroy the people, and completely abolish them. They said one to another, "Let's restore the decayed fortune of our people, and let us fight for our people and the temple."

The congregation gathered together prepared for battle, and they prayed and asked for mercy and compassion. Jerusalem lay empty like the wilderness, and there were none of her children that entered or left. The temple also was pulled down, and the sons of the foreigners held the citadel. nations lived there, and the joy was taken from Jacob, and no one played the pipes or the harps. They assembled and went to Mizpah, near Jerusalem, because Israel had formerly worshiped in Mizpah.

They fasted that day, and put on sackcloth, and they threw ashes on their heads and ripped their clothes. They opened the Torah,[5] to consult it regarding the nations who were consulting the likeness of their idols. They also brought the robes of the priesthood, and the first fruits, and the tithes, and they stirred up the Nazarites,[6] who had finished their days. They cried out with a loud voice to Shamyim, asking, "What will we do with these? Where will we take them? Your temple is torn down and profaned, and your priests are humiliated. See the nations have assembled against us, to destroy us, and you know what they plan against us. How will we be able to stand against them, if you don't help us?"

Then they sounded the trumpets and shouted out in a loud voice. After this, Judas organized captains over the people, including captains over thousands, and over hundreds, and over the fifties, and over tens. He told those who were building houses, and those who were engaged, and were planting vineyards, and were afraid, that each should return to his own house, according to the law.

The camp moved and camped on the south side of Emmaus, and Judas ordered, “Arm yourselves and be valiant. See that you are ready in the morning, that you may fight with the nations who have assembled against us, to destroy us and our temple. It is better for us to die in battle than to see the troubles of our people and our temple. Nevertheless, as the will of Shamayim, so he will do!”

1st Maccabees: Chapter 3 Note

1 Codex Vaticanus: anabaseôs Baethôrôn (ΑΝΑΒΑϹΕΩϹ ΒΑΙΘΩΡΩΝ). Translation: ascent of house of Horon

Beth Horon was a city in Judea, recorded in a number of ancient texts, including Beit-Choron (בֵּית־חוֹרֹן) in the Masoretic text, and Båtå Ḥwåwrn ([illegible]) in Egyptian Texts from the 3rd Intermediate Period. Choron was an ancient Canaanite god the of the underworld, called Hrn (𐎈𐎗𐎐) in the Ugaritic Texts from the Late Bronze Age. He is likely also the Greek god Charon (Χάρων). The ancient Roman historian Diodorus Siculus believed the Greeks had imported the god Charon from the Egyptian due to the similarities of names and iconography, however, the Egyptian god was itself imported from Canaan.

2 Codex Vaticanus: Phylistiim (ΦΥΛΙϹΤΙΙΜ). Translation: Palestinians (or Pelesets)

The Peleseti were an ancient people based in the region of the modern Gaza Strip of the Palestinian Territories. The earliest surviving mention of them is from the reliefs of the Temple of Ramses III at Medinet Habu in Egypt that dates back to some time between 1186 and 1155 BC, in which they were called Pwråsåtj ([illegible]). They were also known in Akkadian Cuneiform as the kurPalastu (𒆳𒉺𒆷𒀸𒌅).

It is unclear where they came from, however, one theory is that they were the Pala, a Luwian people from the Black Sea coast of Anatolia. The region was an independent country called Palaa (𒉺𒆷𒀀) in the Neshite (Hittite) records from the 1600s BC, however, have become part of the Nesite Empire by the 1500s BC. Around the time the Pelesets invaded Canaan, the Pala were driven from their homeland by the neighboring Kaskians from northeast Anatolia, which supports the connection between the groups, however, it has yet to be proven conclusively.

3 Year 147 of the Seleucid era was 165 BC.

4 Codex Vaticanus: Ammaous (ΑΜΜΑΟΥϹ)

- Codex Sinaiticus: Ammaou (ΑΜΜΑΟΥ)
- Codex Alexandrinus: Ammaoun (ΑΜΜΑΟΥΝ)
- LXX 62: Ammaoum (Αμμαουμ)
- LXX 56: Ammaen (Αμμαειν)
- LXX 58: Emmaous (Εμμαουϲ)

The location of the city of Emmaus is disputed, however, generally considered to be the town of Emmaus Nicopolis east of Jerusalem.

5 Codex Vaticanus: biblion tou nomou (ΒΙΒΛΙΟΝΤΟΥ ΝΟΜΟΥ). Translation: book of the law (or Torah)

1st Maccabees: Chapter 3 Note

6 Codex Vaticanus: naziraeous (ΝΑΖΙΡΑΙΟΥϹ). Translation: Nazirites (or Nazarenes, Nasoreans)

The meaning of this term is debatable. The Jewish interpretation, as defined in the Talmud, was a Jew that took vows to abstain from wine, not cut their hair, and not touch corpses. They are sometimes theorized to be an earlier reference to the Essenes. The term Nazarene was used in the Christian gospels as a title of Jesus, and therefore became the Arabic and Hebrew term for 'Christian,' however, the Mandaeans claimed the term referred to their priesthood, which had once been led by John the Baptist, who had baptized Jesus.

1st Maccabees: Chapter 4

Gorgias took 5000 infantry, and 1000 of the best cavalry, and left from the camp by night, to attack the camp of the Judeans, and slaughter them suddenly. The men from the citadel were his guides.

When Judas heard of it, he and the valiant men with him went to attack the king's army at Emmaus while his forces were absent from the camp. When Gorgias entered Judas' camp at night he found no one there, so he searched for them in the mountains, as said, "These people fled from us!"

At daybreak, Judas was in the plain with 3000 men, who did not have armor or swords. They saw the camp of the nations, that it was strong and well fortified and surrounded by cavalry, and these were experts of war.

Then Judas said to the men that were with him, "Don't fear their numbers, or be afraid of their charge. Remember how our fathers were saved in the Papyrus Sea[1] when Pharaoh chased them with an army. Now let's cry out to Shamayim, and see if he will have mercy on us, and remember the covenant with our fathers, and destroys this army before us this day, so that all the nations may know that there is one who saves Israel."

When the foreigners lifted their eyes and saw them coming against them, they left the camp to battle. Those who were with Judas sounded their trumpets, and they attacked, and the nations were surprised and fled to the plain. They slaughtered all those that were slow with the sword, and they chased them from Gazer[2] and to the plains of Edom,[3] and Ashdod[4] and Jamnith[5] and they slaughtered 3000 of them.

When he was done, Judas returned from chasing them with his army, and said to the people, "Don't be greedy for the plunder as there is still a battle before us. Gorgias and his army are near us in the mountains, but stand now against our enemies, and defeat them, and after this, you may boldly take the plunder."

When Judas was still speaking, a detachment appeared, coming out of the mountains. They saw that their army had been put to flight, and that the Judeans were burning the camp, for the smoke that was seen showed what had happened. When they saw these things, they were afraid, and when they also saw the army of Judas in the plain ready for battle, they all fled to the lands of the nations.

Judas returned to plunder the tents, where they seized a great deal of gold and silver, and the Hyacinthus, purple of the sea, and other great riches. After this, they went home and sang songs of thanksgiving, and praised Shamayim, because he was good, and because his mercy endures forever. Israel had been saved that day.

The nations that had escaped went and told Lysias what had happened. When he heard of it, he was confused and discouraged because he did not expect the events in Israel to have happened, nor had things that the king commanded him happened. The next year, therefore, Lysias gathered together 60,000 of the best infantry, and 5000 cavalry, that he might conquer them. They traveled to Edom and camped at Beth Zur,[6] and Judas met them with 10,000 men.

When he saw the mighty army, he prayed, "Blessed are you, savior of Israel, who stopped the violence of the mighty warrior by the hand of your servant David and gave the army of foreigners into the hands of Jonathan, the son of Saul, and his armor-bearer. Deliver this army to the hands of your people Israel, and let them be confused in their power and cavalry. Make them have no courage, and cause the boldness of their strength to fall away, and let them fear their destruction. Strike them down with the swords of those that love you, and let all those that know your name praise you with thanksgiving."

They attacked and slaughtered about 5000 men of the army of Lysias. When Lysias saw his army fleeing, and the boldness of Judas' soldiers, and how they were ready either to live or die valiantly, he went into Antioch, and gathered together a company of foreigners, and having made his army greater than it was, he intended to return into Judea.

Then Judas said to his brothers, "See how our enemies are scared. Let's go cleanse and dedicate the temple."

For this, all the army assembled and went up into Mount Zion. When they saw the temple desolate, and the altar profaned, and the gates burnt down, and shrubs growing in the court like in a forest, or on a mountain, and the priests' chambers pulled down, they ripped their clothes, and made great lamentation, and threw ashes on their heads, and fell down flat to the ground on their faces, and blew an alarm with the trumpets, and cried out to Shamayim.

Then Judas appointed certain men to fight against those that were in the fortress until he had cleansed the sanctuary. He chose blameless priests devoted to the law, and they cleansed the temple and removed the defiled stones into an unclean place. When as they consulted what to do with the altar of burnt offerings, which was profaned, and they thought it best to pull it down, in case it should be a reproach for them because the nations had defiled it. They pulled it down and stacked up the stones in the mountain of the temple in a convenient place until there could come a prophet to show what should be done with them.

They took unhewn stones according to the law, and built a new altar like the former, and rebuilt the temple and the things that were within the temple, and sacred the courts. They also made new holy vessels, and into the temple, they took the candlestick, and the altar of burnt offerings and of incense, and the table. On the altar, they burnt incense, and the lamps that were on the candlestick they lighted, that they might give light in the temple. Furthermore, they set the loaves on the table, and spread out the veils, and finished all the works which they had begun to make.

On the twenty-fifth day of the ninth month, which is the month of Kislev, in the year 148,[7] they rose up in the morning and offered sacrifices according to the law on the new altar of burnt offerings, which they had made. What at one time the nations had profaned, on that day it was rededicated with songs, cisterns, harps, and cymbals. Then all the people fell on their faces, worshiping and praising Shamayim, who had given them great success. They kept the dedication of the altar for eight days and offered burnt offerings with gladness, and sacrificed the sacrifice of deliverance and praise.

They also built the porch in the front of the temple with crowns of gold, and with shields, and the gates and the chambers they renewed, and hanged doors on them. There was a great celebration among the people, for that the insult of the nations was behind them. Moreover, Judas and his brothers with the whole congregation of Israel, ordained that the days of the dedication of the altar should be kept in their season from year to year for eight days, from the twenty-fifth day of Kislev, with joy and celebration. At that time they also rebuilt Mount Zion with high walls and strong towers around, in case the nations should come and tear it down as they had done before. They set up a garrison there to keep it and fortified Beth Zur to protect it, that the people might have a defense against Edom.

1st Maccabees: Chapter 4 Notes

1 Codex Vaticanus: thalassê erythra (ΘΑΛΑΣΣΗΕΡΥΘΡΑ). Translation: Erythraean Sea

The Greek term is not geographically specific, allowing for the Israelites to have passed from Egypt to the wilderness at any point in the Red Sea or even the Gulf of Aden. The Greek name appears to be a translation of the Persian term Erostras, which referred to the entire Persian Gulf, Red Sea, and the Indian Ocean. The Greeks were likely referring to the Gulf of Suez, however, this was known to the ancient Egyptians as the 'Sea of Calm,' which is what the Israelites would have called it if that was where they were.

The Greeks transliterated the name as the Sea of Siph (Θαλασσης Σιφ) in the Codex Vaticanus' translation of Judges, confirming that the name Swf was in the Aramaic text they worked from. The Aramaic term swf (𐡎𐡅𐡐) and Phoenician term swf (𐤎𐤅𐤐), both meaning papyrus plants were adopted from the Egyptian term ṯwfj (𓍿𓅱𓆑𓇋𓇋𓇅), which referred to papyrus, papyrus plants, and papyrus marshes. The Masoretic Text uses the later Hebrew version of the name ym swp (ים סוף) in other books, meaning Sea of Papyrus.

The Egyptian term continued to be used into the Classical era as the Coptic words čoouf (ϫοουϥ), conf (ϭονϥ), and comf (ϭομϥ), all meaning papyrus. Conversely, the Egyptian name of the Red Sea was the Sea of Ḥeḥ (𓁨), meaning 'very large sea' from the Middle Kingdom era onward, however, believed to have originally been named after the ancient Egyptian frog god Heh (𓎛𓎛𓅱). As the Greek translation of

Erythrean Sea is anachronistic, the translation of Papyrus Sea is imported from the Masoretic Text.

As the Greek translation of Erythrean Sea is anachronistic, the translation of Papyrus Sea is imported from the Masoretic Text. The Hebrew term 'Sea of papyrus' is not geographically specific either, however, does match the description of the shallow Lake Bardawil which has been a major source for papyrus reeds throughout Egyptian history.

2 Codex Vaticanus: Gazêrôn (ΓΑΖΗΡΩΝ). Translation: Gezer

The town of Gezer (גֶּזֶר) was west of Jerusalem. It had been an Egyptian town known as Kådjr (𓈎𓄿𓆓𓂋𓏤) during the New Kingdom era, and was transferred to the Kingdom of Judah as a dowry according to 3rd Kingdoms (Masoretic Kings).

3 Codex Vaticanus: Idoumaeas (ΙΔΟΥΜΑΙΑΣ). Translation: Edom

• Codex Alexandrinus: Ioudaeas (ΙΟΥΔΑΙΑΣ). Translation: Judea

4 Codex Vaticanus: Azôtou (ΑΖΩΤΟΥ). Translation: Ashdod

5 Codex Vaticanus: Iamnias (ΙΑΜΝΕΙΑϹ). Translation: Jamnith

6 Codex Vaticanus: Baethsouroes (ΒΑΙΘϹΟΥΡΟΙϹ). Translation: Beth-Zur

- Septuagint manuscript 98: Baethôrô (βαιθωρω)
- LXX 340: Bethôr (βεθωρ)

Beth-Zur (בית צור) was a town south of Jerusalem.

7 Year 148 of the Seleucid era was 164 BC.

1st Maccabees: Chapter 5

When the nations around them heard that the altar was rebuilt and the sanctuary restored, it displeased them greatly. They decided to destroy the descendants of Jacob living among them and began to slaughter the people. Then, Judas fought against the children of Esau in Edom at Akrabattene,[1] because they kept lying in wait for Israel, and he defeated them soundly, and destroyed their courage, and plundered their lands. He remembered the injury of the children of Baean,[2] who had been a trap and a snare to the people, in that they ambushed them along the roads. He trapped them in their towers, and besieged them, and slaughtered them completely, and burnt the towers of that place with fire, and all that was within them.

Afterward, he traveled over to the Ammonites, where he found a mighty force, and many people following Timothy their captain. He fought many battles with them until eventually they were defeated before him, and he slaughtered them. After he had captured Jazar and the towns belonging to it, he returned to Judea.

The nations who were in Gilead assembled together against the Israelites that were in their region to destroy them, but they fled to the fortress of Dathema, and sent letters to Judas and his brothers, saying, "The nations around us are allied against us to destroy us, and they are preparing to come and take the fortress in which we are hiding. Timothy is the captain of their army. Come and save us from their hands, for many of us have been slain. All our brothers that were in the lands of Tobiah[3] have been put to death. Their wives and their children have been taken away as captives, and their belongings had also been taken. They have killed about 1000 men."

While these letters were being read, more messengers came from Galilee with their clothes ripped, who reported on, "Those of Acre,[4] and Tyre, and Sidon, and all of the nations in Galilee are allied against us, and will destroy us."

When Judas and the people heard these words, a great congregation assembled, to discuss what they should do for their brothers that were in trouble. Then Judas said to Simon his brother, "Choose men, and go and save your brothers that are in Galilee, and I and Jonathan, will go into the country of Gilead."

He left the captains of the people, Joseph the son of Zachariah, and Azariah, with the remnants of the army in Judea to hold it. He commanded them, "Take charge of these people, and don't make war against the nations until we return."

To Simon, he gave 3000 men to go into Galilee, and to Judas 8000 men for the land of Gilead. Simon went into Galilee, where he fought many battles with the nations so that the nations were scared of him. He chased them to the gates of Acre, and they slaughtered about 3,000 Greeks and took plunder from the lands.

Those that were in Galilee, and in Arbatta,[5] with their wives and their children, and all that they had, he captured as slaves and brought them back to Judea in great joy. Judas the one called the hammer and his brother Jonathan crossed the Jordan, and traveled three days' journey in the wilderness, where they met with the Nabateans,[6] who came to them peacefully and told them everything that happened to their brothers in the land of Gilead, that many of them have been blockaded within Bozrah and Bosor, in Alema and Chaspho, Maked and Carnaim (all these being fortified cities) and those that were trapped in the rest of the cities in the country of Gilead. They were getting ready to attack the strongholds the next day and take and destroy all these men in one day.

As a result, Judas and his army turned suddenly from the road in the wilderness to Bozrah, and when he had captured the city, he murdered all the men by the edge of the sword, and took all their property, and burnt down the city with fire. From there he moved by night and traveled until he came to the fortress. In the morning they looked out, and there was an uncountable number of people carrying ladders and other war machines to take the fortress, and they attacked them. When Judas saw that the battle had begun, and the cry of the city went up to Shamayim, with trumpets, and a great sound, he said to his army, "Fight this day for your brothers."

He went out behind them in three companies, who sounded their trumpets, and cried with prayer. Then the army of Timothy, knowing that it was the hammer, fled from him, and he slaughtered them in great numbers, and killed on that day about 8000 men. After this, Judas traveled to Alema, and after he had assaulted it he captured and killed all the men, and took all the plunder from it, and burnt it with fire. From there he went and captured Kasphor, Maked, Bosor, and the other cities of the country of Gilead.

After these things, Timothy amassed another army and besieged Raphon beyond the stream. So Judas sent men to spy on the army, who returned with word, saying, "All the nations around us have allied themselves, and amassed a great army. He has also hired the Arabs to help them and they have camped across the brook, ready to come and fight against you."

On hearing this Judas went out to meet them, and Timothy said to the captains of his army, "When Judas and his army approaches the brook if he crosses over first to attack us, we will not be able to defend against him, for he will be mighty and defeat us. But, if he is afraid, and camps beyond the river, we will cross over to him, and defeat him."

When Judas came to the stream, he had the scribes of the people remain by the stream, and commanded them, "Allow no man to remain in the camp, but let all come to the battle."

He crossed over first to them, and all the people behind him, then all the nations, being scared of him, threw away their weapons and fled to the temple that was at Karnaim. But they took the city and burnt the temple with all who were in it, and so Karnaim was conquered, and they could not defend themselves from Judas.

Judas gathered together all the Israelites that were in the country of Gilead, from the small and the great, with their wives and children and goods, a very large company, to go to the land of Judah. When they came to Ephron, (this was a great city along the road they traveled, and very well fortified) they could not turn from it, either to the right or the left, but needed to pass through the middle of it. The people of the city locked them out and blocked the gates with stones.

Judas sent a message to them in a peaceful message, saying, "Let us pass through your land and go into our own country, and we will not hurt any of you. We will only pass through on foot," however, they would not open to him.

Therefore Judas sent a proclamation throughout the army, that every man should pitch his tent where he was. So the soldiers camped there and attacked the city all day and night until eventually the city was delivered into his hands, and then he killed all the men with the edge of the sword, and razed the city, and plundered it, and passed through the city over the dead bodies. After this, they crossed the Jordan into the great plain before Beth Shan.[7]

Judas gathered together those who came behind, and exhorted the people until they came into the land of Judea. They went to Mount Zion with joy and gladness, where they offered burnt offerings because none of them were killed and they had returned in safety.

While Judas and Jonathan were in the land of Gilead, and Simon his brother in Galilee near Acre, Joseph ben Zachariah, and Azariah, captains of the garrisons, heard of the valiant acts and warlike deeds which they had done.

Therefore they said, "Let us also earn a name, and go fight against the nations that are around us."

When they had given orders to the garrison that was with them, they went towards Jamnith, and Gorgias and his men came out of the city to fight against them. Joseph and Azariah were put to flight and chased to the borders of Judea, and about 2000 men were slaughtered on that day from the people of Israel. And so there was a great defeat among the Israelites because they were not obedient to Judas and his brothers, but wanted to do some valiant act. Moreover, these men had not come of the seed of those, by whose hand deliverance was given to Israel.

Judas and his brothers were greatly renowned before all of Israel, and of all the nations, wherever their name was heard of, as the people assembled before them with joyful praise. Afterward, Judas went out with his brothers and fought against the children of Esau in the land towards the south, where he attacked Hebron, and the villages around it, and pulled down the fortress, and burnt the towers around it. From there, he traveled into the land of the nations and passed through Samaria. At that time certain priests desiring to show their valor were slain in battle, as they went out to fight poorly. So Judas turned to Ashdod in the land of the nations, and when he had pulled down their altars and burnt their statues with fire and plundered their cities he returned into the land of Judea.

1st Maccabees: Chapter 5 Notes

1 Codex Vaticanus: Acrabattênên (ΑΚΡΑΒΑΤΤΗΝΗΝ)

2 Codex Vaticanus: Baean (ΒΑΙΑΝ)

3 Codex Vaticanus: Toubiou (ΤΟΥΒΙΟΥ). Translation: Tobiah

4 Codex Vaticanus: Ptolemaedos (ΠΤΟΛΕΜΑΙΔΟϹ). Translation: Ptolemais, Acre

The city of Acre (עכו / عكا), in northern modern Israel, was known as Antiochia Ptolemaes (Αντιόχεια Πτολεμαΐς), and simplified as Ptolemaes (Πτολεμαΐς) during the Hellenic era. The earlier Canaanite name was Ôk (𐤏𐤊), which the Greeks had transliterated as Acê (Ἄκη) before conquering the region. As the Ptolemais is not commonly used anymore, the ancient and modern name of Acre is used.

5 Codex Vaticanus: Arbattoes (ΑΡΒΑΤΤΟΙϹ)

- Codex Sinaiticus: Arbanoes (ΑΡΒΑΝΟΙϹ)
- Codex Alexandrinus: Arbactoes (ΑΡΒΑΚΤΟΙϹ)
- Codex Venetus: Arbatnoes (ΑΡΒΑΤΝΟΙϹ)
- LXX 93: Drabyttoes (δραβυττοις)
- LXX 542: Acrabatoes (ακραβατοις)
- LXX 55: Arabaoes (αραβαοις)

This is generally accepted as the town of Arraba (عرّابة), near in the northern area of the Palestinian West Bank. The city has existed since at least the Egyptian New Kingdom era, when it was known as Rubutu ([illegible]), listed as one of the towns the king of Egypt ceded to the Habiru in the Amara Letters. It appears to have been continuously inhabited, and was known as Arubbot (אֲרֻבּוֹת) in the Masoretic book of Kings, although the name does not appear to have been in the Aramaic version of Kings that formed the bases of the Greek translation.

6 Codex Vaticanus: Nabataeoes (ΝΑΒΑΤΑΙΟΙϹ).
Translation: Nabateans

The Nabateans were an Arabian people who occupied the region to the east of the Jordan in the 2nd century BC.

7 Codex Vaticanus: Baethsan (ΒΑΙΘϹΑΝ). Translation: Beth Shan

- LXX 93: Bêthsan (βηθσαν)
- LXX 340: Bethsan (βεθσαν)
- LXX 106: Baethaan (βαιθααν)

1st Maccabees: Chapter 6

About that time, King Antiochus was traveling through the high countries and heard it said that Elymais[1] in the country of Persia had a city greatly renowned for riches, silver, and gold. That there was in it a rich temple which was covered in gold and contained breastplates and shields, which had been left there by Alexander, the son of Philip, the Macedonian king, who ruled first among the Greeks.

He wanted to sack the city and plunder it, but he was not able to because those in the city had warning, and rose against him in battle, so he fled, and departed from there with great sadness, and returned to Babylon. Then someone came and brought him the news in Persia, that the armies which he sent to the land of Judea, were put to flight, and that Lysias, who went out first with a great power was driven away by the Judeans. That they were strengthened by the armor, weapons, and plunder, they had captured from the armies that they had destroyed.

Also that they had pulled down the abomination, which he had set up on the altar in Jerusalem, and that they had surrounded the sanctuary with high walls, like previously, and what happened in Beth Zur.

When the king heard these words, he was astonished and angry, and he laid him down on his bed and fell sick in his grief because it had not happened to him before.

He continued there for many days, for his grief grew greater, and he made an account in case he should die. Therefore, he called for all his friends, and said to them, "The sleep is gone from my eyes, and my heart fails. I thought to myself, 'What troubles have I come into? How great the flood of misery, in which I am now! I was bountiful and beloved in my power. But now I remember the evils that I did in Jerusalem, and that I took all the vessels of gold and silver that were there, and sent armies to destroy the inhabitants of Judea without a cause. I saw therefore that this was the cause of these troubles that have come on me, and, look, I perish with great grief in a strange land."

Then he called for Philip, one of his friends, who he made ruler over all his realm, and gave him the crown, robe, signet, so he could raise his son Antiochus V Eupator, and educate him for the kingdom. King Antiochus IV Epiphanies died there in the year 149.[2] When Lysias heard that the king was dead, he established Antiochus V Eupator his son, who he had raised since he was young to reign in his place.

About this time, those who were in the tower, locked up the Israelites near the temple, and wanted to hurt them and strengthen the nations. Therefore Judas, intending to destroy them, called all the people together to besiege them. They united and besieged them in the year 150,[3] and he made catapults to shoot against them, and other engines.

Some of those that were besieged escaped, helped by unlawful men of Israel, and they went to the king, and said, "How long will it be until you execute judgment, and avenge our brothers? We were willing to serve your father and did as he wanted, and to obey his commandments, which is the reason those from our nation besiege the tower and are alienated from us. Moreover, as many of us as they could catch they killed, and plundered our inheritance. Not only have they stretched out their hand against us, but also against their neighbors. Look, today they are besieging the tower at Jerusalem, to capture it, and they have also fortified the sanctuary, and also Beth Zur. Therefore, if you do not prevent them quickly, they will do greater things than these, and you won't be able to rule them."

Now when the king heard this, he was angry and gathered together all his friends, and the captains of his army, and those that were in charge of the horses. Bands of hired soldiers also came to him from other kingdoms, and isles of the sea, so that the number of his army was 100,000 infantry, and 20,000 cavalry, and 32 war-elephants. These went through Edom and besieged Beth Zur, which they assaulted many days, making war machines, but they of Beth Zur came out, and burnt them with fire, and fought valiantly.

On hearing this, Judas left the tower, and camped in Beth Zachariah, near the king's camp. The king rose very early and marched fiercely with his army towards Beth Zachariah, where his armies prepared for battle and sounded the trumpets. To provoke the elephants to fight, they showed them the juice of grapes and mulberries which looked like blood. They divided the beasts among the armies, and for each elephant, they appointed 1000 men, armed with coats of mail, and with helmets of brass on their heads, and besides this, for every beast were assigned 500 of the best cavalry. These remained ready at all times, wherever the beast was, and wherever the beast went, they followed and did not leave them. On the beasts, there were fortified towers made of wood, which covered all of them, and were clamped tight to them. There were also on each of them 32 strong men, that fought on them, besides the Indian that controlled him.

As for the rest of the cavalry, they set half of them on each side of the army, to relay commands of what to do, and being spread among the ranks. When the sun shone on the shields of gold and brass, the mountains glistened and shined like lamps of fire. Part of the king's army was spread on the high mountains, and part in the valleys below, and they marched in order. Therefore, all that heard the noise of their multitude, and the marching of the company, and the rattling of the harness, ran, for the army was very great and mighty.

Then Judas and his army approached and attacked, and 600 of the king's men were slaughtered. Eleazar, called Watcher, saw that one of the beasts, armored with a royal harness was higher than all the rest, and assuming the king was on him, put himself in jeopardy so that he might save his people and be known forever. He ran at him courageously through the middle of the battle, killing on the right hand and the left, so that they were divided from him into both sides. When done, he crept under the elephant and stabbed him underneath, killing him, and the elephant fell on him and killed him.

The rest of the Judeans, seeing the strength of the king and the violence of his forces, ran away from them. Then the king's army went on to Jerusalem to meet them, and the king besieged Judea and besieged Zion. But with those who were in Beth Zur, he made peace, as they came out of the city because they had no food there to endure the siege, as it was a year of rest in the land. So the king captured Beth Zur and set a garrison there to keep it. As for the sanctuary, he besieged it many days and set their artillery with engines and catapults to throw fire and stones, and ballistas to shoot arrows. They also made their engines to combat the engines and held them off for a long season. Yet, in the end, they ran out of food, (as that it was the seventh year, and they in Judea that were delivered from the nations, had eaten up all the stores) There were few left in the sanctuary, because the famine prevailed against them, and they were ready to flee, every man to his home.

At that time Lysias heard that Philip, who Antiochus IV Epiphanies while still living had appointed to bring up Antiochus his son to be king, had returned from Persia and Media with the forces that had gone with the king, and that he was trying to seize control of the government. Therefore, he quickly gave orders to depart, and said to the king, to the commanders of the forces, and to the men, "We daily grow weaker, our food supply is scant, the place against which we are fighting is strong, and the affairs of the kingdom press urgently upon us. Now, therefore, let us make peace with these men, and with all their nation, and negotiate with them so they will live by their laws as they did before. They are disgruntled and have done all these things because we abolished their laws."

The king and the princes agreed, and therefore he sent to them to make peace, and they accepted it. Also, the king and his officers made an oath with them, whereby they left the stronghold. Then the king entered into Mount Zion, but when he saw the strength of the place, he broke his oath that he had made, and commanded to pull down the wall around it. Afterward, he departed quickly and returned to Antioch, where he found Philip to be ruling the city, and he fought against him and captured the city by force.

1st Maccabees: Chapter 6 Notes

1 Codex Vaticanus: Elymaes (ελυμαις)

- Codex Sinaiticus: en Lymaes (ενλυμαις)
- Codex Alexandrinus: en Elymaes (ενελυμαις).

Translation: in Elymaes

- LXX 728: Lymaes (λυμαεις)
- LXX 381: en Lymaes (εν λυμαεις). Translation: in Lymaes
- LXX 311: polis en Elymaes (πολις εν ελυμαισ). Translation: city in Elymaes

Elymais was the name of a semi-independent kingdom in the region of modern Khuzestan, Iran. It succeeded from the rule of the Parthians in 147 BC. During Antiochus IV Epiphanies's reign, it was still at least nominally part of his empire. The capital city of Susa, is likely where the temple referenced was located.

2 Year 149 of the Seleucid era was 163 BC.

3 Year 150 of the Seleucid era was 162 BC.

1st Maccabees: Chapter 7

In the year 150, Demetrius, the son of Seleucus departed from Rome, and came to a city on the coast with a few men, and ruled there. As he entered the palace of his ancestors, his forces had captured Antiochus and Lysias, to bring them under his control. When he found out, he said, "Don't let me see their faces," so his army killed them.

When Demetrius[1] took his seat on the throne of his kingdom, there came to him all the wicked and unlawful men of Israel led by Alcimos[2] who wanted to be a high priest. They accused the people before the king, saying, "Judas and his brothers have murdered all your friends, and driven us out of our own land. Now, therefore, send some man who you trust, and let him go and see what havoc he has made among us in the king's land, and let him punish them with all those who aid them."

Then the king chose his friend Bacchides,[3] who ruled beyond the river, and was a great man in the kingdom, and faithful to the king. He sent him with that wicked Alcimos, who he declared high priest, and commanded that he should take vengeance against the Israelites. They departed and came with a great power into the land of Judea, where they sent messengers to Judas and his brothers with peaceful words deceitfully. But they did not pay attention to their words, as they saw that they had come with a great force. Then amassed with Alcimos and Bacchides a company of scribes, to record justice.

Now the Hasideans were the first among the Israelites that wanted peace from them, as they said, "One that is a priest of the seed of Aaron has come with this army, and he will do us no harm."

So he spoke to them, peacefully, and swore to them, saying, "We will not harm you or your friends."

When they believed him, he took sixty men and killed them in one day, according to the words which he wrote, "The flesh of your saints have been thrown out, and their blood they shed around Jerusalem," but there was no one to bury them.

The fear and dread of them fell on all the people, who said, "There is neither truth nor righteousness in them, as they have broken the treaty and oath that they made."

After this, Bacchides left Jerusalem and pitched his tents in Beth Zaith[4] where he sent for and captured the men that had ignored him, and also some of the people, and when he had slaughtered them, he threw them into a great pit. Then he placed the country under Alcimos's administration and left with him a force to support him, and then Bacchides went to the king, and Alcimos took the position of the high priest. To him, all the troubled people contended, who, after they had taken the land of Judah into their hands, created many problems in Israel.

When Judas saw all the mischief that Alcimos and his company had done among the Israelites, even more than the nations, he went out to all the frontiers of Judea and took vengeance against those who had revolted from him, so that they dared not go out into the country anymore. On the other side, when Alcimos saw that Judas and his company had taken the upper hand, and knew that he was not able to survive their army, he returned to the king and said all the worst things about those who he could. The king sent Nicanor,[5] one of his honorable princes, a man that hated the Israelites with an order to destroy the people.

Nicanor traveled to Jerusalem with a great army, and sent a messenger to Judas and his brothers with deceitfully friendly words, saying, "Let there not be a battle between us. I will come with a few men, that I may see you in peace," then he came to Judas, and they saluted one another peacefully, however, the enemies were prepared to capture Judas by violence.

Once it became known to Judas, that he came to him in deceit, he was very afraid of him, and would not see his face again. Nicanor also, when he saw that his plans were discovered, went out to fight against Judas beside Caphar-salama,[6] where about 5,000 of Nicanor's men were slaughtered, and the rest fled into the City of David.

After this, Nicanor went up to Mount Zion, and some of the priests and certain elders of the people came out of the temple, to salute him peacefully, and to show him the burnt sacrifice that was offered for the king. But he mocked them, and laughed at them, and abused them shamefully, and spoke proudly, and swore in his anger, saying, "Unless Judas and his army is given into my hands now, I will return and burn down this temple." Then he left in a great rage.

Then the priests entered, and stood before the altar in the temple, weeping, and saying, "You chose this temple to be called by your name and to be a house of prayer and petition. Take vengeance on this man and his army, and let them fall by the sword. Remember their blasphemies, and don't allow them to continue any longer."

Nicanor left Jerusalem and camped in Beth Horon, where an army from Syria met him. But Judas camped in Adasa with 3000 men, and there he said, "When the messages who were sent from the king spoke blasphemy, your messenger went out and slaughtered 185,000 Assyrians. Now, destroy this army before us today, so the rest may know that he has spoken blasphemously against your temple, and judge you him according to his wickedness."

On the thirteenth day of the month of Adar[7] the armies met in battle, but Nicanor's army was defeated, and he himself was the first one killed in the battle. When Nicanor's army saw that he was slain, they threw away their weapons and fled. They chased after them for a day, from Adasa to Gazer, sounding the alarm behind them with their trumpets. They came out of all the towns around Judea, and trapped them, so that they, turning back against them who pursued, were all slaughtered by the sword, and not one of them was left alive. Afterward, they took the plunder and the victims and cut off Nicanor's head, and his right hand, which he stretched out so proudly, and brought them back, and mounted them up near Jerusalem. The people rejoiced greatly, and they kept that day a day of great celebration. Moreover, they ordered to keep this day annually, on the thirteenth of Adar.

Afterward, the land of Judea was in peace for some time.

1st Maccabees: Chapter 7 Notes

1 Codex Vaticanus: Dêmêtrios (ΔΗΜΗΤΡΙΟϹ)

Between 161 and 150 BC Demetrius I Soter was the ruler of the Seleucid Empire based in Syria.

2 Codex Vaticanus: Alcimos (ΑΛΚΙΜΟϹ)

3 Codex Vaticanus: Bacchidên (ΒΑΚΧΙΔΗΝ)

4 Codex Vaticanus: Bêthzaeth (ΒΗΘΖΑΙΘ). Translation: Beth Zaith

5 Codex Vaticanus: Nicanora (ΝΙΚΑΝΟΡΑ). Translation: Nicanor

6 Codex Vaticanus: Chapharsalama (ΧΑΦΑΡϹΑΛΑΜΑ)

- Codex Sinaiticus: Pharsalama (ΦΑΡϹΑΛΑΜΑ)
- Codex Alexandrinus: Charpharsarama (ΧΑΡΦΑΡϹΑΡΑΜΑ)
- LXX 542: Chapharsarama (χαφαρσαραμα)
- Septuagint ms. 62: Charsarama (χαρσαραμα)
- LXX 46: Charsaram (χαρσαραμ)
- Septuagint ms. 56: Phagath Rama (φαγαθ ραμα)

1st Maccabees: Chapter 7 Notes

7 Codex Vaticanus: Adar (ⲁⲇⲁⲣ). Translation: Adar

The month of Adar is the twelfth month of the Hebrew ecclesiastical year, corresponding to late February and early March on the Gregorian calendar.

1st Maccabees: Chapter 8

Judas had heard of the fame of the Romans, that they were mighty and valiant men, and they would gladly accept any that allied themselves to them and make a peace treaty with all that came to them, and that they were men of great valor. It was also told to him of their wars and noble acts which they had done among the Galatians,[1] and how they had conquered them and brought them under tribute, and what they had done in the land of Spain,[2] for the conquest of the mines of the silver and gold which are there, and that by their policies and patience they had conquered the entire land, though it was very far from them, and the kings that also came against them from the farthest parts of the earth until they had conquered them, and given them great victories so that the rest gave them tribute every year.

Besides this, how they had defeated Philip in battle, and Perseus, king of the Greeks, along with others that had risen against them, and had conquered them. How also Antiochus the great king of Asia, who came against them in battle, having 120 elephants, with cavalry, and chariots, and a great army, was conquered by them. How they took him alive and agreed that he and those that ruled after him should pay a great tribute, and give forces, and that which was agreed on, and the lands of India, Media, and Lydia and of the greatest countries, which they took from him, and gave to King Eumenes. Also how the Greeks had determined to come and destroy them, and that they, having found out sent against them a certain captain, and through fighting with them killed many of them, and carried away their wives as captives, and their children as plunder, and took possession of their lands, and pulled down their strongholds, and brought them to be their slaves until today. It was also told to him, how they destroyed and brought under their dominion all other kingdoms and isles that resisted them, but with their friends and those relying on them they kept amity, and that they had conquered kingdoms both far and near, as all that heard of their name were afraid of them.

Also, regarding who they helped to seize kingdoms and then reign, and who they displaced. Finally, they were greatly exalted. Yet even with all this, none of them wore a crown or was clothed in purple, to be praised. Moreover, how they had made for themselves a senate house, in which three hundred and twenty men sat in council daily, consulting for the people so they might be well ruled. That they committed their government to one man every year, who ruled over all their country, and that all were obedient to that one, and that there was no envy or emulation among them.

In consideration of these things, Judas chose Eupolemus the son of John, the son of Accos, and Jason the son of Eleazar, and sent them to Rome, to make a treaty of friendship and confederacy with them, and to ask them to free them, as they saw the kingdom of the Greeks oppressed Israel with servitude.

They traveled to Rome, which was a very great journey, and entered into the senate, where they spoke and said,

> "Judas the one called the hammer, with his brothers, and the Judeans have sent us to you, to make an alliance and peace with you, and that we might be listed as your allies and friends."

That matter pleased the Romans greatly. This is the copy of the letter which the senate wrote back, in tables of brass, and sent to Jerusalem, that they might have from them a memorial of peace and confederacy:

> "Great victory to the Romans and to the Judeans, by sea and by land forever! The sword and enemy also be far from them! If they come first, any war against the Romans or any of their allies throughout all their dominion, the Judeans will help them, at the appointed time, with all their hearts. Neither will they give anything to those that make war against them, or aid them with food, weapons, silver, or ships, as it is determined by the Romans, but they will keep their agreement without taking anything. In the

same manner also, if war comes first against the nation of the Judeans, the Romans will help them with all their heart, at the appointed time. Neither will food be given to those who take part in the war against them, or weapons, or silver, or ships, as determined by the Romans. They will keep their agreement, and that without deceit."

By these articles, the Romans made a treaty with the Judeans. From then onward, neither party will think to meet to add or remove anything, they may do it at their pleasure, and whatever they will add or take away will be ratified. As regards the evil that Demetrius did to the Judeans, they wrote to him, "You made your yoke heavy on our friends and allies the Judeans. If therefore they complain again against you, we will do them justice, and fight with you by sea and by land."

1st Maccabees: Chapter 8 Notes

1 Codex Vaticanus: Galataes (ΓΑΛΑΤΑΙϹ). Translation: Galatians

The Galatians were Gauls (from ancient France), who were hired as mercenaries by the Greeks, and ultimately settled in central Anatolia (modern Turkey) in the 3rd century BC. In 189 BC, the Romans defeated the Galatians.

2 Codex Vaticanus: Spanias (ϹΠΑΝΙΑϹ). Translation: Spain

1st Maccabees: Chapter 9

When Demetrius heard the Nicanor and his army were slaughtered in battle, he sent Bacchides and Alcimos into the land of Judea the second time, and with them the main force of his army. They traveled along the road that leads in through Galgal[1] and pitched their tents near Maesaloth,[2] which is in Arbela,[3] and after they had captured it, they killed many people. In the first month of the year 152,[4] they camped near Jerusalem, and from there they moved and went to Berean,[5] with 20,000 infantry and 2,000 cavalry.

Judas had pitched his tents at Elasa,[6] and 3,000 chosen men with him, who when they saw the multitude of the other army, was so great they were very afraid, and many abandoned the army, so many in fact that no more then eight hundred men were left. When Judas saw that his army sneaked away and that the battle was on him, he was very concerned and distressed, as he had no time to gather more together. To those that remained, he said, "Let's rise and attack our enemies, we may be able to defeat them."

They refused him, saying, "We will never be able! Let's save our lives instead for now, and we will return with our brothers, and fight against them, as we are only a few."

Then Judas said, "God forbid that I should do this, and flee from them! If our time has come, let us die bravely for our brothers, and let us not stain our honor!"

With that, the army of Bacchides moved out of their camp and assembled near them, their cavalry divided into two troops, with their slingers and archers traveling before the army, and those who marched in the vanguard were all mighty men. As for Bacchides, he was in the right-wing, so the army drew near on the two parts, and sounded their trumpets.

They of Judas' side, also sounded their trumpets, so that the earth shook at the noise of the armies, and the battle continued from morning until night. Now when Judas saw that Bacchides and the strength of his army were on the right side, he took with him all the strongest men who defeated the right-wing and chased them to the hills of Ashdod.

When those in the left-wing saw that those in the right-wing were defeated, they followed Judas and those that were with him hard on their heels. A great battle followed, in which many were killed on both parts. Judas also was killed, and the remnants fled.

Then Jonathan and Simon took Judas their brother and buried him in the sepulcher of his fathers in Modi'in. They mourned him, and all Israel made great lamentation for him, and mourned many days, saying, "How has the valiant man fallen, who delivered Israel?"

As for the other things concerning Judas and his wars, and the noble acts which he did, and his greatness, they are not written, as they were too many. After the death of Judas the wicked began to put out their heads in all the lands of Israel, and there arose up all those that worked iniquity. In those days also was there a very great famine, due to the civil war in the country. Then Bacchides chose the wicked men and made them lords of the country. They searched for Judas' friends and brought them to Bacchides, who took vengeance on them and tortured them. There was a great torment across Israel like there had not been since the time of the prophets.

For this reason, all of Judas' friends came together, and said to Jonathan, "Since your brother Judas died, we have no man like him to attack our enemies, and Bacchides, and attack those of our nation that don't support us. Now, therefore, we have chosen you today to be our prince and captain in his place, that you may fight our battles."

At this, Jonathan took the governance on him at that time and rose up in place of his brother Judas. When Bacchides heard of it, he wanted to kill him. Then

Jonathan and Simon his brother, and all that were with him found out. They fled into the wilderness of Teqoa[7] and camped by the water of the pool of Asphar.[8] When Bacchides heard it, he traveled to Jordan with his entire army on the sabbath day.

Jonathan had sent his brother John, a captain of the people, to beg his friends the Nabataeans, that they might leave with them their property, which was great. But the children of Iambri[9] came out of Madaba,[10] and captured John, and all that he had, and took it away.

Later, word came to Jonathan and Simon his brother, that the children of Iambri made a great marriage, and were bringing the bride from Nadabath with a great train, as being the daughter of one of the great princes of Canaan.[11] They remembered John their brother, and went up and hid in the mountain, where they watched, and saw there was a lot happening and a great carriage arrived, and the bridegroom came out with his friends and brothers to meet them with drums, and musical instruments and many weapons. Then Jonathan and those that were with him attacked them from the place where they had lain in ambush and slaughtered them. Many fell dead, and the remainders fled into the mountains, and they took all their plunder. Therefore the marriage turned into mourning and the noise of their celebration to lamentation.

When they had fully avenged the blood of their brother, they returned to the marshes of Jordan. When Bacchides heard of it, he came on the sabbath day to the banks of the Jordan with a great force. Then Jonathan said to his company, "Let us go up now and fight for our lives, as it is not today like it was in the past. For, look, the battle is before us and behind us, and the water of Jordan on this side and that side, and also the marshes and the woods, neither is there a place for us to run. Therefore cry now to Shamayim, that you may be saved from the hand of your enemies!"

With that they attacked, and Jonathan reached out his hand to kill Bacchides, but he ran away from him. Then Jonathan and those that were with him fled into the Jordan and swam across to the other bank, and the others did not cross the Jordan with them. About 1,000 from Bacchides' side were killed that day. Afterward, Bacchides returned to Jerusalem and repaired the fortified cities in Judea, the fortresses of Jericho, Emmaus, Beth Horon, Bethel, Timnath, Phar'athon,[12] and Tephon. These he fortified with high walls, and gates and with bars. In them, he stationed a garrison, so they might harass Israel.

He also fortified the cities Beth Zur, and Gazer, and the citadel, and put forces in them, and provisions of food. He also took the chief's sons in the country as hostages and put them in the citadel in Jerusalem. In the year 153,[13] in the second month, Alcimos commanded that the wall of the inner court of the temple should be pulled down, and he also pulled down the works of the prophets. As he began to pull them down, even at that time Alcimos was plagued and his work stopped, for his mouth was silenced and he was paralyzed so he could no longer say anything, or give orders concerning his temple, and Alcimos died at that time in great agony.

When Bacchides saw that Alcimos was dead he returned to the king, and the land of Judea was in peace for two years. Then all the lawless men plotted, saying, "See how Jonathan and his company are at peace and live without care, therefore we will bring Bacchides here, who will capture them all in one night!"

They went and consulted with him. Then he moved, and a great army came along, and sent letters privately to his supporters in Judea, telling them to capture Jonathan and his men, but they were unable to do it as their plan became known. Jonathan's men seized about fifty of the men of the country who were leaders in the plot and killed them. Jonathan with his men, and Simon, withdrew to Beth Basi in the wilderness. He rebuilt the parts of it that had been demolished, and they fortified it.

When Bacchides found out, he gathered together all his army and sent word to those that were in Judea. Then he went and laid siege against Beth Basi, and they attacked it for an entire season with war machines. Jonathan left his brother Simon in the city and went out himself into the country with several men. He attacked Odomera[14] and his brothers, and the children of Phasiron in their tents. When he began to attack them and came up with his forces, Simon and his company left the city, and destroyed the war machines, and fought against Bacchides, who was defeated by them, and they afflicted him greatly, as his counsel and works were in vain. Therefore he was very angry at the wicked men that gave him counsel to come into the country, and he killed many of them and decided to return to his own country.

When Jonathan heard, he sent ambassadors to him, to make peace with him, and exchange prisoners with them. This he accepted and did according to his demands, and swore to him that he would never do him harm all the days of his life. After he had returned to him the prisoners that he had taken previously from the land of Judea, he left for his own land and did not come again into their borders. And so the war ended in Israel, but Jonathan lived at Michmash and began to govern the people, and he murdered the lawless men from out of Israel.

1st Maccabees: Chapter 9 Notes

1 Codex Vaticanus: Galgala (ΓΑΛΓΑΛΑ). Translation: Galgal

- LXX 46: Galaan (ΓΑΛΑΑΝ)
- LXX 311: Galaa (ΓΑΛΑΑ)

Gilgāl (גִּלְגָּל) is the Hebrew word for circle. Archaeologists have discovered several ceremonial stone circles in Canaan that were used between 1200 and 1000 BC for gatherings that are assumed to be religious in nature. As these stone circles are found down in the valleys, unlike the altars at the tops of hills where the Canaanites worshiped, and 'circles' (גלגל) are mentioned throughout the old Hebrew texts, it is assumed they are early Israelite religious centers from before the First Temple was built. According to the Book of Joshua, the Israelites built a stone circle in Samaria after invading Canaan in approximately 1508 BC. By the classical era, a town existed near the stone circle in Judea.

2 Codex Vaticanus: Maesalôth (ΜΑΙϹΑΛΩΘ)

3 Codex Vaticanus: Arbêloes (ΑΡΒΗΛΟΙϹ). Translation: Arbela

4 Year 152 of the Seleucid era was 160 BC.

5 Codex Vaticanus: Bereth (ΒΕΡΕΘ)

- Codex Sinaiticus: Berean (ΒΕΡΕΑΝ)
- LXX 56: Barean (βαρεαν)
- LXX 46: Bessan (βεσσαν)
- LXX 311: Baesa (βαισα)

6 Codex Vaticanus: Elasa (ΕΛΑϹΑ)

7 Codex Vaticanus: Thecôe (ΘΕΚΩΕ). Translation: Teqoa

Teqoa (تقوع) is a Palestinian town south of Jerusalem.

8 Codex Vaticanus: Asphar (ΑϹΦΑΡ)

9 Codex Vaticanus: Iambri (ΙΑΜΒΡΙ)

- Codex Sinaiticus: Ambri (ΑΜΒΡΕΙ)
- Codex Alexandrinus: Iambrin (ΙΑΜΒΡΕΙΝ)
- LXX 106: Iabrim (ιαβρειμ)
- LXX 46: Mambri (Μαμβρι)

10 Codex Vaticanus: Mêdaba (ΜΗΔΑΒΑ). Translation: Madaba

11 Codex Vaticanus: Chanaan (ΧΑΝΑΑΝ). Translation: Canaan

12 Codex Vaticanus: Pharathôn (ΦΑΡΑΘΩΝ)

- Codex Sinaiticus: Phasin (ΦΑCΙΝ)
- LXX 56: Pharathôni (φαραθωνι)
- LXX 93: Pharathô (φαραθω)
- LXX 19: Pharôth (φαρωθ)
- LXX 340: Tharathôn (θαραθων)

The town of Pharathôn was also mentioned in the Book of Judges, chapter 13, where it was transliterated into Hebrew as Pirôātôn (פִּרְעָתוֹן). It is generally transliterated as Pirathon, however, appears to be derived from the Egyptian name Per-Aten, meaning House of Aten. The location of the town is unknown today, however, sometimes theorized to be the Palestinian town of Fara'ata (فرعتا), north of Jerusalem.

13 Year 153 of the Seleucid era was 159 BC.

14 Codex Vaticanus: Odomêra (ΟΔΟΜΗΡΑ)

1st Maccabees: Chapter 10

In year 160,[1] Alexander the son of Antiochus IV Epiphanes went out and captured Acre, for the people had received him, and he ruled there. When King Demetrius heard of it, he gathered together a great army and went out against him to fight. Demetrius sent letters to Jonathan with friendly words and praised him, and said, "Let's first make peace with him, before he joins with Alexander against us, or else he will remember all the evils that we have done against him, and his brothers and his people."

He gave him authority to gather an army, and to provide weapons, that he might aid him in battle. He also commanded that the hostages that were in the tower should be returned to him. Then Jonathan went to Jerusalem, and read the letters in front of all the people, and those that were in the tower, who were very afraid when they heard that the king had given him authority to gather together an army. They in the citadel delivered their hostages to Jonathan, and he returned them to their parents.

After this, Jonathan settled in Jerusalem and began to rebuild and repair the city. He commanded the workmen to build the walls around Mount Zion with square stones for fortification, and they did it. Then the nations, that were in the fortresses which Bacchides had built, fled, in that every man left his place, and returned to his own country. Only at Beth Zur some of those that had abandoned the law and the commandments remained, as it was their place of refuge.

Now when King Alexander had heard what promises Demetrius had sent to Jonathan, and when it was also told him of the battles and noble acts which he and his brothers had done, and of the pains that they had endured, he said, “Will we find another man like him? Now, therefore, we will make him our friend and ally.”

At this he wrote a letter, and sent it to him, saying these words:

> “King Alexander to his brother Jonathan sends greeting,
>
> We have heard of you, that you are a man of great power. Meet and become our friend. Therefore, now today we ordain you to be the high priest of your nation, and to be called the king’s friend, (and with it he sent him a purple robe and a gold crown) and require you to take our side, and keep friendship with us.”

In the seventh month of the year 160, at the feast of the tabernacles, Jonathan put on the holy robe, and gathered together forces, and provided a great deal of armor. When Demetrius heard, he was very angry, and said, “What have we done, that Alexander has prevented us in making amity with the Judeans to strengthen himself? I also will write to them words of encouragement, and promise them dignities and gifts, that I may have their aid."

Therefore, he sent this letter to them:

"King Demetrius to the Judeans sends greeting,

As you have kept treaties with us, and continued in our friendship, not allying yourselves with our enemies, we have heard, and are glad. Therefore continue to be faithful to us, and we will award you well for the things you do on our behalf and will grant you immunity, and give you rewards. Now, I free you and for your sake, I release all the Judeans from tributes, and from the salt taxes, and from crown taxes, and from that which pertains to me, to receive a third of the seed, and half of the fruit of the trees, and I release it from this day on so that they will not be taken from the land of Judea, or of the three governments which are added to it out of the country of Samaria and Galilee, from this day onward forever.

Let Jerusalem and her territory, with the borders of it, bee free from both tithes and tributes. As for the tower which is at Jerusalem, I yield authority over it, and give it to the high priest, that he may set in it such men as he will choose to keep it. Moreover, I freely set at liberty all of the Judeans that were carried off as slaves from the land of Judea into any part of my kingdom, and I order that all my officers send tributes even from their own livestock. Furthermore, I order that all the feasts, and sabbaths, and new moons, and solemn days, and the three days before the feast, and the three days after the feast will all be of immunity and freedom for all the Judeans in my realm. Also, no man will have the authority to meddle with or to molest any of them in any matter. I order further, that there be hired among the king's armies about 30,000 Judeans, who will be paid the same as all the king's forces. Of them, some will be stationed in the king's fortified holds, and some that are trusted will be set over the affairs of the kingdom. I order that their overseers and governors will be from themselves and that they live following their own laws, even as the king has commanded in the land of Judea.

Concerning the three governments that are added to Judea from the country of Samaria, let them be joined with Judea, that they may be considered to be one, or bound to obey any other authority than the high priest's. As for Acre, and the land around it, I give it as a gift to the temple in Jerusalem for the necessary expenses of the sanctuary. Moreover, I give every year 15,000 shekels of silver out of the king's accounts. All the surplus, which the officers had paid in former times, from now on will be given towards the works of the temple. Besides this, the 5,000 shekels of silver, which they took from the uses of the temple out of the accounts year by year, even those things will be released, because they pertain to the priests that minister. Whoever that has fled to the temple at Jerusalem, or are within the liberties of it, having been indebted to the king, or for any other matter, let them be free, and all that they have in my realm. For the building also and repairing of the works of the sanctuary, expenses will be given of the king's accounts. Yes, and for the building of the walls of Jerusalem, and the fortifying around it, expenses will be given out of the king's accounts, as also for the building of the walls in Judea."

When Jonathan and the people heard these words, they gave no credit to them, or accepted them, because they remembered the great evil that he had done in Israel, for he had greatly hurt them. Instead, they were very pleased with Alexander, because he was the first that offered a real peace with them, and they were allied to him always. Then King Alexander gathered a great force and camped near Demetrius. After the two kings had begun to battle, Demetrius's army fled, but Alexander chased after him and defeated them. He continued the battle until the sun went down, and on that day Demetrius was killed. Afterward, Alexander sent ambassadors to Ptolemy,[2] King of Egypt with a message saying:

"As I have come to my realm, and sitting on the throne of my forefathers, and have gained dominion, and overthrown Demetrius, and recovered our country. After I had battled with him, both he and his army was conquered by us, so that we sat in the throne of his kingdom. Now, therefore, let us make a peace treaty, and give me your daughter as wife, and I will be your son-in-law and will treat both you and her according to your dignity."

King Ptolemy answered, "Great is the day in which you return into the land of your fathers, and sat on the throne of their kingdom. Now I will do it for you as you have written. Meet me in Acre, where we may see one another, for I will marry my daughter to you as you desire."

Ptolemy left Egypt with his daughter Cleopatra, and they traveled to Acre in the hundred and sixty-second year where King Alexander met him, he gave to him his daughter Cleopatra,[3] and celebrated her marriage at Acre with great glory, in the manner of kings. Now King Alexander had written to Jonathan, that he should come and meet him, who therefore went honorably to Acre, where he met the two kings and gave them and their friends silver and gold, and many presents, and found favor in their sight.

At that time certain pestilent men of Israel, men of a wicked life, assembled themselves against him, to accuse him, but the king would not hear them. More than that, the king commanded to take off his garments, and clothe him in purple, and they did so. He made him sit by him, and said to his princes, "Go with him to the middle of the city, and proclaim that no man may complain against him in any matter, and that no man trouble him for any reason."

Now when his accusers saw that he was honored according to the proclamation, and clothed in purple, they all fled. So the king honored him, and wrote him among his chief friends, and made him a general and governor. Afterward, Jonathan returned to Jerusalem with peace and joy.

Furthermore, in the year 165,[4] Demetrius the son of Demetrius came out of Crete into the land of his fathers. When King Alexander heard of it, he was concerned and returned to Antioch. Then Demetrius made General Apollonius the governor of Coele-Syria, who gathered together a great army, and camped in Jamnith, and sent a messenger to Jonathan the high priest, saying, "You alone rise up against us, and I am laughed at because of you and insulted. Why do you flaunt your power against us in the mountains? If you trust in your strength, come down and meet us in the plain field, and let us settle the matter together, as the strength of the cities is with me. Ask, and learn who I am, and those that take our side, and they will tell you that your foot is not able to stand before us, for your fathers have twice been put to flight in their land. Therefore now you will not be able to survive the cavalry and such a great force in the plain, where there is neither stone nor flint, or a place to flee to."

When Jonathan heard these words of Apollonius, he was disturbed in his mind and chose 10,000 men, and left Jerusalem, where Simon his brother met him to help him. He pitched his tents near Jaffa, but, those of Jaffa locked him out of the city because Apollonius had a garrison there. Then Jonathan laid siege to it, and those of the city let him in out of fear, and so Jonathan captured Jaffa. When Apollonius heard of it, he took 3,000 cavalry, with a great army of infantry, and went to Ashdod and drew him out into the plain, because he had a great number of cavalry, in which he placed his trust.

Jonathan chased after him to Ashdod, where the armies engaged in battle. Apollonius had left 1000 cavalry in ambush. Jonathan knew that there was an ambush behind him and that they had surrounded his army, and shot arrows at the people, from morning until evening. But the people stood still, as Jonathan had commanded them, and so the enemies' horses became tired. Then Simon brought out his army and attacked the infantry, (as the cavalry were spent) who were defeated by him and fled. The cavalry also, being scattered in the field, fled to Ashdod, and went into Beth Dagon,[5] their idol's temple, for safety. But Jonathan set fire to Ashdod, and the cities around it, and took plunder from the temple of Dagon,[6] and those that had fled into it he burnt in a fire. Therefore, almost 8,000 men were burnt and murdered by the sword.

From then, Jonathan moved his army and camped near Ashkelon, where the men of the city came out and met him with a great ceremony. After this, Jonathan returned with his army to Jerusalem having a great deal of plunder. Now when King Alexander heard these things, he honored Jonathan even more, and sent him a buckle of gold, as were given to those of the king's blood. He also gave him Ekron with the borders of it as a possession.

1st Maccabees: Chapter 10 Notes

1 Year 160 of the Seleucid era was 152 BC.

2 Codex Vaticanus: Ptolemaeon (ΠΤΟΛΕΜΑΙΟΝ). Translation: Ptolemy

In 152 BC, Ptolemy VI Philometor was the king of Egypt.

3 Codex Vaticanus: Cleopatra (ΚΛΕΟΠΑΤΡΑ)

This is a reference to Cleopatra Thea, Ptolemy VI Philometor's 12-year-old daughter.

4 Year 165 of the Seleucid era was 147 BC.

5 Codex Vaticanus: Bêthdagôn (ΒΗΘΔΑΓΩΝ). Translation: Beth Dagon

6 Codex Vaticanus: Dagôn (ΔΑΓΩΝ). Translation: Dagon (Philistine and Canaanite god)

This god's name is also recorded in various other languages, including Akkadian ^{an}Dagana (𒀭𒁕𒂵𒈾), Mari ^{an}Dagan (𒀭𒁕𒂵𒈾), Ugaritic Dgn (𐎄𐎂𐎐), Canaanite Dagun (𐤃𐤂𐤍), and Hebrew Dagon (דָּגוֹן). His exact nature has been debated over the centuries, as little was known about him from the Canaanite and Israelite records before the discovery of the Ugaritic Texts.

The name was once believed to be a reference to a fish god, however, is now recognized as being a non-Canaanite grain god. This was reported in the fragments of Sanchuniathon's writing that have survived to the present, however, disregarded for centuries as it could not be proven. Until the discoveries of the past century, he was mainly known from brief references found in ancient Israelite books, including Joshua, Judges, and Samuel (1st Kingdoms), where he is described as being the god of the Philistines. As these people are now generally accepted to have been settlers from somewhere in the Mediterranean, it is likely a Semitic name that was applied to their own grain god. According to the Greek translation of Sanchuniathon that survives, Dagon was the brother of Cronos, which would be consistent with the relationship described in the Ba'al Cycle, where Dagon is repeatedly referred to as the father of Ba'al Hadad, the Canaanite equivalent of Zeus.

1st Maccabees: Chapter 11

The king of Egypt amassed a great army, like the sand that lies on the seashore, and many ships, and deceptively prepared to seize Alexander's kingdom and unite it to his own. He journeyed into Syria peacefully so those in the cities opened to him, and met him, as King Alexander had commanded them to do, because he was his brother-in-law. Now, as Ptolemy entered into the cities, he stationed in every one of them a garrison of soldiers to hold it.

When he approached Ashdod, they showed him the temple of Dagon that had been burned, and Ashdod and the suburbs that had been destroyed, and the bodies that were laying around it and those that he had burned in the battle. as they had made heaps of them by the road where he would pass. Also, they told the king whatever Jonathan had done, so he might blame him, but the king held his peace. Then Jonathan met the king with great ceremony at Jaffa, where they saluted one another and stayed.

Afterward, Jonathan, when he had traveled with the king to the al-Kabir[1] River, and then returned again to Jerusalem. King Ptolemy therefore, having gained the dominion of the cities from the sea all the way to Seleucia, devised wicked counsel against Alexander. He sent ambassadors to King Demetrius, saying, "Let's make an alliance between us, and I will give you my daughter who Alexander has married, and you will reign in your father's kingdom. I regret that I gave my daughter to him, as he wants to kill me."

He slandered him because he wanted his kingdom, and he took his daughter from him, and gave her to Demetrius, and ignored Alexander, so that their hatred was openly known. Then Ptolemy entered into Antioch, where he set two crowns on his head, the crowns of Asia and Egypt.

In the meantime, King Alexander was in Cilicia because those that lived in that land had revolted from him, but when Alexander heard of this, he came to attack him, and King Ptolemy brought out his army, and met him with a mighty force and put him to flight.

So Alexander fled into Arabia, to hide, and King Ptolemy was exalted, as Zabdiel the Arab chopped off Alexander's head and sent it to Ptolemy. King Ptolemy died on the third day, and they who were in the strongholds were murdered by one another, and Demetrius came to rule in the year 167.[2]

At the same time, Jonathan gathered together those in Judea to capture the citadel in Jerusalem, and he made many war machines against it. Then lawless people, who hated their own people, and went to the king, and told him that Jonathan besieged the citadel. When he heard it, he was angry, and immediately moved to Acre, and wrote to Jonathan, that he shouldn't lay siege to the citadel, but come and speak with him at Acre immediately.

Nevertheless, Jonathan, when he heard this, continued to besiege it, and he assembled some of the elders of Israel and the priests and put his life in peril. He took silver and gold, and clothing, and other various gifts, and went to Acre to the king, where he found favor in his sight. Though certain lawless men of the people had made complaints against him, the king praised him as his predecessors had done before, and promoted him in the sight of all his friends, and confirmed him in the high priesthood, and in all the honors that he had before, and gave him preeminence among his chief friends.

Then Jonathan requested the king, that he would make Judea free from tribute, as also the three governments, with the country of Samaria, and he promised him three hundred talents. So the king consented, and wrote letters to Jonathan of all these things saying:

> "King Demetrius to his brother Jonathan, and to the nation of the Judeans, sends greeting:
>
> We send you a copy of the letter which we wrote to our cousin Lasthenes concerning you, that you might see it. King Demetrius to his father Lasthenes sends greeting.

We are determined to do good to the Judeans, who are our friends and keep covenants with us, because of their goodwill towards us. Therefore we have ratified to them the borders of Judea, with the three governments of Apherema and Lydda and Ramathem, that are added to Judea from the country of Samaria, and all things belonging to them. All will make sacrifices in Jerusalem, instead of the payments which the king received of them annually before, out of the fruits of the earth and of trees. As for other things that belong to us, of the tithes and customs, and also the salt mines, and the crown taxes, which are due to us, we discharge them of them all. Nothing will be required from this time onward forever.

Now, therefore, see that you make a copy of these things, and let it be delivered to Jonathan, and set on the holy mount in a conspicuous place."

After this, when king Demetrius saw that the land was peaceful before him, and that no resistance was made against him, he sent away all his forces, everyone to his own place, except certain bands of foreigners, whom he had gathered from the isles of the nations. therefore all the forces of his fathers hated him. There was one called Tryphon, that had been at Alexander's side before, who, seeing that all the army murmured against Demetrius, went to Simalcue the Arabian that raised Antiochus the young the son of Alexander, and implored him to deliver to him this young Antiochus, that he might reign in his father's place. He told him therefore all that Demetrius had done, and how his soldiers hated him, and he remained there a long time.

In the meantime, Jonathan sent a messenger to King Demetrius, that he would throw those in the citadel out of Jerusalem, and those also in the fortresses, as they fought against Israel. So Demetrius sent to Jonathan, saying, "I will not only do this for you and your people, but I will greatly honor you and your nation, if given the opportunity rule. Now therefore you will do well if you send me men to help me, for all my forces have abandoned me."

On hearing this Jonathan sent 3000 strong men to Antioch, and when they arrived the king was very glad. Those from the city gathered themselves together into the middle of the city, 120,000 men, and would have murdered the king. Therefore the king fled to the court, but those from the city held the streets of the city, and began to fight.

Then the king called to the Judeans for help, who came to him all at once, and dispersing themselves through the city that day killed 100,000 people who lived there. Also, they set fire to the city, and stole much plunder that day, and saved the king. So when those of the city saw that the Judeans had captured the city, their courage was gone, and they made supplication to the king, and cried, saying, "Give us peace and let the Judeans stop attacking us and the city," and with that, they threw down their weapons, and made peace. The Judeans were honored in the sight of the king, and in the sight of all that were in his realm, and they returned to Jerusalem, with great plunder. King Demetrius sat on the throne of his kingdom, and the land was quiet around him. Nevertheless, he lied in all that he had ever said, and estranged himself from Jonathan, and did not reward him according to the benefits which he had received from him, but troubled him greatly. After this Tryphon returned, and with him the young child Antiochus, who was crowned and ruled. Then there gathered around him all the soldiers, who Demetrius had put away, and they fought against Demetrius, who ran away.

Tryphon took the elephants and captured Antioch. At that time young Antiochus wrote to Jonathan, saying, "I confirm you in the high priesthood, and appoint you ruler over the four governments, and to be one of the king's friends."

With this, he sent him golden vessels and permitted him to drink from gold, and to be clothed in purple, and to wear a golden buckle. His brother, Simon, he also made captain from the place called the ladder of Tyre to the borders of Egypt. Then Jonathan went out and passed through the cities beyond the water, and all the forces of Syria gathered themselves to him to help him, and when he came to Ashkelon, they of the city met him honorably. From there he went to Gaza, but those of Gaza locked him out, and therefore he laid siege to it, and burned its suburbs with fire, and plundered them. Afterward, when those of Gaza made supplication to Jonathan, he made peace with them, and took the sons of their chieftains as hostages, and sent them to Jerusalem, and passed through the country to Damascus.

When Jonathan heard that Demetrius' officers had come to Kadesh, which is in Galilee, with a great force, purposing to remove him out of the country, he went to meet them and left Simon his brother in the country. Simon camped near Beth Zur and fought against it a long time, and blockaded it, but they desired to have peace with him, which he granted them, and then drove them out from there, and captured the city, and set a garrison in it. As for Jonathan and his army, they camped at the water of Gennesar, from where they traveled to the plain of Nasor. And, look, the army of foreigners met them in the plain, who, having laid men in ambush for him in the mountains, came themselves against him. So when those who lay in ambush rose out of their places and joined battle, all that were on Jonathan's side fled, and there was not one of them left, except Mattathias the son of Absalom, and Judas the son of Calphi, the captains of the army.

Jonathan ripped his clothes, and threw dirt on his head, and prayed. Afterward returning to battle, he put them to flight, and they ran away. Now when his own men that had fled saw this, they returned again to him, and with him chased them to Kadesh, all the way to their tents where they were camped. There were about 3000 Gentiles killed that day, and Jonathan returned to Jerusalem.

1st Maccabees: Chapter 11 Notes

1 Codex Vaticanus: Eleutherou (ΕΛΕΥΘΕΡΟΥ). Translation: al-Kabir

Eleutheros (Ελεύθερος) was the name of the al-Kabir (الكبير) River, on the modern Lebanese-Syrian border.

2 Year 167 of the Seleucid era was 145 BC.

1st Maccabees: Chapter 12

When Jonathan saw that time had been favorable to him, he chose certain men, and sent them to Rome, to confirm and renew the friendship that they had with them. He sent letters also to the Spartans,[1] and to other places, for the same purpose. So they went to Rome, and entered into the senate, and said, "Jonathan the high priest and the Judeans sent us to you so you would renew the friendship, which you had with them, and the treaty, as in former times. At this, the Romans gave them letters to the governors of every place that they should bring them into the land of Judea peacefully. This is the copy of the letter which Jonathan wrote to the Spartans:

> Jonathan the high priest, and the elders of the nation, and the priests, and the other of the Judeans, to the Spartans their brothers send greeting:
>
> There were letters sent in times past to Onias the high priest from Darius, who ruled then among you, to signify that you are our brothers, as the copy here underwritten does specify. At which time Onias begged the ambassador that was sent honorably, and received the letters, in which declaration was made of the alliance and friendship. Therefore we also, albeit we need none of these things, that we have the holy books of scripture in our hands to comfort us, have nevertheless attempted to send to you for the renewing of brotherhood and friendship, in case we should become foreigners to you altogether, for there has been a

long time passed since you sent to us. We therefore at all times without ceasing, both in our feasts, and other convenient days do remember you in the sacrifices which we offer, and in our prayers, as reason is, and as it becomes us to think on our brothers. We are glad of your honor.

As for ourselves, we have had great troubles and wars on every side, as the kings that are around us have fought against us. We have not been troublesome to you, or our other allies and friends, in these wars, for we have help from Shamayim that helps us, so as we are saved from our enemies, and our enemies are brought underfoot. For this cause we chose Numenius the son of Antiochus, and Antipater he the son of Jason, and sent them to the Romans, to renew the friendship that we had with them and the former treaty. We commanded them also to go to you, and to salute and to deliver you our letters concerning the renewing of our brotherhood. Therefore, now, you will do well to give us an answer to it.

This is the copy of the letter which Oniares sent:

"King Areus of the Spartans, to Onias the high priest, greeting:

It is found in writing, that the Spartans and Judeans are brothers, and that they are of the stock of Abraham.[2] Now, therefore, since this has come to our knowledge, you will do well to write to us of your prosperity. We do write back again to you, that your livestock and goods are ours, and ours are yours We do command our ambassadors to make a report to you on this."

When Jonathan heard that Demetrius' princes had come to fight against him with a greater army than before, he left Jerusalem, and met them in the land of Amathis, for he gave them no permission to enter his country. He sent spies also to their camps, who returned and told him that they had decided to come against them in the night. Therefore, as soon as the sun went down, Jonathan commanded his men to watch, and to be armed, so all night long they would be ready to fight. Also, he sent out sentinels around the army. But when the enemies heard that Jonathan and his men were ready for battle, they were afraid and trembled in their hearts, and they started fires in their camp and fled. Jonathan and his company did not know it until the morning, as they saw the lights burning.

Then Jonathan chased after them but did not catch them, as they had crossed over the al-Kabir River. Therefore Jonathan turned to the Arabians, who were called Zabadeans, and attacked them, and plundered them. Leaving there, he went to Damascus and passed through all the country.

Simon also went out and passed through the country to Ashkelon, and the holds near there, from where he turned back to Jaffa and captured it. He had heard that they would deliver the hold to those that took Demetrius' side, and therefore he set a garrison there to keep it. After this Jonathan went home again, and called the elders of the people together, consult with them about building strongholds in Judea, and making the walls of Jerusalem higher, and raising a great mount between the tower and the city, to separate it from the city, that so it might be alone, that men might neither sell nor buy in it. At this they came together to build up the city, as part of the wall towards the brook on the east side had fallen and they repaired that which was called Caphenatha. Simon also set up Adida in Sephela, and made it strong with gates and bars.

Now Tryphon went about to get the kingdom of Asia, and to kill Antiochus the king, that he might set the crown on his own head. Yet he was afraid that Jonathan would not allow him, and that he would fight against him, therefore he searched for a way to capture Jonathan, that he might kill him. So he moved to Beth Shan, and then Jonathan went out to meet him with 40,000 men chosen for the battle and traveled to Beth Shan.

When Tryphon saw Jonathan came with so great a force, he dared not stretch his hand against him, but received him honorably, and commended him to all his friends, and gave him gifts, and commanded his soldiers to be as obedient to him, as to himself. To Jonathan also he said, "Why have you brought all these people to such great trouble, seeing there is no war between us? Send them home again, and choose a few men to wait on you, and come with me to Acre, for I will give it to you, and the rest of the strongholds and forces, and all that take any orders from me. I will return and leave, for this is the reason I came.

Jonathan believed him and did as he commanded, and sent away his army, who returned to the land of Judea. He kept only 3,000 men with himself, from which he sent 2,000 into Galilee, and 1,000 stayed with him. Now as soon as Jonathan entered into Acre, those of Acre locked the gates and captured him and all those that came with him they killed with the sword.

Then Tryphon sent an army of infantry and cavalry into Galilee, and to the great plain to destroy all Jonathan's army. But when they heard that Jonathan and those who were with him were captured and killed, they encouraged one another, got into formation, and prepared to fight. They therefore that chased them, seeing that they were ready to fight for their lives, turned away again. After which, they all returned into the land of Judea peacefully, and there they mourned Jonathan, and those that were with him, and they were very afraid. All Israel made great lamentation.

Then all the nations that were around wanted to destroy them, as they said, “They have no captain, or any to help them, now, therefore, let’s make war against them, and erase their memory from among men.”

1st Maccabees: Chapter 12 Notes

1 Codex Vaticanus: Spartiataes (ⲥⲡⲁⲣⲧⲓⲁⲧⲁⲓⲥ). Translation: Spartans

2 Codex Vaticanus: Abraam (ⲁⲃⲣⲁⲁⲙ). Translation: Abraham

This is the second reference to Abraham via his older Aramaic name Abram, however, it is not clear why the Spartans would have considered themselves descendants of Abraham. The Spartans generally considered themselves descendants of Hêraclês (Ἡρακλῆς), whose birth name was Alcaeos (Ἀλκαῖος) or Alcidês (Ἀλκείδης), and who more famously known in English via his Latin name Hercules. It is difficult to imagine how anyone could confuse Abraham with Hercules.

1st Maccabees: Chapter 13

When Simon heard that Tryphon had gathered together a great army to invade the land of Judea and destroy it, and he saw the people were terrified and trembling, he went up to Jerusalem, and gathered the people together, and said, "You all know what great things I and my brothers, and my father's house have done for the laws and the temple, and the battles and troubles that we have seen. All my brothers were killed for Israel's sake, and I am left alone. Now, therefore, it is far from me, that I should spare my own life in any time of trouble, as I am no better than my brothers. Doubtless, I will avenge my nation, and the temple, and our wives, and our children, for all the nations are gathered to destroy us with great hatred."

When the people heard these words, their breath was revived. They answered with a loud voice, saying, "You will be our leader instead of Judas and Jonathan your brothers. Fight our battles, and whatever you command us we will do."

He gathered together all the soldiers and rushed to finish the walls of Jerusalem, and he fortified all around it. He sent Jonathan ben Absalom and a great force to Jaffa, who drive out those that remained there. So Tryphon moved from Acre with a great force to invade the land of Judea, and Jonathan was with him as a prisoner. But Simon pitched his camp at Adidoes[1] in the plain.

When Tryphon knew that Simon had risen instead of his brother Jonathan, and meant to battle with him, he sent messengers to him, saying, "We have Jonathan your brother in custody. He owes to the king's treasurer, concerning the cost that was committed to fighting him. Now send a hundred talents of silver, and two of his sons as hostages, that when he is free he may not revolt from us, and we will let him go."

Subsequently, Simon, although he knew that they were lying to him, sent the silver and the children, in case the people should start hating him. Who might have said, 'Because I did not send the silver and the children, Jonathan has died.' So he sent them the children and 100 talents, but Tryphon had lied and would not let Jonathan go. After this Tryphon came to invade the land, and destroy it, traveling by the road that leads to Adora,[2] but Simon and his army marched against him in every place, wherever he went. Now, those who were in the citadel sent messengers to Tryphon, so that he should rush and come to them by the wilderness, and send them food.

Therefore Tryphon prepared his cavalry to come that night, but a great snowfall fell, and he could not come. So he departed and traveled into the country of Gilead.

When he approached Bascama[3] he killed Jonathan, who was buried there. Afterward, Tryphon returned and went into his own land. Then Simon went, and took the bones of Jonathan his brother, and buried them in Modi'in, the city of his forefathers.

All Israel lamented for him and mourned him many days. Simon also built a monument on the sepulcher of his father and his brothers, and raised it high to be seen, with cut stones behind and in front. He also built seven pyramids, one next to another, for his father, and his mother, and his four brothers. In these, he made cunning devices, around which he set great pillars, and on the pillars, he made all their armor for an eternal memorial. In addition to the armor, be carved ships so they might be seen by all who sail on the sea. This is the sepulcher which he made at Modi'in, and it stands yet to this day.[4]

Tryphon dealt deceitfully with the young king Antiochus and killed him, and he ruled in his place, and crowned himself king of Asia, and brought a great calamity on the land. Then Simon built up the strongholds in Judea and surrounded them with high towers, and great walls, and gates, and bars, and stored up food within. Moreover, Simon chose men, and sent word to King Demetrius, that he should give the land an immunity, because of all that Tryphon took as plunder. King Demetrius answered:

> "King Demetrius to Simon the high priest, and friend of kings, as also to the elders and nation of the Judeans, sends greeting:
>
> The golden crown, and the scarlet robe, which you sent to us, we have received, and we are ready to make a steadfast peace with you, yes, and to write to our officers, to confirm the immunity which we have granted. Whatever agreements we have made with you will stand, and the strongholds, which you have built, will be your own. As for any oversight or fault committed to this day, we forgive it, and the crown tax also, which you owe us. If there were any other taxes paid in Jerusalem, it will no longer be paid. Look, those who are among you who wish to be in our court, let then be registered, and let there be peace between us."

And so the yoke of the nations was taken away from Israel in the year 170.[5] Then the people of Israel began to write their agreements and contracts, in the first year of Simon the high priest, the governor, and leader of the Judeans. In those days Simon camped against Gaza and besieged it and all around. He also made a war machine, and set it by the city, and battered a certain tower, and captured it. They who were in the engine leaped into the city, and there was a great uproar in the city. The people of the city ripped their clothes, and climbed on the walls with their wives and children, and cried with a loud voice, begging Simon to grant them peace. They said, "Don't deal with us according to our wickedness, but according to your mercy."

Simon was appeased by them and stopped fighting against them, but threw them out of the city, and cleansed the temples in which the idols were, and so entered into it with songs and thanksgiving. He put all uncleanness out of it, and placed such men there that would follow the law, and made it stronger than it was before, and built a palace for himself there. They also of the tower in Jerusalem were locked in, so they could neither come out, or go into the country, or buy, or sell. Therefore they were in great distress for lack of food, and a great number of them died by starvation.

Then they called out to Simon, begging him to be at one with them, which he granted them, and when he had thrown them out of there, he cleansed the tower from pollution, and entered into it the twenty-third day of the second month in the year 171,[6] with thanksgiving, and branches of palm trees, and with harps, and cymbals, and with viols, and hymns, and songs, because there was destroyed a great enemy of Israel.

He ordained that that day should be kept every year with a celebration. Moreover, the hill of the temple that was by the tower he made stronger than it was, and there he lived with his company. When Simon saw that

John his son was a valiant man, he made him captain of all the armies, and he lived in Gazer.

1st Maccabees: Chapter 13 Notes

1 Codex Vaticanus: Adidoes (ΑΔΙΔΟΙϹ)

- Codex Sinaiticus: Adinoes (ΑΔΕΙΝΟΙϹ)
- Codex Venetus: Alim oes (ΑΛΙΜΟΙϹ)

2 Codex Vaticanus: Adôra (ΑΔΩΡΑ)

3 Codex Vaticanus: Bascama (ΒΑϹΚΑΜΑ)

- LXX 19: Bascania (βασκανια)

4 Josephus reported the pyramids and ships were still there around 200 years later, however, they have not been found to date.

5 Year 170 of the Seleucid era was 142 BC.

6 Year 171 of the Seleucid era was 141 BC.

1st Maccabees: Chapter 14

In the year 172,[1] King Demetrius gathered his armies together and went into Media to get help to fight against Tryphon. But when Arsaces,[2] the king of Persia and Media, heard that Demetrius had entered within his borders, he sent one of his princes to capture him alive. He went and attacked the army of Demetrius, and captured him, and brought him to Arsaces, who made him his ward.

As for the land of Judea, it was quiet all the days of Simon, for he worked for the good of his nation, so his authority and honor pleased them. As he was honorable in all his acts, so in this, he took Jaffa as a haven, and made a harbor for the isles of the sea, enlarged the borders of his nation, and recovered the country, gathered together a great number of captives, and had the dominion of Gazer, and Beth Zur, and the tower, out of which he took all uncleanness, and none resisted him.

Then they returned to their lands in peace, and Eretz gave her increase and the trees of the field their fruits. The old men sat in the streets discussing the good things, and the young men put on glorious and warlike apparel.

He provided food for the cities and set them in all manner of munition so that his honorable name was renowned to the ends of the world. He made peace in the land, and Israel rejoiced with great joy, for every man sat under his vine and his fig tree, and there was none to attack them. Neither was there any left in the land to fight against them, even the kings themselves were overthrown in those days. Moreover, he strengthened all those of his people that were brought low, and he searched out the law, and every denier of the law and wicked person he took away. He beautified the temple and multiplied vessels of the temple.

When it was heard in Rome, and as far as Sparta, that Jonathan was dead, they were very sad. As soon as they heard that his brother Simon was made high priest in his place and ruled the country, and the cities there, they wrote to him in tables of brass, to renew the friendship and alliance which they had made with Judas and Jonathan his brothers, and the things that were written were read before the congregation in Jerusalem.

This is the copy of the letter that the Spartans sent:

> The rulers of the Spartans, with the city, to Simon the high priest, and the elders, and priests, and rest of the Judeans, our brothers, send greeting:
>
> The ambassadors that were sent to our people certified us of your glory and honor, therefore we were glad they came. They registered the things that they spoke in the council of the people in this manner. Numenius the son of Antiochus, and Antipater the son of Jason, the Judeans' ambassadors, came to us to renew the friendship they had

with us. It pleased the people to entertain the men honorably, and to put the copy of their message in the public records, so the Spartans might have a memorial of it. Furthermore, we have written a copy to Simon the high priest.

After this, Simon sent Numenius to Rome with a great shield of gold weighing 1000-minas to confirm the alliance with them. When the people heard, they said, "What thanks will we give to Simon and his sons? For he, and his brothers and the house of his father have established Israel, and chased away and slaughtered their enemies before them, and confirmed their independence?"

So then they wrote it in tables of brass, which they set on pillars on Mount Zion, and this is the copy of the writing:

On the eighteenth day of the month Elul, in the year 172, being the third year of Simon the high priest at Asaramel in the great congregation of the priests, and people, and rulers of the nation, and elders of the country were these things notified to us. As there have often been wars in the country, in which for the maintenance of their sanctuary, and the law, Simon the son of Mattathias, of the posterity of Joarib, together with his brothers, put themselves in jeopardy, and resisting the enemies of their nation did their nation great honor.

After that, Jonathan, having gathered his nation together, and been their high priest, was added to his people, and their enemies prepared to invade their country, that they might destroy it, and lay hands on the sanctuary. At which time Simon rose up, and fought for his nation, and spent much of his own wealth, and armed the valiant men of his nation and gave them wages, and fortified the cities of Judea, together with Beth Zur, that lies on the borders of Judea, where the armor of the enemies had been before, but he set a garrison of Judeans there. Moreover, he fortified Jaffa, which lies on the sea, and Gazer, which borders on Ashdod, where the enemies had lived before, but he placed Judeans there, and furnished them with all things convenient for the reparation.

The people, therefore, sang the acts of Simon, and to what glory he thought to bring his nation, made him their governor and chief priest, because he had done all these things, and for the justice and faith which he kept to his nation, and for that he wanted by all means to exalt his people. For in his time things prospered in his hands, so that the gentiles were driven out of the country, and also those who were in the city of David, in Jerusalem, who had made themselves a tower, out of which they came to polluted the sanctuary, and did much damage in the holy place, but he housed Judeans there, and fortified it for the safety of the country and the city, and raised the walls of Jerusalem.

King Demetrius also confirmed him in the high priesthood according to those things, and made him one of his friends, and honored him with great honor. For he had heard it said that the Romans had called the Judeans their friends and allies and brothers and that they had entertained the ambassadors of Simon honorably. Also that the Judeans and priests were very pleased that Simon should be their governor and high priest forever until there should arise a faithful prophet. Moreover that he should be their captain and should take charge of the sanctuary, to set them over their works, and the country, and the armor, and over the fortresses, and that he should take charge of the sanctuary. Besides this, that he should be obeyed by every man, and that all the writings in the country should be made in his name, and that he should be clothed in purple, and wear gold.

Also that it should be lawful for none of the people or priests to break any of these things, or to speak against him or to gather an assembly in the country without him, or to be clothed in purple, or wear a buckle of gold. Whoever should do otherwise, or break any of these things, he should be punished.

So all the people dealt with Simon and did as has been said. Then Simon accepted it and was very pleased to be high priest, and captain and governor of the Judeans and priests, and to defend them all. So they commanded that this writing should be put in tables of brass and that they should be set up within the area around the temple in a conspicuous place. Also that the copies of it should be stored up in the treasury, to the end that Simon and his sons might have them.

1st Maccabees: Chapter 14 Notes

1 Year 172 of the Seleucid era was 140 BC.

2 Codex Vaticanus: Arsacên (ΑΡϹΑΚΗΝ). Translation: Arsaces

The Arsacid Dynasty ruled Parthia between 247 BC and 224 AD. The Arsacid king in 140 BC was Mithridates I.

1st Maccabees: Chapter 15

Antiochus the son of Demetrius the king sent letters from the isles of the sea, to Simon the priest and prince of the Judeans, and to all the people. The contents were this:

King Antiochus to Simon the high priest and prince of his nation, and to the Judeans, greeting:

As certain pestilent men have usurped the kingdom of our fathers, and my purpose is to challenge it again, that I may restore it to the old estate, and to that end have gathered a multitude of foreign soldiers together, and prepared warships. My meaning also being to go through the country, that I may avenge those who have destroyed it, and made many cities in the kingdom desolate, now, therefore, I confirm to you all the oblations which the kings before me granted you, and whatever gifts besides they granted. I permit you also to coin silver for your country with your stamp. As concerning Jerusalem and the temple, let them be free, and all the armor that you have made, and fortresses that you have built, and keep in your hands, let them remain to you. If anything is, or will be, owing to the king, let it be forgiven from this time on forever. Furthermore, when we have obtained our kingdom, we will honor you, and your nation, and your temple, with great honor, so that your honor will be known throughout the world.

In the year 174,[1] Antiochus went into the land of his fathers, at which time all the forces came together to him, so that few were left with Tryphon. Therefore being chased by king Antiochus, he fled to Dora, which lies on the seashore, for he saw that troubles came on him all at once, and that his forces had abandoned him. Then Antiochus attacked Dora, having with him 120,000 soldiers, and 8,000 cavalry. When he had surrounded the city, and joined ships close to the town on the coast, he attacked the city by land and by sea, and did not allow any to go out or in.

In the meantime, Numenius came with his forces from Rome, having letters for the kings and countries, in which were written these things:

> "Lucius, consul of the Romans to King Ptolemy, greeting:
>
> The Judean ambassadors, our friends and allies, came to us to renew the old friendship and alliance, being sent from Simon the high priest, and from the people of Judea they brought a shield of gold of 1000 minas. We thought it good therefore to write to the kings and countries, that they should do them no harm, or fight against them, their cities, or countries, or even aid their enemies against them. It seemed also good to us to receive the shield from them. If therefore, there is any pestilent fellows, that have fled from their country to you, return them to Simon the high priest, that he may punish them according to their own law."

He also wrote the same things to King Demetrius, and to Attalus, Ariarathes, Arsaces, and to all the countries, and Sampsames, the Spartans, Delos, Myndus, Sicyon, Caria, Samos, Pamphylia, Lycia, Halicarnassus, Rhodes, Phaselis, Cos, Side, Arvad, Gortyna, Cnidus, Cyprus, and Cyrene. A copy they wrote to Simon the high priest. King Antiochus camped against Dora the second day, assaulting it continually, and making war machines, by which means he sealed up Tryphon, so he could neither go in or out. At that time Simon sent him 2,000 chosen men to aid him, and also silver, and gold, and a great deal of armor. Nevertheless, he would not receive them, but broke all the treaties which he had made with him before, and became strange to him.

Furthermore, he sent to him Athenobius, one of his friends, and said to him:

> "You hold Jaffa and Gazer, with the tower that is in Jerusalem, which are cities of my realm. The borders you have ruined, and done great damage in the land, and seized dominion of many places within my kingdom. Now, therefore, return the cities which you have taken, and the tributes of the places, which you have gained dominion outside the borders of Judea, or else give me five hundred talents of silver for them, and for the damage that you have done, and for the tributes of the cities another 500 talents. If not, we will come and fight against you."

Athenobius the king's friend came to Jerusalem, and when he saw the glory of Simon, and the cupboard of gold and silver plates, and his great entourage, he was astonished and told him the king's message. Then Simon answered, and said to him, "We have neither taken other men's land, or held that which belongs to others, but the inheritance of our forefathers, which our enemies had wrongfully taken possession of. Therefore, we, having the opportunity, recaptured the inheritance of our forefathers. Whereas you demand Jaffa and Gazer, even though they did great harm to the people in our country, yet will we give you a hundred talents for them."

Athenobius did not answer him not a word, but returned in a rage to the king, and reported to him what was said, and of the glory of Simon, and of all that he had seen, and the king was exceeding angry.

In the meantime, Tryphon fled by ship to Orthosias. Then the king made Cendebeus captain of the sea coast, and gave him an army of infantry and cavalry, and commanded him to move his army towards Judea. He also commanded him to build up Cedron, and to fortify the gates, and to war against the people, but as for the king himself, he chased Tryphon. So Cendebeus came to Jamnith and began to provoke the people and to invade Judea, and to take the people prisoners, and kill them.

When he had built up Cedron, he set cavalry there, and an army of infantry, to the end that issuing out they might make roads on the way to Judea, as the king had commanded him.

1st Maccabees: Chapter 15 Notes

1 Year 174 of the Seleucid era was 138 BC.

1st Maccabees: Chapter 16

John went up from Gazer and told Simon his father what Cendebeus had done. Then Simon called his two oldest sons, Judas and John, and said to them, "I, and my brothers, and my father's house have since my youth until this day fought against the enemies of Israel, and things have prospered so well in our hands, that we have delivered Israel often. Now I am old, and you, by God's mercy, are old enough. You, instead of me and my brothers, will go and fight for our nation, and may the help of Shamiyim be with you."

So he chose out of the country 20,000 soldiers with cavalry, who went out against Cendebeus, and rested that night at Modi'in. When they rose in the morning and went into the plain, saw a mighty army both of infantry and cavalry coming against them, and there was a water brook between them. So he and his people camped near them, and when he saw that the people were afraid to go over the water brook, he went first over himself, and then the men saw him and crossed after him. He divided his men, and set the cavalry in the middle of the infantry, for the enemies' cavalry were great in numbers. Then they sounded with the holy trumpets, and Cendebeus and his army were put to flight so that many of them were slaughtered, and the remainder got to the stronghold.

At that time, John's brother Judas was wounded, but John still chased after them, until he came to Cedron, which Cendebeus had built. They fled all the way to the towers in the fields of Ashdod, and so he burnt it with fire so that there were slaughtered from among them about 2,000 men. Afterward, he returned to the land of Judea in peace. Moreover in the plain of Jericho, Ptolemy the son of Abubus was made captain, and he had a great abundance of silver and gold, as he was the high priest's son-in-law. Therefore his heart being lifted, he thought to take the country for himself and consulted deceitfully against Simon and his sons to destroy them.

Simon was visiting the cities that were in the country, and taking care to organize them well, at which time he came down himself to Jericho with his sons Mattathias and Judas, in the year 177,[1] in the eleventh month, called Shevat,[2] where the son of Abubus receiving them deceitfully into a little stronghold called Dok,[3] which he had built. He held a great banquet, and he had men hidden there. When Simon and his sons had drunk a lot, Ptolemy and his men rose up, and took their weapons, and attacked Simon in the banqueting hall, and killed him, and his two sons, and some of his slaves. In doing this, he committed great treachery and repaid evil for good. Then Ptolemy wrote these things, and sent a message to the king, that he should send him an army to aid him, and he would deliver to him the country and cities.

He sent others also to Gazer to kill John, and to the tribunes, he sent letters to come to him, that he might give them silver, and gold, and rewards. Others he sent to take Jerusalem, and the mountain of the temple. Now, one had run before to Gazer and told John that his father and brothers were murdered, and he said, "Ptolemy has sent us to kill you also."

When he heard it, he was very astonished, and so he seized those who had come to destroy him, and killed them, for he knew that they wanted to take him away. As concerning the rest of the acts of John, and his wars, and worthy deeds which he did, and the building of the walls which he made, and his activities, look, these are written in the chronicles of his priesthood, from the time he was made high priest after his father.

1st Maccabees: Chapter 16 Notes

1 Year 177 of the Seleucid era was 135 BC.

2 Codex Vaticanus: Sabat (ⲥⲁⲃⲁⲧ). Translation: Shevat

The month of Shevat (שְׁבָט) is the eleventh month of the Hebrew ecclesiastical year, corresponding to late January and early February on the Gregorian calendar.

3 Codex Vaticanus: Dôc (ⲇⲱⲕ). Translation: Dok

2nd Maccabees: Chapter 1

To the brothers, the Egyptian Judahites,[1] greeting from the Jerusalem Judahites[2] and greetings from Judea,[3] peace and good fortune. God[4] be gracious to you, and remember the covenant that he made with Abraham, Isaac, and Jacob,[5] his faithful servants. Give you all a heart to serve him, and to do his will, with good courage and a willing mind.[6] Open your hearts in his law and commandments, and send you peace, and hear your prayers, and be at one with you, and never forsake you in time of trouble. We are here praying for you.

When Demetrius[7] reigned, in the year 169,[8] we the Judeans, wrote to you of the extreme trouble that came on us in those years, from the time that Jason and his army revolted from the holy land and the kingdom, and burnt the gate, and shed innocent blood, then we prayed to the Lord.[9] We offered sacrifices and fine grains, and lit the lamps, and set out the loaves. Now make sure you observe the feast of tabernacles in the month Kislev,[10] in the year 188.[11]

Those in Jerusalem and in Judea, and the senate, and Judah Aristobulus[12] the teacher[13] of King Ptolemy,[14] who was from the family of the anointed priests, to the Egyptian Judahites.

As God has delivered us from great dangers, we thank him highly, for taking our side in the battle against a king. He drove away those that fought outside the sacred city. When the leader had traveled to Persia with an army that seemed invincible, they were killed in the temple of Nanaya[15] by the deceit of Nanaya's priests. For Antiochus,[16] as though he would marry her, came into the place, and his friends that were with him, to receive silver in the name of a dowry. When the priests of Nanaya had set out, and he was entered with a small company into the compass of the temple, they locked the temple as soon as Antiochus had come in. Opening a secret door in the roof, they slung stones like thunder-bolts, and struck down the captain, cut them in pieces, chopped off their heads, and threw them to those who were outside.

Blessed in every way is the god who has brought judgment upon those who have behaved impiously. Ever since, on the twenty-fifth day of Kislev, we have celebrated the purification of the temple. We thought it necessary to notify you, so you also might keep it as the feast of the tabernacles and of the fire, which was given to us when Nehemiah,[17] who built the temple and the altar, offered sacrifices. When our forefathers were led into Persia, the priests that were then devout, took the fire of the altar secretly and hid it in a hollow place of a pit without water, where they kept it safe, so that the place was unknown to all men.[18]

Now, after many years, when it pleased God, Nehemiah was sent from the king of Persia, sent from the descendants of those priests that had hidden the fire. However, they told us they found no fire, but instead found thick water.[19] He commanded them to draw it up and to bring it out, and when the sacrifices were prepared, Nehemiah commanded the priests to sprinkle the wood and that laid on it with the water. When this was done, and the time came the sun rose and lit up the darkness, a great fire was started, so that every man marveled. The priests prayed while the sacrifice was consuming, both the priests and every one. Jonathan led, and the rest answering to it, as Nehemiah did.

The prayer was like this:

> Lord Ba'al the god[20] and creator of everything, the fearful and strong and fair and gracious. The only King and Savior. The only benefactor and only justice, and omnipotent[21] and eternal. The savior of Israel from all trouble, and creator of their forefathers, who chose and sanctified them.
>
> Accept this sacrifice for all of the Israelite people, and preserve your own inheritance, and sanctify it. Gather together our scattered people, and save those who are slaves among the nations. Look on them who are despised and ab-

horred, and let the nations know that you are our god. Punish those that oppress us and are full of pride. Plant your people in your sacred place, as Moses had said.

The priests sang songs of thanksgiving. When the sacrifice was consumed, Nehemiah commanded the water that was left should be poured on the great stones. When this was done, a flame was started, but it was consumed by the light that shined from the altar. When this matter was known, it was told the king of Persia, that in the place, where the priests that were led away had hidden the fire, there appeared water, and that Nehemiah had purified the sacrifices therewith. Then the king made the place sacred after he had investigated the matter. The king took many gifts and bestowed on those who he would gratify. Nehemiah called this thing Nephtar,[22] which is as much as to say, purification, but most men call it Naphtha.[23]

2nd Maccabees: Chapter 1 Notes

1 Codex Alexandrinus: Aegypton Ioudaeoes (ΑΙΓΥΠΤΟΝ ΙΟΥΔΑΙΟΙϹ). Translation: Egyptian Judahites

The term used by the Greeks could refer to someone from the tribe of Judah, the land of Judea, or a practitioner of a Jewish religion. In this context, it is referring to the Judahites living in Jerusalem.

2 Codex Alexandrinus: Ierosolymoes Ioudaeoe (ΙΕΡΟϹΟΛΥΜΟΙϹΙΟΥΔΑΙΟΙ). Translation: Jerusalem Judahites

3 Codex Alexandrinus: Ioudaeas (ΙΟΥΔΑΙΑϹ). Translation: Judea

4 Codex Alexandrinus: o theos (ΟΘΕΟϹ). Translation: the God

5 Codex Alexandrinus: Abraam cae Isaac cae Iacôb (ΑΒΡΑΑΜΚΑΙΙϹΑΑΚΚΑΙΙΑΚΩΒ). Translation: Abraham and Isaac and Jacob

6 Codex Alexandrinus: psychê (ΨΥΧΗ). Translation: mind, consciousness

7 Codex Alexandrinus: Dêmêtriou (ΔΗΜΗΤΡΙΟΥ)

Between 185 and 150 BC, Demetrius I Soter was the ruler of the Seleucid Empire based in Syria.

8 Year 169 of the Seleucid era was 143 BC.

9 Codex Alexandrinus: cyriou (ΚΥΡΙΟΥ). Translation: lord

10 Codex Alexandrinus: Chaselef (ΧΑCΕΛΕΥ). Translation: Kislev

- LXX 728: Chasleu (χασλευ)
- LXX 534: Chasaleu (χασαλευ)
- LXX 106: Chaleu (χαλευ)

Kislev is the ninth month of the year in the Hebrew calendar of the time, and the third month in the modern Israeli civil calendar. It corresponds to late November and early December in the Gregorian calendar.

11 Year 188 of the Seleucid era was 124 BC. This reference is likely to the year that the book was sent to Egypt.

12 Codex Alexandrinus: Ioudas Aristoboulô (ΙΟΥΔΑϹ ΑΡΙϹΤΟΒΟΥΛΩ). Translation: Judah Aristobulus

Judah Aristobulus I was the first king of the Hasmonean Kingdom of Judea who reigned between 104 and 103 BC, and the High Priest in Jerusalem. In 124 BC, the year indicated in the book, John Hyrcanus was the High Priest in Jerusalem, and Judah Aristobulus was a religious general, involved in the wars to conquer Sichem, Samaria, Hebron, and Medaba.

13 Codex Alexandrinus: didascalô (ΔΙΔΑϹΚΑΛΩ). Translation: teacher (or master, director)

14 Codex Alexandrinus: Ptolemaeou tou basileôs (ΠΤΟΛΕΜΑΙΟΥ ΤΟΥ ΒΑϹΙΛΕΩϹ). Translation: Ptolemy the king

In 124 BC, Ptolemy VIII Physcon was the king of Egypt. In 124 BC, the long-running feud between Ptolemy VIII Physcon and his wives Cleopatra II, and her daughter and co-wife Cleopatra III, was settled, restoring peace to the lands of Egypt, Syria, and Judea.

15 Codex Alexandrinus: Nanaeas (ΝΑΝΑΙΑϹ). Translation: Nanaya

- LXX 55: Ananeas (ανανεας)
- LXX 19: Anaraeas (αναραιας)

- Codex Bobbiensis: Anania
- Peshitta: Nny (ܢܢܝ)

Nanaya (Ναναια) was the Greek translation of the Aramaic name Nny (𐡍𐡍𐡉), itself the a translation of the Mesopotamian name deityNanaa (𒀭𒈾𒈾𒀀), more commonly called Nanaya today. Nanaya was a minor Sumerian love goddess who was worshiped until the 5th century AD. As the events described took place in Armenia, this is most likely a reference to Nane (Նանէ), the Armenian version of Nanaya.

16 Codex Alexandrinus: Antiochos (ΑΝΤΙΟΧΟϹ). Translation: Antiochus

This is a reference to Antiochus IV Epiphanes, king of the Seleucid Kingdom of Syria between 175 and 164 BC. He died while campaigning in Armenia, in the year 164 BC.

17 Codex Alexandrinus: Neemian (ΝΕΕΜΙΑΝ). Translation: Nehemiah

- LXX 106: Nemian (Νϭμιαν). Translation: Nehemiah

According to the books of Ezra, Nehemiah was sent to Jerusalem by King Artaxerxes of the Persian Empire to restore order in 384 BC, after Artaxerxes II had reunited all of his empire other than Egypt, which he was preparing to invade. When he launched the invasion, it was one of the largest armies the world had ever seen, with over 200,000

Persian soldiers participating in the invasion. Nevertheless, Artaxerxes's massive invasion of Egypt was a complete failure, which led to the Great Satraps' Revolt, of 372 BC, which saw many of the governors rebel against the king they saw as weak.

The Great Satraps' Revolt began the same year that Nehemiah left Jerusalem to serve the king again, supporting the fact that he had rebuilt the walls of Jerusalem as part of Artaxerxes' plans to reconquer Egypt, and once that venture had failed, returned to help the king suppress the ensuing revolt. In the last two chapters of 2nd Ezra and Masoretic Ezra, Nehemiah reports that after twelve years in Jerusalem, he left to return to the king in the 32nd year of King Artaxerxes, 372 BC, and then returned later to resume his position in Jerusalem. Nehemiah was recorded as evicting the High Priest Eliashib after his return and attempting to suppress corruption, as well as building the temple and other buildings in Jerusalem.

18 The reference to the eternal fires first shows up in the books of Ezra and does not appear to have been a part of Judaism prior to the Persian era. The rest of the chapter is clearly referencing fire-worship and not anything described in the Torah. Either the reference is to a referent religion that was practiced in the Temple of Solomon, or to Nehemiah attempting to import Zoroastrianism to Judea.

As Nehemiah was sent to restore the temple in Jerusalem by the king of Persia, and the royal family was Zoroastrian at the time, this is the logical conclusion, however, there are elements found in the Canaanite religion and in Israelite folklore that suggest Ba‘al worshipers believed in genies. These genies were made of fire and electricity, as described in Ezekiel, and helped built the Temple of Ba‘al on Mount Zephon in the Ugaritic Texts, as well as King Solomon's Palace in the mountains of Lebanon. As King Solomon's temple was originally dedicated to Ba‘al and Asherah, it is possible that there was some kind of genie worship taking place there before King Josiah's reforms.

19 Codex Alexandrinus: ydôr pachy (ΥΔΩΡΠΑΧΥ). Translation: water thick

• Codex Venetus: ydôr tachy (υδωρ ταχυ). Translation: quick thick

20 Codex Alexandrinus: Cyrie Cyrie o theos (ΚΥΡΙΕΚΥΡΙΕΟ ΘΕΟϹ). Translation: Lord Lord the god

This term was also used in the Book of Ezekiel, which suggests that Nehemiah was the one that brought the Book of Ezekiel to Judea from Babylonia in 384 BC. If Nehemiah did believe that the ancient Israelite religion was Zoroastrian, it would explain why the early version of the Book of Ezekiel was added to Judaism, as Ezekiel himself thought very little of the Judahites.

In any event, the term Lord Lord, could only have been translated from Adon Ba‘al (𐡀𐡃𐡍 𐡁𐡏𐡋𐡀) in the Aramaic texts the Greeks translated Ezekiel from, as both adon and ba‘al translate as ‘lord.’ As this letter has Aramaic loanwords, and the Judean Judahites and Egyptian Israelites corresponded in Aramaic, it is logical to conclude the letter was written in Aramaic, and, therefore, it included the term Lord Ba‘al.

21 Codex Alexandrinus: pantepoptês (ΠΑΝΤΕΠΟΠΤΗϹ)
Translation: omnipotent

22 Codex Alexandrinus: nephthar (ΝΕΦΘΑΡ)

- LXX 55: ephthar (εφθαρ)

This appears to be a Greek transliteration of nptyrå (𐡍𐡐𐡈𐡉𐡓𐡀), a passive and reflexive counterpart of ptyrå (𐡐𐡈𐡉𐡓𐡀), the Aramaic term for the Passover. This suggests an attempt to reinterpret the Passover, and related firstborn sacrifice, known as the peṭer (פֶּטֶר) in the Masoretic Text, as a sacrifice in Naphtha. Given the details in Exodus, and the later amendments to the law requiring the sacrifice of the firstborn in Leviticus and Deuteronomy, it suggests the reinterpretation could only have taken place during an era when the Torah was not in wide circulation, supporting it happening during the Persian era.

23 Codex Alexandrinus: nephthar (ⲛⲉⲫⲑⲁⲣ)

- LXX 62: nephtha (νεφθα)
- LXX 46: nephthe (νεφθε)
- LXX 107: nephthai (νεφθαι)

Naphtha is a flammable liquid hydrocarbon mixture, either produced from natural gas condensates, petroleum distillates, and the distillation of coal tar and peat. In the ancient Persian empire, crude oil was also used as naphtha. Naphtha was used to keep the eternal fires of the Zoroastrian religion burning. The word naphtha, in various forms, had existed in the Middle East for thousands of years by the time this letter was written, and the author appears to be implying the Hebrews in Jerusalem had turned it into a sacred term by his time. Petroleum was known to the Neo-Babylonian as naptu (𒈾𒀊𒌅), which appears to be the source of the Aramaic neptā (𐡍𐡐𐡈𐡀), Avestan napta (𐬥𐬀𐬞𐬙𐬀), Greek naphtha (νάφθα), Hebrew nēpət (נֵפְט), and Arabic naft (نفط).

2nd Maccabees: Chapter 2

It is also found in the records, that Jeremiah the prophet commanded those who were taken away, to take the fire, as it has been foretold how the prophet, having given them the law, ordered them not to forget the commandments of the Lord, and that they shouldn't err in their minds when they saw silver and gold statues with their ornaments. With other such speeches, he encouraged them, that the law shouldn't leave from their hearts.

It was also in the writing that ordered the tabernacle and the box, and the prophet commanded and they carried and followed to the sacred mountain where Moses had gone up and had seen the inheritance of God. When he arrived Jeremiah discovered a temple in the caves, and the tabernacle, box, and the altar of incense were hidden there, and the entrance was hidden in a passage. Some of those following him entered to mark the path but were not able to find it.

When Jeremiah found out, he rebuked them, saying, "The place will be unknown until the time that God gathers his people together again and show them mercy. Then the Lord will reveal these things, and the glory of the Lord will be seen, and the cloud[1] as Moses saw it, and like when Solomon was worthy to see the place he chose for greatness."[2]

It was made clear, and Wisdom[3] possessed him and he made a sacrifice of inauguration, and completed the temple like when Moses prayed to the Lord, and fire came down from Shamayim[4] to consume the sacrifices. And when Solomon prayed and the fire came down from the sky and consumed the burnt offerings. Moses said, 'Because the sin offering was not to be eaten, it was consumed.' Also, when Solomon prayed, and down came the fire and consumed the sacrifice."

This was explained in the records and in the memorandums from Nehemiah,[5] and how he founded and gathered a library and collected together the books of the kings, and the prophets, and of David, and the letters of the kings concerning the curses.

Likewise, Judah has also collected all the books that had been lost because of the war we had, and they are with us, therefore, if you need them, send people to fetch them for you. Therefore, as we are about to celebrate the purification, we have written to you, so you will also keep the same days. It is God who saved all his people, and gave them all a heritage and the kingdom and priesthood and the temple, as he promised through the law. We have hope in God, that he will soon show mercy on us, and gather us together out of every land under the sky into the holy place, for he has delivered us out of great troubles, and has purified the place.

The story of Judas the Hammer,[6] and his brothers, and the purification of the great temple, and the dedication of the altar, and the wars against Antiochus Epiphanes,[7] and Eupator[8] his son. From the will of Shamayim, came into being the zealousness and bravely of the Judeans, so that, being only a few, they conquered the whole country, and chased the barbarian[9] hordes, and reclaimed the temple again and are legendary all the world over. They freed the city and restored the laws which were abandoned, and restored the Lord after he graciously showed them favor.

All these things, which were written by Jason of Cyrene[10] in five volumes, we will condense into one abridged volume. For considering the infinite number, and the difficulty which they find that desire to look into the narrations of the story, for the variety of the matter, and we have been careful, that those that will read may have delight, and that those that are desirous to commit to memory might have ease, and that all into whose hands it comes might have profit.

For us, who have taken on us this painful labor of abridging, it was not easy, but a matter of sweating and loss of sleep. Even as it is not easy for him that prepares a banquet and seeks the benefit of others, and yet for the pleasure of many, we will gladly undertake these great pains. Leaving the author the exact handling of every particular, and laboring to follow the rules of an abridgment. For as the master-builder of a new house must care for the whole building, but he that undertakes to set it out, and paint it, must seek out fit things for the adorning of it, even so, I think it is with us. To cover every point, and go over things at large, and to be detailed in particulars, belongs to the original author of the story. But to use brevity, and avoid much laboring of the work, is to be granted to him that will make an abridgment. Here then will we begin the story. Only adding as much to that has been said, it is a foolish thing to make a long prologue, and to be short in the story itself.

2nd Maccabees: Chapter 2 Notes

1 Codex Alexandrinus: nephelê (ΝΕΦΕΛΗ). Translation: cloud

2 Codex Alexandrinus: topos cathagiasthê megalôs (ΤΟΠΟϹΚΑΘΑΓΙΑϹΘΗΜΕΓΑΛΩϹ). Translation: place cathagiasthe greatness

The word in the middle of the sentence is not Greek or Aramaic, but a transliteration of the Canaanite term htgyysty (𐤄𐤕𐤂𐤉𐤉𐤎𐤕𐤉), meaning 'he chose.' This means the sentence originally read 'place he chose for greatness,' in a Canaanite source text. The term is in a quote of Jeremiah's meaning the quote was taken from a Canaanite (Judahite) copy of a book or letter attributed to Jeremiah.

There were many books attributed Jeremiah and/or his scribe Baruch in the Second Temple era, including the Septuagint's Book of Jeremiah, Peshitta's Book of Jeremiah, Masoretic Book of Jeremiah, Book of Baruch, Lamentations, Letter of Jeremiah, 2nd Baruch, Syriac Apocalypse of Baruch, Letter of Baruch to the Nine and a Half Tribes, Greek Apocalypse of Baruch (3rd Baruch), Paralipomenon of Jeremiah, and Meneo 4th Baruch. Some of these books are attributed to Jeremiah in one language, and Baruch in another language. Translations of the various books have survived in Armenian, Greek, Hebrew, Syriac, Old Slavonic, Ge'ez, and Romanian, but not in Canaanite. Nevertheless, Jeremiah was in Jerusalem before the Assyrians conquered the Kingdom of Judah, and so would have been writing in Canaanite. This story does not appear in any of the surviving books of Jeremiah or Baruch, which means there was at least one other book or letter attributed to Jeremiah in Judea during the Greek Era.

3 Codex Alexandrinus: Sophian (ϹΟΦΙΑΝ). Translation: Sophia (wisdom)

4 Codex Alexandrinus: ouranou (ΟΥΡΑΝΟΥ). Translation: Uranus (Greek sky god), the vaulted sky

Uranus was used as a translation of the ancient Canaanite and Israelite sky-god name. His name was spelled as Šmm (𐎌𐎎𐎎) in Ugaritic and Šamuu (𒊓𒈬𒌋𒌋) in Akkadian cuneiform during the bronze age, and later during the iron age Šmm (𐤌𐤌𐤔) in Phoenician, Šmyn (𐡍𐡉𐡌𐡔) in Aramaic, and Šāmáyim (שָׁמַיִם) in Hebrew. His earlier Sumerian and Akkadian name was Ān (𒀭), meaning both 'god' and 'sky,' as well as 'star.' The constellation Orion was known to in Akkadian as the asterism of úruān (𒌋𒊒𒀭), meaning 'Light of An,' and the asterism was believed to represent the god An. This term was subsequently absorbed into Greek as the name Orion during the Greek Dark Age, after the collapse of the Mycenaean civilization, as the name has not been documented in Linear-B, the script of the Mycenaeans.

The name Ān (𒀭), is also the likely origin of the name of Moses' god Ôn (Ὢν) in the Septuagint, which is later used in the Septuagint's Book of Hosea as a translation of the name of the god referred to in the Masoretic version as Āwen (אָוֶן).

The Temple of Ôn / Āwen continued to be in use until the time of Hosea, who denounced it. The Canaanites and early Israelites worshiped several sky gods, including Beth El, Ba‘al Hadad, and Shamayim / An, who were worshiped in the Temple of Solomon until King Josiah's reforms changed the national god of Judah to Yahw, the early iron age Edomite god. As the Judean rebels would not have been worshiping the Greek version of the sky god, the Hebrew name Shamayim is used.

5 No writings of Nehemiah are believed to have survived to the present There is a Book of Nehemiah in Catholic and Protestant Bibles, however, it is the second half of the Septuagint's 2nd Ezra, and Masoretic Ezra-Nehemiah. It is possible that it was excerpted from an older book of Nehemiah, as Ezra did live later than Nehemiah, however, it does not include the details found in 2nd Maccabees.

6 Codex Alexandrinus: Ioudan ton Maccabaeon (ΙΟΥΔΑΝ ΤΟΝΜΑΚΚΑΒΑΙΟΝ). Translation: Judas the hammer

The nickname Maccabeus is derived from the Aramaic word for 'hammer,' mkkbå (𐡀𐡁𐡊𐡊𐡌).

7 Codex Alexandrinus: Antiochon ton Epiphanê (ΑΝΤΙΟΧΟΝΤΟΝΕΠΙΦΑΝΗ). Translation: Antiochus Epiphanes

This is accepted as King Antiochus IV Epiphanes, ruler of the Seleucid Dynasty between 175 and 164 BC.

8 Codex Alexandrinus: Eypatora (ΕΥΠΑΤΟΡΑ). Translation: Eupator

This is accepted as King Antiochus V Eupator, ruler of the Seleucid Dynasty between 164 and 161 BC.

9 Codex Alexandrinus: barbara (ΒΑΡΒΑΡΑ). Translation: barbarians

10 Codex Alexandrinus: Iasônos tou Cyrênaeou (ΙΑϹΩΝΟϹ ΤΟΥΚΥΡΗΝΑΙΟΥ). Translation: Jason the Cyrenian

Jason of Cyrene's original five-volume work is considered lost, and the only surviving work based on it is 2nd Maccabees.

2nd Maccabees: Chapter 3

While the sacred city was inhabited peacefully, and the laws were followed again because of the piety of the High Priest Onias,[1] and his hatred of wickedness, it happened that even the kings themselves honored the place and glorified the temple with their best gifts. Even King Seleucus of Asia,[2] from his own revenue, paid all the expenses connected with the service of the sacrifices.

When Simon of the tribe of Benjamin was made governor of the temple, he disagreed with the high priest about the administration of the city marketplace. When he could not convince Onias, he went to Apollonius Thraseas,[3] who was then governor of Coele-Syria and Phoenicia, and told him that the treasury in Jerusalem was full of an uncountable sum of silver, and that they did not belong to the account of the sacrifices, but that it was possible for them to fall under the control of the king.

When Apollonius met the king, he told him of the silver about which he had been informed. The king chose Heliodorus, who was in charge of his affairs and sent him with commands to effect the removal of the silver. Heliodorus at once set out on his journey, ostensibly to make a tour of inspection of the cities of Coele-Syria and Phoenicia, but in fact to carry out the king's purpose. When he had arrived at Jerusalem and had been kindly welcomed by the high priest of the city, he told about the disclosure that had been made and stated why he had come, and he inquired whether this really was the situation.

Then the high priest told him that there was silver saved up for the relief of widows and fatherless children and that some of it belonged to Hyrcanus son of Tobiah, a man of great dignity, and not as that dishonest Simon had misrepresented. The sum was in all, 400 talents of silver, and 200 of gold. He said that it was completely impossible that wrong should be done to those people who had trusted in the sacredness of the place and in the sanctity and inviolability of the temple which is honored throughout the whole world.

But Heliodorus, because of the king's commandment said, "It must be confiscated into the king's treasury," so he appointed a day, and went in to direct the inspection of these funds. There was no great distress throughout the whole city, but the priests prostrated themselves before the altar in their priests' vestments, called to Shamayim, to he who made a law concerning things given to be followed, that they should be preserved safely, for it had committed to them to be kept. Whoever would have looked at high priest then, would have been wounded his heart, for his countenance and the changing of his color showed the inward agony of his mind.

Terror and trembling had come over the man, which plainly showed to those who looked at him the pain lodged in his heart.

People also hurried out of their houses in crowds to make a general supplication because the holy place was about to be brought into contempt. Women, dressed with sackcloth under their breasts, crowded into the streets. Some of the girls who were kept indoors ran together to the gates, and some to the walls, while others peered out of the windows, and holding their hands up to Shamayim, they all prayed. It would have concerned any man to see them falling down at that time, the crowds of all kinds, and the fear of the high priest being in such an agony.

While they were calling on the omnipotent Lord[4] to keep the things committed in trust safe and ensure those that had committed them. Nevertheless, Heliodorus went on with that which had been decreed. When he arrived at the treasury with his guards, then the spirits of all the powerful dynasties manifested greatly, causing that all of them became bold toward the collectors, stricken down by the god Sabaoth,[5] and became faint with terror.

There appeared to them a horse with a terrible rider on it, adorned with very beautiful clothes, and it ran fiercely and attacked Heliodorus with its forefeet, and it looked like he who rode on the horse wore armor made completely of gold. Moreover, two other young men appeared before him, notable in strength, excellent in beauty, and in fine apparel, who stood by him on either side, and scourged him continually, and wiped him many times.

Heliodorus fell suddenly to the ground and was surrounded with great darkness, but those who were with him picked him up and put him into a stretcher. And so he who had come with a great caravan and with all his guards into the treasury, they carried out being unable to help himself with his weapons, and they acknowledged the power of God. While he lay prostrate, speechless because of the divine intervention and deprived of any hope of recovery, they praised the Lord who had miraculously honored his place, the temple which previously was full of fear and trouble, but when the omnipotent Lord appeared. Then immediately some of Heliodorus' friends begged Onias, that he would call on the Highest[6] to grant him his life as he lay close to death.

The high priest, suspecting the king should conclude that some treachery had been done to Heliodorus by the Judeans, offered a sacrifice for the health of the man. While the high priest was making the offering, the same young men in the same clothing appeared and stood beside Heliodorus, saying, "Give Onias the high priest great thanks, as for his sake the Lord has granted you life. Seeing that you have been scourged by Shamayim, declare to all men the mighty power of God," then they disappeared.

So Heliodorus offered sacrifice to the Lord, and made great vows to him that had saved his life and saluted Onias, returned with his army to the king. Then he testified to all men the works of the greatest god which he had seen with his eyes. When King Heliodorus, who might decide send another fit man once again to Jerusalem, said, "If you have any enemy or traitor, send him there, and you will receive him well scourged, if he escapes at all, for there certainly is a place of the god of forces. He who is housed in the sky has his eye on that place and defends it, and he beats and destroys those that come to hurt it."

The matters concerning Heliodorus, and the taking of the treasury, ended because of this.

2nd Maccabees: Chapter 3 Notes

1 Codex Alexandrinus: Oniou (ΟΝΙΟΥ). Translation: Onias

There were several High Priests called Onias, or Oniyyo (ונִיו), during the Greek era. Onias I was the son of Jaddua, mentioned in 2nd Ezra (Masoretic Ezra) as being in Jerusalem during the era of Ezra circa 350 BC. Josephus recorded that Onias I was the high priest in the era of Alexander the Great, meaning sometime between 333 and 323 BC. Onias II was the high priest from sometime between before 222 BC until 219 BC. He was described by Josephus as being a greedy man who refused to pay tribute to King Ptolemy III Euergetes, which led to problems for the Judeans. Onias III was the grandson of Onais II, who was high priest between 199 and 175 BC. Onais III's son Onais IV, built the Temple in Leontopolis, Egypt 154 BC, after Judas the Hammer made Alcimos the high priest in Jerusalem.

2 Codex Alexandrinus: Seleucon ton tês Asias basilea (ϹΕΛΕΥΚΟΝ ΤΟΝ ΤΗϹ ΑϹΙΑϹ ΒΑϹΙΛΕΑ). Translation: Seleucus the Asian King

This is accepted as a reference to Seleucus IV Philopator, king of the Seleucid Empire between 187 and 175 BC. Judea had rebelled against the Ptolemys in 200 BC, and joined the Seleucid Empire, under the rule of Antiochus III the Great. Both Antiochus III the Great and his son Seleucus IV Philopator invested in Judea.

3 Codex Alexandrinus: Apollônion Tharseou (ΑΠΟΛΛΩΝΙΟΝΘΑΡϹΕΟΥ). Translation: Apollonius Thraseas (or courageous)

4 Codex Alexandrinus: pancratê cyrion (ΠΑΓΚΡΑΤΗ ΚΥΡΙΟΝ). Translation: omnipotent Lord

5 Codex Alexandrinus: theou dynamin (ΘΕΟΥΔΥΝΑΜΙΝ). Translation: god forces

This appears to be the translation of the term ål ṣbåwt (אל צבאות), meaning 'god of forces' in Hebrew, or ålhå ṣbåwt (אלהא צבאות), meaning 'god of desires' in Aramaic. Given that the following paragraph describes the the Phrygian god Sabazdiôs (ΣΑΒΑΖΔΙΟΣ), the horseman of the sky, it indicates that the original text read God Sabaoth. There are several parallels between the terms used Israelite texts and the Phrygian god Sabazios. Both were described as flying on some sort of animal, Sabazios on a Pegasus, and the Lord on a cherub, which appears to be the Judahite interpretation of a sphinx. According to the Greek philosopher Strabo, in the 1st century AD, Sabazios was the Phrygian version of the Greek god Zagreus, who was also described in Greek philosophy as being the 'highest god.'

6 Codex Alexandrinus: ypsiston (ΥΨΙϹΤΟΝ). Translation: highest

2nd Maccabees: Chapter 4

Regarding Simon, who was mentioned before, who had betrayed his own country over silver, and slandered Onias, saying that it was he who had incited Heliodorus and had been the real cause of the misfortune. He dared to call him a traitor to the government, he who was the benefactor of the city, and his own nation because he was too zealous of the laws. Their hatred went so far, that one of Simon's faction committed murders. Onias, seeing the danger of this struggle and that Apollonius Menestheus,[1] as the governor of Coele-Syria and Phoenicia, raged and his hatred of Simon increased. He went to the king, not to be an accuser of his countrymen, but seeking the good of all, both public and private. For he saw that without the king's attention public affairs could not again reach a peaceful settlement and that Simon would not stop his foolish.

When Seleucus died and Antiochus who was named Epiphanes[2] succeeded to the kingdom, Jason the brother of Onias obtained the high priesthood through corruption, promising the king in a meeting 360 talents of silver, and an ongoing revenue of 80 talents. Besides this, he promised to assign 150 more, if he might have authority to set up a gymnasium[3] for training the youths and to enroll the men of Jerusalem citizens of Antiochus.[4]

He set aside the existing royal concessions to the Judeans, secured through John the father of Eupolemus, who went on the mission to establish friendship and alliance with the Romans, and he destroyed the lawful ways of living and introduced new customs contrary to the law. He gladly built a gymnasium right under the citadel, and he induced the noblest of the young men to wear the Greek hat. There was such an extreme of Hellenization and an increase in the adoption of foreign ways because of the surpassing wickedness of Jason, who was ungodly and no high priest!

The priests had no courage to serve at the altar anymore, but despised the temple and neglecting the sacrifices, instead of rushed to partaker in the unlawful exercise in the wrestling area, and of playing the game of discus. They did not honor their forefathers but honored the Greeks highest of all. Because of this, a very great disaster came on them, and those whose ways of living they admired and wished to imitate completely became their enemies and punished them. It is not a minor thing to ignore the divine laws, and the time that followed proved this.

Now when the Olympiad Games[5] were held at Tyre, and the king was present, this ungracious Jason sent envoys from Jerusalem, who were Antiochians, to carry three hundred drachmas of silver for the sacrifice of

Melqart.[6] Even the bearers thought it was not fit to bestow on this sacrifice, because it was inappropriate, but should be reserved for other purposes. Therefore, this silver was intended by the sender for the sacrifice to Melqart, but by the decision of its carriers, it was applied to the construction of galleys.

When Apollonius Menestheus was sent to Egypt for the coronation of King Philometor,[7] Antiochus, understanding him not to be effective at taking care of his business, provided for his safety, and he traveled to Jaffa,[8] and from there to Jerusalem, where he was honorably received by Jason and the city. He entered with torchlight and a great cheer, and then afterward traveled with his army to Phoenicia.

Three years later, Jason sent Menelaus, the brother of Simon, to carry the silver to the king and to complete the records of essential business. But when he brought to the king, he had praised himself for the with an air of authority, and secured the high priesthood for himself, outbidding Jason by 300 talents of silver. So he came with the king's mandate, possessing no qualification for the high priesthood, but having the hot temper of a cruel tyrant and the rage of a savage wild beast.

Jason, who after supplanting his own brother was supplanted by another man, was driven as a fugitive into the land of the Ammonites. Menelaus gained the office, but as for the silver that he had promised to the king, he did not collect it. When Sostratus the captain of the citadel kept requesting payment, for the collection of the revenue was his responsibility, the two of them were summoned by the king on account of this issue. Menelaus left his brother Lysimachus in his place in the priesthood, and Sostratus left Crateta, in command of the Cypriots.

While these things were happening, those of Tarsus and Mallus[9] rebelled because they were given to Antiochis,[10] the king's concubine. Then the king went quickly to settle the trouble, leaving Andronicus, a man of high rank, to act as his deputy. Menelaus, thinking he had obtained a suitable opportunity, stole some of the gold vessels of the temple and gave them to Andronicus, and other vessels he had sold to Tyre and the neighboring cities. When Onias became fully aware of these acts he publicly exposed them, having first withdrawn to the Sanctuary of Daphne[11] near Antioch.

Menelaus took Andronicus aside and urged him to kill Onias, and resorting to treachery offered him sworn pledges and gave him his right hand, and in spite of his suspicion persuaded Onias to come out of the sanctuary, and then, with no regard for justice, he immediately killed him. Because of this, not only the Judeans but also many other nations took great indignation and were much grieved for the unjust murder of the man.

When the king had returned from Cilicia, the Judeans that were in the city, and some of the Greeks that also abhorred the event, complained that Onias was murdered without reason. Antiochus was deeply sorry, and moved to pity, and wept because of the moderation and good conduct of the deceased Becoming enraged, he immediately stripped off the purple robe from Andronicus, tore off his garments, and led him about the whole city to that very place where he had committed the outrage against Onias, and there he executed the cursed murderer. So the Lord rewarded him his punishment, as he had deserved.

When many acts of sacrilege had been committed in the city by Lysimachus with the connivance of Menelaus, and when reports of them had spread abroad, the populace gathered against Lysimachus, because many of the gold vessels had already been stolen. The common people rose filled with rage, and Lysimachus armed about 3000 men and launched an unjust attack, under the leadership of a certain Auranus, a man advanced in years and no less advanced in folly. When the Judeans became aware of Lysimachus' attack, some picked up stones, some blocks of wood, and others took handfuls of the ashes that were lying about and threw them in wild confusion at Lysimachus and his men. As a result, they wounded many of them, and killed some, and put them all to flight. The temple robber himself they killed close by the treasury.

Charges were brought against Menelaus because of this incident.

When the king came to Tyre, three men sent by the senate presented the case before him, but Menelaus, being now convicted, promised Ptolemy Dorymenes a substantial bribe if he would win over the king. Therefore, Ptolemy taking the king aside into a certain gallery, as it was to take the air, changed his mind, in that he dismissed Menelaus from the accusations, who notwithstanding was the cause of all the problems, and those poor men, who, if they had told their cause before the Scythians would have been judged innocent, them he condemned to death.

And so those who had spoken for the city and the villages and the sacred vessels quickly suffered the unjust penalty. Therefore even the Tyrians, showing their hatred of the crime, provided magnificently for their funeral. But Menelaus, because of the cupidity of those in power, remained in office, growing in wickedness, having become the chief traitor against his fellow citizens.

2nd Maccabees: Chapter 4 Notes

1 Codex Alexandrinus: Apollônion Menestheseôs (ΑΠΟΛΛΩΝΙΟΝΜΕΝΕϹΘΕϹΕΩϹ)

- Codex Venetus: Apollônion Maenesthae (ΑΠΟΛΛΩΝΙΟΝΜΑΙΝΕϹΘΑΙ)
- Codex Bobbiensis: Apollonion Naestei

The alternate transliteration of this name indicates that there was more than one translation of this book into Greek, and the Vetus Latina translation was likely made separately.

2 Codex Alexandrinus: Antiochou tou prosagoreuthentos Epiphanous (ΑΝΤΙΟΧΟΥΤΟΥΠΡΟϹΑΓΟΡΕΥΘΕΝΤΟϹ ΕΠΙΦΑΝΟΥϹ). Translation: Antiochus of address Epiphanes

3 Codex Alexandrinus: exousias autou gymnasion (ΕΞΟΥϹΙΑϹΑΥΤΟΥΓΥΜΝΑϹΙΟΝ). Translation: authority his gymnasium

Jason's request to Antiochus was to set up an Olympiad Games in Jerusalem.

4 Enrolling the Judeans as citizens of the Seleucid Empire, would have meant their being treated as Greeks, and not a conquered people, however, it would have also meant their loss of autonomy, and right to follow their own customs and laws. Therefore, these actions of the High Priest Jason, precipitated the entire Maccabean Revolt, and all subsequent interactions between the Judeans and Greeks and ultimately

Romans, culminating in the destruction of the Second Temple.

5 Codex Alexandrinus: pentaetêricou agônos (ΠΕΝΤΑΕΤΗΡΙΚΟΥ ΑΓΩΝΟϹ). Translation: every four (five inclusive) years competition

The modern version of the Olympic Games moves from city to city, however, in the Hellenic world, each major city held its own games every four years. The most famous was the Olympic Games, held at Mount Olympus, from which the term Olympiad was derived, meaning 'four year period.'

6 Codex Alexandrinus: Êracleous (ΗΡΑΚΛΕΟΥϹ). Translation: Hercules

The patron god of Tyre was the Canaanite god Melqart (𐤌𐤋𐤒𐤓𐤕), who the Greeks equated with Heracles. Heracles (Ἡρακλῆς), which meant 'Pride of Hera,' was the title of the Greek god Alcaeus (Αλκαῖος), who the Romans later adopted as Hercules. There was more than one Heracles in Greek mythology, the one from the age of the Titans, and the later son of Zeus. Classical-Era Greeks believed the hero from the age of the Titans was the Canaanite Lord of Tyre, Melqart. The Temple of Melqart in Tyre is one of the few buildings Alexander the Great spared when he razed the city, as he was a Hercules worshiper, and viewed Melqart as Hercules. In this translation, the Canaanite name of the god is restored.

7 Codex Alexandrinus: Philomêtoros (φιλομητορος). Translation: Philometor

Ptolemy VI Philometor was coronated as the king of Egypt in 180 BC.

8 Codex Alexandrinus: Ioppên (ιοππην). Translation: Jaffa

9 Codex Alexandrinus: Tarsis cae Mallôtas (ταρσεισκαι μαλλωτας). Translation: Tarsus and Mallus

Tarsus and Mallus were two cities in Cilicia, in south-central modern Turkey.

10 Codex Alexandrinus: Antiochidi (αντιοχιδι). Translation: Antiochis

- LXX 106: Antiochian (αντιοχειαν)

11 Codex Alexandrinus: topon epi Daphnês (τοπον επι δαφνης). Translation: place of Daphne, office of Daphne

Daphne was a Greek naiad, a type of nymph (spirit) associated with wells or fountains.

2nd Maccabees: Chapter 5

At about the same time, Antiochus launched his second invasion of Egypt. It happened then, that throughout the city, for almost forty days, there appeared golden-clad horsemen charging through the air, in companies fully armed with lances and drawn swords, troops of horsemen drawn up, attacks and counterattacks made on this side and on that, brandishing of shields, massing of spears, hurling of missiles, the flash of golden trappings, and armor of all sorts.

Every man prayed that that apparition might turn to good.

When a false rumor arose that Antiochus was dead, Jason took no less than 1000 men and suddenly made an assault upon the city. When the troops upon the wall had been forced back and at last the city was being taken, Menelaus took refuge in the citadel. Jason kept relentlessly slaughtering his fellow citizens, not realizing that success at the cost of one's kindred is the greatest misfortune, but imagining that he was setting up trophies of victory over enemies and not over fellow countrymen. He did not gain control of the government, however, and in the end, got only disgrace from his conspiracy, and fled again into the country of the Ammonites.

Finally, he met a miserable end. Accused before Aretas the ruler of the Arabs, fleeing from city to city, pursued by all men, hated as a rebel against the laws, and abhorred as the executioner of his country and his fellow citizens, he was cast ashore in Egypt, and he who had driven many from their own country into exile died in exile, having embarked to go to the Spartans[1] in hope of finding protection because of their kinship. He who had thrown out many to lie unburied, had no one to mourn for him. He had no funeral of any sort and no place in the tomb of his fathers.

When news of what had happened reached the king, he took it to mean that Judea was in revolt. So, raging inwardly, he left Egypt and took the city by storm, and commanded his soldiers to cut down relentlessly everyone they met and to slay those who went into the houses. Then there was the killing of young and old, destruction of boys, women, and children, and slaughter of virgins and infants. Within the total of 80,000 destroyed in three days, 40,000 in hand-to-hand fighting, and as many were sold into slavery as were killed. Not content with this, Antiochus dared to enter the most sacred temple in all the world, guided by Menelaus, who had become a traitor both to the laws and to his country. He took the sacred vessels with his polluted hands and swept away with profane hands the votive offerings which other kings had made to enhance the glory and honor of the place.

Antiochus was elated in spirit and did not perceive that the Lord was angered for a little while because of the sins of those who dwelt in the city and that therefore he was disregarding the holy place. If it had not happened that they were involved in many sins, this man would have been scourged and turned back from his rash act as soon as he came forward, just as Heliodorus was, whom Seleucus the king sent to inspect the treasury. The Lord did not choose the nation for the sake of the holy place, but the place for the sake of the nation.

Therefore the place itself shared in the misfortunes that befell the nation and afterward participated in its benefits, and what was forsaken in the wrath of the omnipotent was restored again in all its glory when the great ruler[2] became reconciled. Antiochus carried away 1800 talents from the temple, and rushed back to Antioch, thinking in his arrogance that he could sail on the land and walk on the sea because his mind was elated.

He left governors to punish the people. In Jerusalem, Philip, a Phrygian[3] by birth and by nature more barbarous than the men who appointed him. In Gerizim,[4] Andronicus. In addition, he left Menelaus, who lorded it over his fellow citizens worse than the others did in his malice toward the citizens of Judea. Antiochus sent Apollonius, the captain of the Mysians, with an army of

22,000, and commanded him to murder all the grown men and to sell the women and boys as slaves.

When this man arrived in Jerusalem, he pretended to be peaceably disposed and waited until the holy sabbath day, then, when he found the Judahites not working. He commanded his men to arm themselves, and he killed all those who were observing the sabbath. They ran through the city with weapons, and killed great numbers of people. Judas the Hammer, with about nine others, escaped into the wilderness and lived in the mountains like animals with his company, who only ate wild plants so that they might not become unclean.

2nd Maccabees: Chapter 5 Notes

1 Codex Alexandrinus: Lacedaemonious (ΛΑΚΕΔΑΙΜΟΝΙΟΥϹ). Translation: Lacedaemonians, Spartans

Lacedaemonia was the ancient Greek name for the land the Spartans lived in. The Spartans were also listed as being relatives of the Judahites in 1st Maccabees, although this is not supported by the genealogies of the patriarchs in the Torah. As the term Lacedaemonians is obscure in modern English, the translation Spartans is used.

2 Codex Alexandrinus: megalou despotou (ΜΕΓΑΛΟΥ ΔΕϹΠΟΤΟΥ). Translation: great despot (or tyrant)

3 Codex Alexandrinus: Philippon to men genos Phryga (ΦΙΛΙΠΠΟΝΤΟΜΕΝΓΕΝΟϹΦΡΥΓΑ). Translation: Philip a man descended from Phrygia.

As Philip was listed as being the governor in Jerusalem, and Andronicus was the governor at Gerizim, the implication is that the positions were religious governors. The appointment of a Phrygian by the Greeks was likely because the Phrygians worshiped Sabazios (ΣΑΒΑΖΙΟΣ) who the Greeks viewed as another version of the Judean god Sabaôth (Σαβαώθ). Sabazios and Sabaoth were both considered to be versions of Dionysus by the Greeks, which explains the presence of Dionysus worship in the temple of Jerusalem in the next chapter.

4 Codex Alexandrinus: Garizin (ΓΑΡΙΖΙΝ). Translation: Gerizim

Mount Gerizim (הַר גְּרִזִּים / جَبَل جَرِزِيم / ࠄࠓࠂࠓࠆࠉࠌ), in the modern Palestinian West Bank, is the holy mountain of the Samaritans. The Samaritan priesthood maintains a temple on Mount Gerizim at the time that they believed was the original Solomon's Temple. It was destroyed between 113 and 110 BC by John Hyrcanus, the High Priest of the Temple in Jerusalem when he enslaved the Samaritan people.

The Roman General Pompey free the Samaritans and other peoples enslaved by the Judeans in 63 BC, and the Samaritans returned to Gerizim and rebuilt the temple. Pontius Pilate later attacked Gerizim and slaughtered the Samaritans in the nearby town of Tirathana in circa 35 AD, believing there were artifacts of Moses hidden in the Gerizim Temple. The Samaritans, who were pacifists, complained to Lucius Vitellius the Elder, the Roman governor of Syria, and the Roman Senate removed Pontius Pilate from his office. The Samaritans became the largest religion in Roman Palestine after the Second Roman-Jewish War, however, in 555 AD they revolted from the Byzantine Empire over attempts to forcibly convert them to Christianity, and were massacred. The Byzantines destroyed the Gerizim Temple, and only a few hundred Samaritans survived the genocide.

2nd Maccabees: Chapter 6

Not long after this, the king sent an Athenian senator to compel the Judahites to abandon the laws of their fathers, and not to follow the laws of God, and to pollute the temple in Jerusalem, calling it the temple of Zeus of Olympus,[1] and the temple on Gerizim, the temple of the god El.[2] The beginning of these problems was very and terrible for the people, as the temple was filled with celebrations and reveling by the foreigners, who entered with their friends and women into the holy places, and also brought in things that were not lawful. The altar also was filled with profane things, which the law forbids. Men could not keep the sabbath, nor feasts of his forefathers, nor call himself a Judahite.

On the monthly celebration of the king's birthday, the Judeans were taken and forced to partake in the sacrifices. When the Dionysia[3] feast came, they were compelled to walk in the procession to honor Sabaoth,[4] wearing wreaths of ivy.

At the suggestion of Ptolemy, a decree was issued to the neighboring Greek cities, that they should adopt the same policy toward the Judahites and make them partake of the sacrifices, and those who did not choose to change over to Greek customs should be killed. One could see, therefore, the misery that had come upon them.

A man could have seen the misery that had come on them then, as there were two women that brought in for having circumcised their children. These women they publicly paraded about the city, with their babies hung at their breasts, then hurled them down headlong from the wall. Others who had assembled in the caves nearby, to observe the seventh day secretly, were betrayed to Philip and were all burned together, because their piety kept them from defending themselves, in view of their regard for that most sacred day.

Now, I urge those who read this book not to be depressed by such calamities but to recognize that these punishments were designed not to destroy but to discipline our people. In fact, not to let the impious alone for long, but to punish them immediately, is a sign of great kindness. For in the case of the other nations the ruler waits patiently to punish them until they have reached the full measure of their sins, but he does not deal in this way with us, in order that he may not take vengeance on us afterward when our sins have reached their height.

Therefore he never withdraws his mercy from us. Though he disciplines us with calamities, he does not forsake his own people. Let what we have said serve as a reminder; we must go on briefly with the story.

Eleazar, one of the scribes in high position, an old man with a noble presence, was being forced to open his mouth to eat pork.

But he, welcoming death with honor rather than life with pollution, went up to the rack of his own accord, spitting out the meat, as men should do, who have the courage to refuse things that are not right, even over the natural love of life. Those who were in charge of that unlawful sacrifice took the man aside, because of their long acquaintance with him, and privately urged him to bring food from his own provisions, appropriate for him to use, and pretend that he was eating the flesh of the sacrificial meal which had been commanded by the king so that by doing this he might be saved from death, and be treated kindly on account of his old friendship with them.

But making a high resolve, worthy of his years and the dignity of his old age and the gray hairs which he had reached with distinction and his excellent life even from childhood, and moreover, according to the sacred and God-created law, he declared himself quickly, telling them to send him to Hades.

"Such pretense is not worthy of our time of life," he said, "or many of the young should suppose that Eleazar in his ninetieth year has gone over to an alien religion, and through my pretense, for the sake of living a short time longer, they should be led astray because of me, while I defile and disgrace my old age. For even if for the present I should avoid the punishment of men, yet whether I live or die I shall not escape the hands of the omnipotent. Therefore, by manfully giving up my life now, I will show myself worthy of my old age and leave to the young a noble example of how to die a good death willingly and nobly for the revered and holy laws."

When he had said this, he went immediately to the rack.

And those who a little before had acted toward him with goodwill now changed to ill will, because the words he had uttered were in their opinion sheer madness. When he was about to die under the blows, he groaned aloud and said, "It is clear to the Lord in his holy knowledge that, though I might have been saved from death, I am enduring terrible sufferings in my body under this beating, but in my mind, I am glad to suffer these things because I fear him."

So in this way he died, leaving in his death an example of nobility and a memorial of courage, not only to the young but to the great body of his nation.

2nd Maccabees: Chapter 6 Notes

1 Codex Alexandrinus: Dios Olympiou (ΔΙΟϹΟΛΥΜΠΙΟΥ). Translation: Zeus of Olympus

2 Codex Alexandrinus: Dios Dio (ΔΙΟϹΔΙΟ). Translation: Zeus (or god) god

- LXX 106: Dios Dioxenou (Διος Διοξενου). Translation: Zeus god of hospitality
- LXX 55: Dios Dioxeniou (Διος Διοξενιου). Translation: Zeus god of hospitality
- LXX 771: Dios Xeniou (Διος Ξενιου). Translation: Zeus Xenios (or of hospitality)

While Dios (Διὸς) is considered an alternate form of Zeús (Ζεύς), and Xenios (Ξενιος) was a well documented epithet of Zeus, it is possible that the Aramaic text the Greeks translated referred to the 'God of Heaven,' and a 'foreign god,' as xeniou (ξενίου) is also the genitive singular of Xenias (Ξενίας), a proper name which meant 'foreigner,' or 'alien.'

However, based in the oldest surviving version of the text, the Codex Alexandrinus, the term is simply 'god god,' which in this context would refer to the god El (𐤀𐤋), whose temple had been associated with nearby Bet El since the time of Abraham. Based on the opposing of 'god El' and 'foreign god' it appears that one translation was made by a Samaritan, while the other was made by a Jew, as the Samaritans had a temple on Mount Gerizom dedicated to El, which the Jews in Jerusalem rejected. As the Codex Alexandrinus is the oldest surviving codex the translation of god El is used, however, 'foreign god,' or 'Zeus of hospitality' might have been the original phrase.

3 Codex Alexandrinus: Dionysiôn (ΔΙΟΝΥϹΙΩΝ).
Translation: Dionysia

There were two Dionysia festivals the Greeks held annually, the Rural Dionysia at the winter solstice, somewhat similar to the Christian Christmas festival, and the City Dionysia at the vernal equinox, similar to the Christian Easter festival. These festivals celebrated the death and rebirth of Dionysus, the god of agriculture, at the beginning and end of winter. Several similarities have been noted to the Egyptian annual Festival of Osiris, which was practiced in Egypt since at least the Old Kingdom era, suggesting the Greeks adopted the festival from the Egyptians.

As this would have been the City Dionysia, then it would have happened at the time of the Passover / Pesach. Additional parallels have been noted between the god Osiris and the Canaanite god Leḥem (𐤋𐤇𐤌 לֶחֶם / ࠋࠇࠌ / ܠܚܡ), the god of both bread and life, suggesting that the wave offering ceremony and requirement to drink wine during the seder meal at Passover / Pesach, which falls around vernal equinox, was another interpretation of the ancient Festival of Osiris. Whether it originated as a Canaanite interpretation of the Festival of Osiris or not, it would have been interpreted as a local variation of the City Dionysia during Greek rule of Judea, supporting the connection between Dionysus and the Judean god in the interpretatio graeca.

4 Codex Alexandrinus: Dionysô (ΔΙΟΝΥϹѠ). Translation: Dionysus (or Sabaoth, Sabazious)

• LXX 64: Dionysiô (Διονυσιω). Translation: Dionysus (or Sabaoth, Sabazious)

Dionysus was the Greek name of the Judean god Sabaoth (Σαβαώθ) before the Battle of Rafah, in 217 BC, according to 3rd Maccabees. Dionysus was also the Greek name of the Phrygian and Thracian god Sabazios (ΣΑΒΑΖΙΟΣ), explaining why Philip the Phrygian would have been appointed to rule Jerusalem. The name Sabaoth (Σαβαώθ) was later translated into Hebrew as ṣbåwt (צבאות), meaning 'armies,' which is likely a direct translation of the Aramaic term. The fact that Dionysus was the Greek name of Sabaoth and Sabazios was recorded by the many Classical Era scholars, including Strabo, Diodorus Siculus, Tacitus, Lydus, Cornelius Labeo, and Plutarch. As the original work of Jason would have been written in Aramaic or Phoenician, the Canaanite name is restored in this translation.

2nd Maccabees: Chapter 7

It also happened that seven brothers with their mother were taken, and forced by the king to taste pork, violating the law, and were tortured with scourges and whips. One of them spoke up and said, "What would you ask or learn from us? We are ready to die, rather than to break the laws of our forefathers."

Then the king became enraged and commanded pan and cauldrons be heated, which were immediately heated, and he commanded to cut out the tongue of him that spoke up and to cut off his arms and legs while the rest of his brothers and his mother watched. Once he was mutilated, he commanded that while he was still alive, he be taken to the fire, and fried in a pan. As the smell from the pan spread, which took some time, they told one another to die bravely, saying "Lord the god[1] sees us, and in truth is happy because of us, as Moses[2] in his song, which he witnessed to their them, saying, 'He will be comforted in his servants.'"

After the first brother had died in this way, they brought forward the second for their sport. They tore off the skin of his head with the hair, and asked him, "Will you eat rather than have your body punished limb by limb?"

He replied in the language of his forefathers, saying, "No," and therefore he was also tortured like the first was.

With his last breath, he said, "You remove us from this life in a fury, but the Cosmic King[3] will resurrect us who have died for his laws, to everlasting life."

After him, the third was mocked, and when he was questioned, he put out his tongue and held out his hands bravely, saying courageously, "These I had from Shamayim, and for his laws I disdain them, and from him, I hope to get them back again."

As a result, the king himself and those with him were astonished at the young man's spirit, for he regarded his sufferings as nothing. When he too had died, they maltreated and tortured the fourth in the same way. when he was near death, he said, "One cannot but choose to die at the hands of men and to cherish the hope that God gives of being raised again by him. But for you, there will be no resurrection to life!"

Next, they brought forward the fifth and tortured him. But he looked at the king, and said, "Because you have authority among men, mortal though you are, you do what you please. But do not think that God has forsaken our people. Keep on, and see how his mighty power will torture you and your descendants!"

After him, they brought the sixth also, who being ready to die said, "Do not be deceived without cause, for we allowed these things ourselves, by having sinned against our god, and therefore marvelous things are done to us. But don't think that you can take in your hands to fight against God and that you will escape unpunished."

The mother was especially admirable and worthy of honorable memory. Though she saw her seven sons perish within a single day, she bore it with good courage because of her hope in the Lord. She encouraged each of them in the language of their fathers. Filled with a noble spirit, she fired her woman's reasoning with a man's courage, and said to them, "I do not know how you came into being in my womb. It was not I who gave you life and breath, nor I who set in order the elements within each of you. Therefore the Creator of the world, who shaped the beginning of man and devised the origin of all things, will in his mercy give life and breath back to you again since you now forget yourselves for the sake of his laws."

Antiochus felt that he was being treated with contempt, and he was suspicious of her reproachful tone. The youngest brother being still alive, Antiochus not only appealed to him in words, but promised with oaths that he would make him rich and enviable if he would turn from the ways of his fathers and that he would take him for his friend and entrust him with public affairs. Since the young man would not listen to him at all, the king called the mother to him and urged her to advise the youth to save himself. After much urging on his part, she undertook to persuade her son.

But, leaning close to him, she spoke in their native tongue as follows, deriding the cruel tyrant, "My son, have pity on me. I carried you nine months in my womb, and nursed you for three years, and have reared you and brought you up to this point in my life, and have taken care of you. I beseech you, my child, to look at the heaven and the earth and see everything that is in them, and recognize that God did not make them out of things that existed. Likewise, mankind also comes into being. Do not fear this butcher, but prove worthy of your brothers. Accept death, so that in God's mercy I may get you back again with your brothers."

While she was still speaking, the young man said, "What are you waiting for? I will not obey the king's command, but I obey the command of the law that was given to our fathers through Moses. But you, who have contrived all sorts of evil against the Hebrews,[4] will certainly not escape the hands of God.

We are suffering because of our own sins, and if our living Lord is angry for a little while, to rebuke and discipline us, he will again be reconciled with his own servants. However, you, unholy man, you most despicable of all men, do not be elated in vain and puffed up by uncertain hopes, when you raise your hand against the children of Shamayim. You have not yet escaped the judgment of the almighty, all-seeing God. Our brothers after enduring a brief suffering have drunk of eternally flowing life in God's covenant, but you, through the judgment of God, will receive just punishment for your arrogance. I, like my brothers, give up body and life for the laws of our fathers, appealing to God to show mercy soon to our nation and by afflictions and plagues to make you confess that he alone is God, and through me and my brothers to bring to an end the wrath of the omnipotent which has justly fallen on our whole nation."

The king fell into a rage, and handled him worse than the others, being exasperated at his scorn. So he died in his integrity, putting his whole trust in the Lord. Last of all, the mother died, after her sons. This is enough about the eating of sacrifices and the extreme tortures.

2nd Maccabees: Chapter 7 Notes

1 Codex Alexandrinus: Cyrios o theos (ΚΥΡΙΟϹΟΘΕΟϹ). Translation: Lord the god

- LXX 19: Cyrie o theos (κυριε ο θεος). Translation: Lord the god
- LXX 311: theos Cyrios (θεος κυριος). Translation: god Lord

2 Codex Alexandrinus: Môysês (ΜΩΥϹΗϹ). Translation: Moses

3 Codex Alexandrinus: cosmou basileus (ΚΟϹΜΟΥ ΒΑϹΙΛΕΥϹ). Translation: cosmic (or universal) king

4 Codex Alexandrinus: Ebraeous (ΕΒΡΑΙΟΥϹ). Translation: Hebrews (or Eberites)

2nd Maccabees: Chapter 8

Judas, also called the Hammer, and his companions secretly entered the villages and summoned their kinsmen and enlisted those who had continued following the Judaean religion, and so they gathered about 6,000 men.

They called on the Lord, to look upon the people who were oppressed by all, and to have pity on the temple which had been profaned by ungodly men, and to have mercy on the city which was being destroyed and about to be leveled to the ground, and to hearken to the blood that cried out to him, and to remember also the lawless destruction of the innocent babies and the blasphemies committed against his name, and to show his hatred of evil.

Once the Hammer had his army organized, the Gentiles could not withstand him, for the wrath of the Lord had turned to mercy. Striking without warning, he would set fire to towns and villages. He captured strategic positions and put to flight not a few of the enemy. He found the nights most advantageous for such attacks. And talk of his valor spread everywhere.

When Philip saw that the man was gaining ground little by little, and that he was pushing ahead with more frequent successes, he wrote to Ptolemy, the governor of Coele-Syria and Phoenicia, for aid to the king's government. Ptolemy promptly appointed Nicanor the son of Patroclus, one of the king's chief friends, and sent him, in command of no fewer than twenty thousand Gentiles of all nations, to wipe out the whole race of Judea. He associated with him Gorgias, a general and a man of experience in military service. Nicanor decided to make up for the king the tribute due to the Romans, 2000 talents, by selling the captured Judeans into slavery.

Therefore immediately sent to the cities on the seacoast, inviting them to buy Judean slaves and promising to hand over ninety slaves for a talent, not expecting the judgment from the omnipotent that was about to overtake him. Word came to Judas concerning Nicanor's invasion, and when he told his companions of the arrival of the army, those who were cowardly and distrustful of God's justice ran off and got away.

Others sold all their remaining property, and at the same time prayed to the Lord to rescue those who had been sold by the ungodly Nicanor before he ever met them, if not for their own sake, yet for the sake of the covenants made with their fathers, and because he had called them by his holy and glorious name. The hammer gathered his men together, to the number six thousand, and exhorted them not to be frightened by the enemy and not to fear the great multitude of Gentiles who were wickedly coming against them, but to fight valiantly, and to remember the damage they had unjustly done to the temple, and the torture of the derided city, and besides, the overthrow of their ancestral way of life.

"They trust in arms and acts of daring," he said, "but we trust in the omnipotent God, who is able with a single nod to strike down those who are coming against us and even the whole world."

Then he told them of the times when help came to their ancestors, both the time of Sennacherib,[1] when 185,000 died, and, he told them what help their forefathers had found. He told them of the battle that they had in Babylonia with the Galatians,[2] and how the Macedonians were confused, and only 8,000 destroyed 120,000 because of the help that they had from Shamayim, and so they took great plunder.

With these words, he filled them with good courage and made them ready to die for their laws and their country, and then he divided his army into four parts. He appointed his brothers also, Simon and Joseph and Jonathan, each to command a division, putting fifteen hundred men under each. Besides, he appointed Eleazar to read aloud from the holy book, and gave the watchword, "God's help," then, leading the first division himself, he joined battle with Nicanor. With the omnipotent as their ally, they slaughtered more than 9,000 of the enemy, and wounded and disabled most of Nicanor's army, and forced them all to flee.

They captured the silver of those who had come to buy them as slaves. After pursuing them for some distance, they were obliged to return because the hour was late. For it was the day before the sabbath, and for that reason, they did not continue their pursuit. When they had collected the arms of the enemy and stripped them of their plunder, they kept the sabbath, praising and thanking the Lord, who had preserved them for that day and allotted it to them as the beginning of mercy.

After the sabbath, they gave some of the spoils to those who had been tortured and to the widows and orphans, and distributed the rest among themselves and their children. When they had done this, they made common supplication and prayed the merciful Lord to be wholly reconciled with his servants.

In encounters with the forces of Timothy and Bacchides, they killed more than twenty thousand of them and got possession of some exceedingly high strongholds, and they divided very much plunder, giving to those who had been tortured and to the orphans and widows, and also to the aged, shares equal to their own. Collecting the arms of the enemy, they stored them all carefully in strategic places and carried the rest of the spoils to Jerusalem. They killed the commander of Timothy's forces, a most unholy man, and one who had greatly troubled the Judeans. While they were celebrating the victory in the city of their fathers, they burned those who had set fire to the sacred gates, Callisthenes and some others, who had fled into one little house; so these received the proper recompense for their impiety.

The triple-accursed Nicanor, who had brought 1000 merchants to buy the Judeans, having been humbled with the help of the Lord by opponents whom he regarded as of the least account, took off his splendid uniform and made his way alone like a runaway slave across the country until he reached Antioch, having succeeded chiefly in the destruction of his own army! Thus he who had undertaken to secure tribute for the Romans by the capture of the people of Jerusalem proclaimed that the Judans had a defender and that therefore the Judahites were invulnerable, because they followed the laws ordained by him.

2nd Maccabees: Chapter 8 Notes

1 Codex Alexandrinus: Sennachêrim (ϹΕΝΝΑΧΗΡΙΜ). Translation: Sennacherib

- Codex Venetus: Senachirim (ϹΕΝΑΧΙΡΕΙΜ)
- LXX 671: Senachêrim (ϲεναχηριμ)
- LXX 74: Senachirim (ϲεναχειριμ)
- LXX 107: Sennachêrim (ϲενναχηριμ)
- LXX 29: Sennacherim (ϲενναχεριμ)
- LXX 542: Sennachirim (ϲενναχειριμ)
- LXX 771: Sennachirêm (ϲενναχειρημ)
- LXX 46: Boêthian (βοηθειαν)
- LXX 311: Antileuin (αντιληυιν)

Sennacherib was the king of the Assyrian Empire between 705 and 681 BC, who campaigned in Judah. According to 4th Kingdoms (Masoretic Kings), King Hezekiah of Judah paid the Assyrians 300 talents of silver, and 30 talents of gold to leave Jerusalem, a price so high that he had to empty the city's vaults and strip the Temple of Solomon of its gold and silver. Then, according to 4th Kingdoms, Sennacherib marched against Jerusalem anyway, but a messenger killed the Assyrian army, which is what Judas was apparently referring to. The Greek historian Herodotus reported that the Assyrians had disbanded their camp after their camp became overrun with mice.

2 Codex Alexandrinus: Galatas (ΓΑΛΑΤΑϹ). Translation: Galatians (or Gauls)

The Galatians were Gauls (from ancient France), who were hired as mercenaries by the Greeks, and ultimately settled in central Anatolia (modern Turkey) in the 3rd century BC.

2nd Maccabees: Chapter 9

Around that time, Antiochus[1] was retreating in disarray from lands of the Persians,[2] as he had entered the city of Persepolis[3] and tried to rob the temples and control the city. Therefore the people rushed to the rescue with arms, and Antiochus and his men were defeated, resulting in Antiochus fleeing from the inhabitants and shamefully retreating. When he arrived in Ecbatana,[4] news came to him of what had happened to Nicanor and the forces of Timothy. Then flying into a rage, he decided to avenge the Judahites the injury done by those who had put him to flight, so he ordered his charioteer to drive without stopping until he completed the journey. But the judgment of heaven rode with him! For in his arrogance he said, "When I get there I will make Jerusalem a cemetery of Judahites."

However, the omniscient Lord the god of Israel struck him with an incurable and invisible plague. As soon as he had boasted these words a pain of the bowels that was incurable came to him, and great pain in the insides, which were mostly just, as he had tortured other men's bowels with many and strange tortures. Yet he did not in any way stop his insolence but was even more filled with arrogance, breathing fire in his rage against the Judahites, and giving orders to hasten the journey. And so it came about that he fell out of his chariot as it was rushing along, and the fall was so hard as to torture every limb of his body. And so, he who had just been thinking that he could command the waves of the sea, in his superhuman arrogance, and imagining that he could weigh the high mountains in a balance, was brought down to earth and carried in a litter, making the power of God manifest to all. Worms grew out of the body of this wicked man, and while he was still living in anguish and pain, his flesh rotted away, and because of his stench, the whole army felt revulsion at his decay. Because of his intolerable stench, no one was able to carry the man who a little while before had thought that he could reach the stars of the sky.

It was then that, broken in spirit, he began to lose much of his arrogance and come to his senses under the scourge of God, for he was tortured with pain every moment. When he could not endure his own stench, he uttered these words, "It is right to be subject to God, and no mortal should think that he is equal to God."

This wicked person vowed also to the Lord, who no longer showed mercy on him, saying that the sacred city (to which he was traveling in a rush to pull it to the ground and to make it a mass-grave), that he would set it free, and as touching the Judahites, who he had judged not worthy even enough to be buried, but to be thrown out with their children to be devoured by the birds and wild animals, he would make them all equals to the citizens of Athens. The holy temple, which before he had plundered, he would decorate with great gifts, and return all the sacred vessels along with many more, and out of his own revenue defray the cost of the sacrifices. Even that he also would become a Judahite, and go through all the civilized world declaring the power of God. But all this his pains would not cease, for the judgment of God had justly come upon him, he gave up all hope for himself and wrote to the Judeans the following letter, in the form of a supplication. This was its content:

> To his worthy Judean citizens, Antiochus their king and general sends hearty greetings and good wishes for their health and prosperity:
>
> If you and your children are well and your affairs are as you wish, I am glad. As my trust is in Shamayim, I remember with affection your esteem and goodwill. On my way back from the region of Persia I suffered an annoying illness, and I have deemed it necessary to take thought for the general security of all. I do not despair of my condition, for I have good hope of recovering from my illness, but I observed that my father, on the occasions when he made expeditions into the upper country, appointed his successor, so that, if anything unexpected happened or any unwelcome news came, the people throughout the realm would not be troubled, for they would know to whom the government was left.
>
> Moreover, I understand how the princes along the bor-

ders and the neighbors to my kingdom keep watching for opportunities and waiting to see what will happen. So I have appointed my son Antiochus to be king, whom I have often entrusted and commended to most of you when I rushed off to the upper provinces, and I have written to him what is written here. For I am sure that he will follow my policy and will treat you with moderation and kindness.

And so the murderer and blasphemer, having endured the more intense suffering, such as he had inflicted on others, came to the end of his life by a most pitiable fate, among the mountains in a foreign land. Philip, who was raised with him, carried his body home, and then, being afraid of the son of Antiochus, went to Ptolemy VI Philometor[5] in Egypt.

2nd Maccabees: Chapter 9 Notes

1 Codex Alexandrinus: Antiochos (ΑΝΤΙΟΧΟϹ).
Translation: Antiochus

This story is also told in 1st Maccabees, where the king in question is identified as Antiochus IV Epiphanes (Ἀντίοχος Ἐπιφανὴς), who ruled the Seleucid Empire between 175 and 164 BC.

2 Codex Alexandrinus: Persida topôn (ΠΕΡϹΙΔΑΤΟΠΩΝ).
Translation: Persian lands

1st Maccabees reports this raid took place against Elymais (Ἐλυμαὶς), a semi-independent kingdom in the region of modern Khuzestan, Iran. The following lines of 2nd Maccabees report it was in the region around Persepolis, farther east.

3 Codex Alexandrinus: Persepolin (ΠΕΡϹΕΠΟΛΙΝ).
Translation: Persepolis

- Codex Venetus: Persipolin (ΠΕΡϹΙΠΟΛΙΝ)
- LXX 74: Persopolin (περσοπολιν)
- LXX 93: Persaipolin (περσαιπολιν)
- LXX 19: Persaeos Polin (περσαιος πολιν). Translation:

Persian city

1st Maccabees reports this raid took place against Elymais (Ἐλυμαὶς), a semi-independent kingdom in the region of modern Khuzestan, Iran. Persepolis was the old southern capital of the Persian Empire, located in Fars, Iran. By the time of Antiochus IV Epiphanes, the city of Persepolis appears to have been abandoned and the capital of the province had moved north to Istakhr. This anachronism suggests that the account in 1st Maccabees was more accurate than the account in 2nd Maccabees. Additionally, there was a revolt in Elymais around the time that Antiochus IV Epiphanes would have died, supporting his raid having been against Susa and not Persepolis.

4 Codex Alexandrinus: Ecbatana (ΕΚΒΑΤΑΝΑ)

- LXX 106: Ebtana (εβτανα)

The name Ecbatana is derived from the Median word for capital, and there appears to have been more than one location designated as Ecbatana during the Median Empire. When the Persians conquered Media, they made the contemporary Ecbatana their northern capital. This Ecbatana was important throughout the Persian era, and a major city throughout the Seleucid and Parthian Empires. If Antiochus withdrew from Susa to Ecbatana, which is believed to have been at Tepe Hegmataneh in the Zagros Mountains, it suggests that the route to Seleucia, near modern Baghdad, had been blocked by the Elymaites.

2nd Maccabees: Chapter 9 Notes

5 Codex Alexandrinus: Ptolemaeon ton Philomêtora (ΠΤΟΛΕΜΑΙΟΝΤΟΝΦΙΛΟΜΗΤΟΡΑ). Translation: Ptolemy the Philometor

Ptolemy VI Philometor was the King of Egypt between 180 and 164 BC, and again between 163 and 145 BC.

2nd Maccabees: Chapter 10

The hammer and his division, with the Lord guiding them, captured the temple and the city and tore down the chapels and the altars which the foreigners had built in the streets. Having cleansed the temple, they made another altar of sacrifice, and then, striking fire out of flint, they offered sacrifices, after a lapse of two years, and they burned incense and lighted lamps and set out the showbread. When they had done this, they fell prostrate and begged the Lord that they might never again fall into such misfortunes, but that, if they should ever sin, they might be disciplined by him with patients and not be handed over to blasphemous and barbarous nations.

On the same day that the foreigners profaned the temple, the purification of the sanctuary took place, that is, on the twenty-fifth day of the same month, which was Chislev. They celebrated it for eight days with rejoicing, in the manner of the feast of booths, remembering how not long before, during the feast of booths, they had been wandering in the mountains and caves like wild animals. They ivy-wreathed wands and beautiful branches and also fronds of palm, they offered hymns of thanksgiving to him who had given success to the purifying of his own temple. They ordained by a common statute and decree, that in every year those days should be kept by the whole nation of the Judahites.

This was the end of Antiochus, who was called Epiphanes.

Now, we will tell the acts of Antiochus Eupator,[1] who was the son of this wicked man, covering briefly the troubles and the wars. When he had gained the crown, he appointed Lysias over the affairs of the government and to be chief governor of Coele-Syria and Phoenicia. Ptolemy who was called Macron chose rather to do justice for the Judeans for the wrong that had been done to them and endeavored to continue peacefully with them. When he was accused before Eupator by the king's friends. He heard himself called a traitor at every turn because he had abandoned Cyprus, which Philometor had entrusted to him, and had gone over to Antiochus Epiphanes. Unable to command the respect due to his office, he took poison and ended his life.

When Gorgias became governor of the region, he hired a force of mercenaries and promoted war continually with the Judeans. Once the Edomites[2] who had control of important strongholds, were harassing the Judeans, they accepted those who were banished from Jerusalem and continued the war.

The hammer and his men, after making solemn supplication and beseeching God to fight on their side, rushed to the strongholds of the Edomites, assaulting them vigorously, they gained possession of the places and defeated all who fought upon the wall, and slew those whom they encountered, killing no fewer than 20,000.

When no less than 9,000 took refuge in two very strong towers well equipped to withstand a siege, the Hammer left Simon and Joseph, and also Zacchaeus and his men, a force sufficient to besiege them; and he himself set off for places where he was more urgently needed. But the men with Simon, who were greedy, were bribed by some of those who were in the towers, and when they receiving 70,000 drachmas, let some of them sneak away.

When word of what had happened came to the Hammer, he gathered the leaders of the people, and accused these men of having sold their brethren for silver by setting their enemies free to fight against them. He executed those who were found to be traitors and immediately captured the two towers. Having great success with his weapons, and in all things he took in hand, he slaughtered more than 20,000 in the two holds.

Now Timothy, who the Judeans had defeated before, gathered a tremendous force of mercenaries and collected the cavalry from Asia in no small number. He came on, intending to take Judea by storm. As he drew near, Maccabeus and his men sprinkled dust upon their heads and girded their wastes with sackcloth, in supplication to God. Falling upon the steps before the altar, they prayed to him to be gracious to them and to be an enemy to their enemies and an adversary to their adversaries, as the law declares.

And rising from their prayer they took up their arms and advanced a considerable distance from the city, and when they came near to the enemy they halted. Just as dawn was breaking, the two armies joined battle, the one having as pledge of success and victory not only their valor but their reliance upon the Lord, while the other made rage their leader in the fight. When the battle became fierce, there appeared to the enemy from heaven five resplendent men on horses with golden bridles, and they were leading the Judeans, and surrounded the Hammer and protecting him with their own armor and weapons, they kept him from being wounded. They showered arrows and thunderbolts[3] upon the enemy, so that, confused and blinded, they were thrown into disorder and cut to pieces. 20,500 were slaughtered among the infantry and 600 cavalry.

As for Timothy himself, he fled into a stronghold, called Gazara, where Chereas was governor. Those who were with the Hammer laid siege to the fortress courageously fro four days. Those who were within, trusting to the strength of the place, blasphemed greatly and said terrible things. On the dawn of the fifth day, twenty young men in the army of the Hammer, fired with anger because of the blasphemies, bravely stormed the wall and with savage fury cut down everyone they met.

Others followed them in, and while they were busy with those who were within, they set fire to the towers, and fires burnt the blasphemers alive. Others broke open the gates, and, having captured in the rest of the army, took the city, and killed Timothy, who was hidden in a cistern, and Chereas his brother, along with Apollophanes. When they had accomplished these things, with hymns and thanksgivings they blessed the Lord who shows great kindness to Israel and gives them the victory.

2nd Maccabees: Chapter 10 Notes

1 Codex Alexandrinus: Ypaton Antiochon (ΥΠΑΤΟΝ ΑΝΤΙΟΧΟΝ). Translation: Ypaton Antiochus

- Codex Venetus: Eypatora Antiochon (ΕΥΠΑΤΟΡΑ ΑΝΤΙΟΧΟΝ). Translation: Eupator Antiochus

Antiochus V Eupator was the king of the Seleucid Empire between 164 and 161 BC.

2 Codex Alexandrinus: Idoumaeoe (ΙΔΟΥΜΑΙΟΙ). Translation: Edomites

- LXX 106: Ioudaeoe (ιουδαιοι). Translation: Judahites

3 Codex Alexandrinus: ceraunous (κεραυνους). Translation: thunderbolts (or lightning)

2nd Maccabees: Chapter 11

Soon after this, Lysias, the king's guard and cousin, who also managed his affairs, took great displeasure at what was done. He gathered about 80,000 cavalry, and attacked the Judeans, intending to make the city a home for Greeks, and to seize plunder from the temple, and to sell the high priesthood every year like the chapels in other nations. He took no account whatever of the power of God, but was elated with his 10,000 infantry, and his thousands of cavalry, and his 80 elephants. He entered Judea and approached Beth-Zur which was a fortified place about five leagues from Jerusalem, and pressed it hard.

When the Hammer and his men got word that Lysias was besieging the strongholds, they and all the people, with lamentations and tears, begged the Lord to send a brave messenger[1] to save Israel. Then the Hammer took weapons and encouraged the others that would jeopardize themselves with him, to help their brothers and they went out together in a willing mind. As they were in Jerusalem, there appeared before them on horseback one in white clothing and golden armor. Then they praised the merciful God together and took heart in that they were ready not only to fight with men, but with most cruel beasts, and to pierce through walls of iron.

They marched onward in their armor, having a helper from Shamayim, for the Lord was merciful to them, and charging like lions against their enemies, they killed 11,000 infantry, and 1,600 cavalry, and put all the others to flight. Many of those who were wounded escaped naked, and Lysias himself fled and escaped in shame. As he was a man of understanding, considered the losses he'd had, and considered that the Hebrews could not be defeated, because the omniscient God helped them, he sent word to them, offering them reasonable conditions, and promised that he would persuade the king that he needed to be a friend to them.

The Hammer, having regard for the common good, agreed to all that Lysias urged. For the king granted every request on behalf of the Judeans which the Hammer delivered to Lysias in writing. The letter written to the Judeans by Lysias was like this:

Lysias to the Judeans, greeting:

John and Absalom, who were sent by you, have delivered your signed communication and have asked about the matters indicated therein. I have informed the king of everything that needed to be brought before him, and he has agreed to what was possible. If you will maintain your goodwill toward the government, I will endeavor for the future to help promote your welfare. Concerning these matters and their details, I have ordered these men and my representatives to confer with you.

Be well.

Year 148,[2] Corinthian Dios,[3] day 24.

The king's letter stated this:

King Antiochus to his brother Lysias, greeting,

Since our father has gone on to the gods, we desire that the subjects of the kingdom be undisturbed in caring for their own affairs. We understand that the Judeans would not submit to our father, or to be converted to the customs of the Greeks, but prefer their own way of living and ask that their own customs be allowed them. Therefore, since we choose that this nation should also be free from disturbance, our decision is that their temple be restored to them and that they live according to the customs of their ancestors. You will do well, therefore, to send a messenger to them, and grant them peace, that when they are told of our thoughts, they may be of good comfort, and forever be cheerful about their own affairs.

The letter of the king to the nation of Judea was like this:

King Antiochus to the senate of the Judeans and to the other Judahites, greeting,

If you farewell, we have our desire, and we are also in good health.

Menelaus informed us that you wish to return home

and look after your own affairs. Therefore, those who leave will have safe passage with security until the thirtieth day of Xanthikos,[4] will have our pledge of friendship and full permission. The Judahites will use their own kind of meats and laws, as before, and none of them will be in any manner be molested for things ignorantly done.

I have sent also Menelaus, that he may comfort you.

Be well.

Year 148, Xanthikos, day 15

The Romans also sent to them a letter containing these words:

Quintus Memmius and Titus Manlius, ambassadors of the Romans, send greeting to the Judeans,

As regards what Lysias the king's cousin has granted, we also recognize. But as to the matters which he decided are to be referred to the king, as soon as you have considered them, send someone promptly, so that we may make proposals appropriate for you. For we are on our way to Antioch. Therefore make haste and send some men, so that we may have your judgment.

Farewell.

Year 148, Xanthikos, day 15.

2nd Maccabees: Chapter 11 Notes

1 Codex Alexandrinus: agathon angelon (ΑΓΑΘΟΝ ΑΓΓΕΛΟΝ). Translation: brave messenger, noble messenger, lucky messenger

2 Year 148 of the Seleucid era was 164 BC.

3 Codex Alexandrinus: Dios Corinthiou (ΔΙΟΣΚΟΡΙΝΘΙΟΥ). Translation: Dios Corinthian

The reference is to the month of Dios on the Corinthian calendar. There was a month of Dios in the Aetolian calendar, used in Corinth and Aetolia, so this is likely the same calendar and month, which was the fourth month of the year. There was also a month of Dios on the Macedonian calendar, which was the first month of the year.

4 Codex Alexandrinus: Xanthicou (ΞΑΝΘΙΚΟΥ)

The month of Xanthikos was the sixth month in the Macedonian calendar.

2nd Maccabees: Chapter 12

When this agreement had been reached, Lysias returned to the king, and the Judeans went about their business. But some of the governors in various places, Timothy and Apollonius the son of Gennaeus,[1] as well as Hieronymus and Demophon, and in addition to these Nicanor the governor of Cyprus, would not let them live quietly and in peace.

The men of Jaffa also did a disrespectful act. They told the Judahites that lived among them to leave with their wives and children in the boats which they had prepared, as though they had meant them no hurt. Those who accepted it according to the common will of the city, desiring to live in peace and suspecting nothing, left on the boats, but when they had gone out into the deep no less than two hundred of them were drowned.

When Judas heard of the cruelty visited on his countrymen, he gave orders to his men to prepare. Calling upon righteous judge God, attacked the murderers of his brethren. He set fire to the harbor by night, and burned the boats, and massacred those who had taken refuge there. Then, because the city's gates were closed, he withdrew, intending to come again and root out the whole community of Jaffa. But when he heard that the men of Yavne[2] wanted to do the same thing to the Judahites that lived among them, he attacked the

Yavnites also at night, and set the port and navy on fire, so that the light of the fire was seen all the way to Jerusalem two 240 stadia away.

When they had traveled from there nine stadia in their journey towards Timothy, no fewer than 5000 Arabs and 500 cavalry from Arabia attacked him. After a hard fight, Judas and his men won the victory, through the help of God. The defeated nomads begged Judas to grant them pledges of friendship, promising to give him cattle and to help his people in all other ways. Judas, thinking that they might really be useful in many ways, agreed to make peace with them, and after receiving his pledges they departed to their tents.

He also built a siege tower to assault the fortified city of Caspin,[3] which was surrounded by walls, and inhabited by people from various countries. Those who were within, relying on the strength of the walls and on their supply of provisions, behaved most insolently toward Judas and his men, railing at them and even blaspheming and saying unholy things. Judas and his men, calling upon the great ruler of the world, who without battering-rams or engines of war overthrew Jericho in the days of Joshua, rushed furiously upon the walls. They captured the city through the will of God, and slaughtered untold numbers, so that the adjoining lake, a quarter of a mile wide, appeared to be running over with blood.

When they had traveled 750 stadia from there, they came to Charax,[4] to the Tobian Judahites.[5] They did not find Timothy in that region, for he had by then departed from the region without accomplishing anything, though in one place he had left a very strong garrison. Dositheus and Sosipater, who were captains under the Hammer, marched out and destroyed those whom Timothy had left in the stronghold, more than ten thousand men. The Hammer arranged his army into divisions, set men in command of the divisions, and rushed after Timothy, who had with him 120,000 infantry and 2,500 cavalry.

When Timothy heard Judas was coming, he sent the women and children and their property to a fortress called Carnion,[6] as it was hard to besiege and difficult to get to. When Judas' first division appeared, terror and fear came over the enemy at the manifestation to them of him who sees all things; and they rushed off in flight and were swept on, this way and that, so that often they were injured by their own men and pierced by the points of their swords. Judas was very diligent in chasing them and killed about 30,000 men. Timothy himself fell into the hands of Dositheus and Sosipater and their men. With great guile, he begged them to let him go in safety because he held the parents of most of them and the brothers of some and would show no consideration to them. After with many words he had confirmed his solemn promise to release them unharmed, they let him go, for the sake of saving their brothers.

Then Judas marched against Carnion and the temple of Atargatis,[7] and slaughtered 25,000 people. After he had put them to flight and then destroyed them, Judas moved his army to Ephron, a fortified city where Lysias lived along with a great multitude from various nations. Strong young men protected the walls and defended them well with a great number of machines and missiles, but when Judas and his army had called on the ruler whose power breaks the strength of his enemies, they captured the city and killed 25,000 of those who lived there.

From there they departed to Scythopolis,[8] which lies six hundred stadia from Jerusalem, but the Judahites who lived there testified that the Scythians[9] had dealt well with them and had treated them kindly in the time of their troubles, they thanked them and desired to remain friends with them.

They returned to Jerusalem, as the feast of the weeks was approaching. After the feast of Pentecost, they went out and attacked Gorgias the governor of Edom, who came out with 3,000 infantry and 400 cavalry. While they were fighting, some of the Judeans were killed, and Dositheos, one of Bakinor's army, who was a strong man on horseback, grabbed hold of Gorgias' coat and pulled him forcefully, and when he would have captured that cursed man alive, a Thracian horseman come along and knocked his head off his shoulders, and Gorgias fled to Marisa.[10] As Esdris and his men had been fighting for a long time and were weary, Judas called upon the Lord to show himself their ally and leader in the battle. In the language of their fathers, he raised the battle cry, with hymns, and then he charged against Gorgias' men when they were not expecting it, and put them to flight.

Then Judas assembled his army and went to the city of Adullam,[11] and on the seventh day was coming on, they purified themselves according to the custom, and they kept the sabbath there. On the next day, as by that time it had become necessary, Judas and his men went to take up the bodies of the fallen and to bring them back to lie with their kinsmen in the sepulchers of their fathers. In the coats of everyone that was killed, they found things consecrated to the idols of the Yavnites, which is forbidden to the Judahites by the law, and it was clear to all that this was why these men had fallen. So they all blessed the ways of the righteous Lord, who reveals the things that are hidden, and they turned to prayer, beseeching that the sin which had been committed might be wholly blotted out. And the noble Judas exhorted the people to keep themselves free from sin, for they had seen with their own eyes what had happened because of the sin of those who had fallen.

He also took up a collection, man by man, a total of 2,000 drachmas of silver, and sent it to Jerusalem to provide for a sin offering. In doing this he acted very well and honorably, taking account of the resurrection. For if he were not expecting that those who had fallen would rise again, it would have been superfluous and foolish to pray for the dead. If he was looking to the splendid reward that is laid up for those who fall asleep in godliness, it was a holy and pious thought. Therefore he made atonement for the dead, that they might be delivered from their sin.

2nd Maccabees: Chapter 12 Notes

1 Codex Alexandrinus: Apollônios o tou Gennaeou (ΑΠΟΛΛΩΝΙΟϹΟΤΟΥΓΕΝΝΑΙΟΥ). Translation: Apollonius the of Gennaeus

2 Codex Alexandrinus: Iamnia (ΙΑΜΝΕΙΑ)

- LXX 46: Iomnia (ιομνια)
- LXX 106: Iomenia (ιομενια)

The port city of Yavne, also called Yibna, Jabneel, Iamnia, and Yavnitesia, has been inhabited since the Hyksos Dynasty of Egyptian.

3 Codex Alexandrinus: Caspin (ΚΑϹΠΙΝ)

The location of this city is unknown today but theorized to be in northern Israel or southern Syria, and near the Jordan River. It is believed to be a different transliteration of the fortified city of Kasphor mentioned in 1st Maccabees. The name Caspin appears to be Persian in origin, meaning the city likely started out as an imperial Persian colony during the Persian rule of Judea. The name is based on the Persian name of the Caspian Sea: Qazvin, meaning the inhabitants likely started out as mercenaries from the lands surrounding the Caspian.

4 Codex Alexandrinus: Characa (ΧΑΡΑΚΑ)

5 Codex Alexandrinus: Toubinous Ioudaeous (ΤΟΥΒΕΙΝΟΥϹΙΟΥΔΑΙΟΥϹ)

- Codex Venetus: Toubianous Ioudaeous (ΤΟΥΒΙΑΝΟΥϹ ΙΟΥΔΑΙΟΥϹ)
- LXX 107: Toubêaenous Ioudaeous (τουβηαινουϲ ιουδαιουϲ)
- LXX 55: Toubiênous Ioudaeous (τουβιηνουϲ ιουδαιουϲ)
- LXX 58: Tôbêinous Ioudaeous (τωβηινουϲ ιουδαιουϲ)
- LXX 106: Bathanênous Ioudaeous (βαθανηνουϲ ιουδαιουϲ)
- LXX 46: Toubianous cae Ioudaeous (τουβιανουϲ και ιουδαιουϲ). Translation: Tobians and Judeans

The Tobian Judahites were likely the followers of the High Priest Tobiah, who Ezra the Scribe threw out of Jerusalem when he arrived in 351 BC. If so, they self-identified as Israelites, not Judahites, the same as the Egyptian Israelites did at the time, both groups being descended primarily from Samaritan Israelites. This suggests that the Hasmoneans were attempting to reunite the Israelites under the leadership of the Judahites, and in the process nationalized all Israelite peoples into the Judahite ethnic group.

6 Codex Alexandrinus: Carnion (ΚΑΡΝΙΟΝ)

- LXX 46: Cranion (κρανιον)

The location of this fortress is unknown today but theorized to be in southern Syria. It is believed to be a different transliteration of the fortified city of Karnaim mentioned in 1st Maccabees. The city of Karnaim was also mentioned in Genesis 14. Eusebius wrote that 'Karnaia' was a large town in Arabia, where tradition stated that Job had lived, and this is generally considered to be a reference to Carnion/Karnaim.

7 Codex Alexandrinus: Atergation (ΑΤΕΡΓΑΤΕΙΟΝ). Translation: Atargatis

- LXX 243: Ergation (εργατειον)

- LXX 311: Atargation Maccabaeos (αταργατιον μακκαβαιος). Translation: Atargatis of Maccabbees

- LXX 534: Atarbation (αταρβατιον)

- LXX 243: Apergation (απεργατιον)

- LXX 771: Acatergation (ακατεργατειον)

- Codex Bobbiensis: Atergation Iudas. Translation: Atargatis of Judas (or Judah)

Atargatis was the main goddess of Northern Syria at the time, also called Ataratheh, Baalat, Derketo, or Deasura.

8 Codex Alexandrinus: Scythopolitae (ϹΚΥΘΟΠΟΛΙΤΑΙ)

Scythopolis was a town in Galilee (modern northern Israel), occupied by Scythians after the fall of the Neo-Assyrian empire. The Scythians briefly occupied all of Assyria's holdings in Canaan, however, were defeated by the Egyptian army, and most Scythians returned to Scythia, north of the Black Sea. Some Scythians did manage to maintain control of Scythopolis until the Persians occupied the region twenty years later, and Scythopolis continued to be a Scythian city until the Greek era. Scythopolis is the site of the modern town of Beit She'an.

9 Codex Alexandrinus: Scythôn (ϹΚΥΘΩΝ)

The Scythians were an ancient Iranian people that lived in southern Russia and Central Asia during the Persian and Greek eras. They often fought in the Persian and Greek armies as mercenaries. They temporarily occupied Canaan, including Judah, after the collapse of the Neo-Babylonian Empire.

10 Codex Alexandrinus: Marisa (ΜΑΡΙϹΑ)

- LXX 311: Samarian (ϲαμαρσιαν)
- LXX 93: Samarian (ϲαμαριαν)
- LXX 106: Marissan (μαρισσαν)

Marisa is now the archaeological mound Tel Marisa in the Bet Guvrin-Marisa National Park in Israel, southwest of Jerusalem.

11 Codex Alexandrinus: Odollam (ΟΔΟΛΛΑΜ)

- LXX 71: Odolam (οδολαμ)
- LXX 534: Sodollan (σοδολλαν)
- LXX 58: Odollan (οδολλαν)
- LXX 771: Odolla (οδολλα)

Adullam was a town just north of Marisa. It was one of the ancient Canaanite holy-cities and the site of David's defeat of Goliath in 2nd Kingdoms.

2nd Maccabees: Chapter 13

In the year 149,[1] Judas was told that Antiochus Eupator was coming with a great force into Judea. With him traveled Lysias, his guard, and governor of his affairs, each of them commanding a Greek army of 110,000 infantry, and 5300 cavalry, and 22 elephants, and 300 chariots armed with hooks. Menelaus also joined them, and with great pretense encouraged Antiochus, not for the sake of his country's welfare but because he hoped to be made governor.

The King of kings aroused the anger of Antiochus against the scoundrel, and when Lysias informed him that this man was to blame for all the trouble, he ordered them to take him to Beroea,[2] and to put him to death by the method which is the custom in that place. There was in that place a tower of 50 cubits high, full of ashes, and it has a rim running around it which on all sides inclines precipitously into the ashes. There they all push to destruction any man guilty of sacrilege or notorious for other crimes. By such a fate it came about that Menelaus the lawbreaker died, without even burial in the earth, and this was eminently just, as he had committed many sins against the altar whose fire and ashes were sacred, he met his death in ashes.

Now the king came in barbarous arrogance to do far worse to the Judeans than had been done in his father's time. When Judas found out, he commanded the multitude to call on the Lord night and day, so that if at any other time he would help them, as they were at the point of being forced from following their law, and from their country, and the holy temple, and not allow the people that had just begun to be restored a little to be in subjected to the blasphemous Gentiles. When they had all done this together and implored the merciful the Lord with weeping and fasting, and lying flat on the ground for three days, Judas, having encouraged them, commanded they should prepare.

Judas, being separated from the elders, decided that before the king's army could enter into Judea and capture the city, to go out and decide the matter by fighting with the help of the Lord. Once he had committed all to the Creator of the world and encouraged his soldiers to fight bravely, even to death, for the laws, the temple, the city, the country, and the commonwealth, he camped by Modi'in.[3] After giving the password to those who were with him, "God's victory,"[4] and with a picked force of the bravest young men, he went in into the king's camp at night and killed about 2,000 men in the camp, and the master of the elephants and those who were with him. They filled the camp with fear and commotion and departed with great success.

This happened, just as day was dawning because the Lord's help protected him.

When the king had seen the bravery of the Judeans, he set as policy capturing the strongholds and marched on Beth-Zur, which was a stronghold of the Judeans, but he lost and was put to flight, as Judas had told those who were in it what was necessary. But Rhodocus, who was in the Judeans' army, gave secret information to the enemy. He was searched for, caught, and put in prison.

The king negotiated with those in Beth-Zur the second time, and they shook hands and departed. He fought with Judas and was defeated, and then heard that Philip, who had been left in charge of his affairs in Antioch was desperately ill and confused, and so negotiated with the Judeans, submitted himself, and swore to all equal conditions, agreed to them, and offered a sacrifice, honored the temple, and dealt kindly with the temple. He accepted the Hammer and made him the principal governor from Acre[5] to Gerar.[6] He traveled to Acre, where the people were angry about the agreements, and raged as they wanted to end the agreements. Lysias sat on the judgment seat, and said as much as could be in defense of the cause, persuaded, pacified, made peace with them, and returned to Antioch.

This was how the king came and left.

2nd Maccabees: Chapter 13 Notes

1 Year 149 of the Seleucid era was 163 BC.

2 Codex Alexandrinus: Beroean (ΒΕΡΟΙΑΝ)

- LXX 71: Berenoean (βερενοιαν)
- LXX 107: Berrhoean (βερροιαν)

Beroia is the ancient name for Veria in Greek Macedonia, one of the most important cities in the ancient Greek civilization, as the second most important city in ancient Macedonia under the Argead Dynasty of Alexander the Great.

3 Codex Alexandrinus: Môdiim (ΜΩΔΙΕΙΜ)

- Codex Venetus: Môdiin (ΜΩΔΙΕΙΝ)
- LXX 58: Modin (Μοδειν)
- LXX 130: Modi (Μοδει)
- LXX 52: Môdeim (Μωδεειμ)
- LXX 93: Môdaem (Μωδαειμ)
- LXX 55: Môdein (Μωδεειν)
- LXX 771: Môdesin (Μωδεσιν)

The village of Modi'in (מודיעין) was also recorded in the Talmud, although its location is unclear.

4 Codex Alexandrinus: theou nicên (ΘΕΟΥΝΙΚΗΝ). Translation: god's victory

- Codex Venetus: theou Nicês (θεου νικης). Translation: god Nike (or victory)
- LXX 19: theou Nicê (θεου ΝΙΚΗ). Translation: god Nike (or victory)

5 Codex Alexandrinus: Ptolemaedos (ΠΤΟΛΕΜΑΙΔΟΣ). Translation: Translation: Ptolemais, Acre

The city of Acre (عكّا / עַכּוֹ), in northern modern Israel, was known as Antiochia Ptolemaes (Αντιόχεια Πτολεμαΐς), and simplified as Ptolemaes (Πτολεμαΐς) during the Hellenic era. The earlier Canaanite name was Ôk (𐤏𐤊), which the Greeks had transliterated as Acê (Ἀκη) before conquering the region. As the Ptolemais is not commonly used anymore, the ancient and modern name of Acre is used.

6 Codex Alexandrinus: Gennêrôn (ΓΕΝΝΗΡΩΝ)

- Codex Venetus: Gerrhênôn (ΓΕΡΡΗΝΩΝ)
- LXX 107: Gerrhêgôn (Γερρηγων)
- LXX 542: Gerdênôn (Γερδηνων)
- LXX 46: Gerênôn (Γερηνων)
- LXX 55: Gerarênôn (Γεραρηνων)

This reference has caused some confusion over the centuries. The word refers to the people from Gerrha, the Greek name for the people in modern Saudi Arabia's Eastern Province, along the western coast of the Persian Gulf, as well as the largest city in the region. Antiochus V Eupator's great-grandfather Antiochus III the Great had marched against the city of Gerrha in 205 and 204 BC, but the rulers of the city had offered a tribute of 500 silver talents, and so he withdrew without conquering it into his empire. If Eupator was recognizing Judas' governorship of everything from Acre on the Mediterranean Sea, to Gerrha on the Persian Gulf, it implies he was trying to secure his southern border by recognizing the Judeans right to rule whatever they could conquer in Arabia.

The Syrian Orthodox church has historically claimed it was a reference to the people of Gezer, an ancient city between Jerusalem and Acre. This assumes the Greek word is a translation error, when the book was translated into Greek from Aramaic. This is consistent with the Syriac Orthodox view that the books of the Septuagint were translated from Aramaic texts before the Hebrew translations were made. The problem with this interpretation, is that the territory Judas was being granted was very small, and did not include either Jerusalem or Modi'in.

Another theory is that the reference was the people of Gerar, a settlement believed to have been in the modern Wadi Sheri'a, in southern modern Israel, east of the Palestinian Gaza Strip. This theory makes the most sense geographically, as the settlement in question would have been near the Egyptian border, which would have created a border between the Seleucid's and Ptolemy's realms. In this case, the Greek translator would have not understood the reference and substituted the more famous land in Eastern Arabia. As this seems like the most probable interpretation, it is the one followed in this interpretation.

2nd Maccabees: Chapter 14

Three years later, Judas was informed that Demetrius,[1] the son of Seleucus, had invaded through the harbor of Tripoli with a great army and navy, and had seized the country and killed Antiochus and Lysias his guard.

Alcimus, who had formerly been high priest but had wilfully defiled himself in the times of separation, realized that there was no way for him to be safe or to have access again to the sacred altar, went to King Demetrius in the year 151,[2] presenting to him a gold crown, and a palm, and besides these some of the customary olive branches from the temple.

Finding the opportunity to further his foolish enterprise, and being invited into counsel by Demetrius, and asked how the Judeans were affected, and what they intended, he answered, "Those of the Judeans that are called Hasideans,[3] whose captain is Judas the Hammer, are keeping up war and stirring up sedition, and will not let the kingdom attain tranquility. Therefore I, being deprived of my forefathers' honor, I mean the high priesthood, have now come here. First, because I am genuinely concerned for the interests of the king, and second because I have regard also for my fellow citizens. For through the folly of those whom I have mentioned our whole nation is now in no small misfortune. Therefore, king, knowing all these things, be thoughtful for our country and our nation which is hard-pressed nation with the gracious kindness which you show to all. For as long as Judas lives, impossible for the government to find peace."

This was no sooner said to him, that others of the king's friends, who were hostile to Judas, further incensed Demetrius. Calling Nicanor, who had been master of the elephants, and making him governor over Judea, he sent him out, with an order to kill Judas, and to scatter those who were with him, and to make Alcimus high priest of the great temple. The Gentiles throughout Judea, who had fled before Judas, flocked to join Nicanor, thinking that the misfortunes and calamities of the Judeans would mean prosperity for themselves.

When the Judeans heard Nicanor was coming, and the gathering of the Gentiles, they sprinkled dust upon their heads and prayed to him who established his own people forever and always upholds his own heritage by manifesting himself. At the command of the leader, they set out from there immediately and engaged them in battle at a village called Dessaou. Simon, Judas' brother, had attacked Nicanor but was somewhat disturbed by the sudden silence of his enemies.

When Nicanor heard of the bravery of those who were with Judas, and the courageousness that they fought for their country, dared not test it with his sword, and so he sent Posidonius, Theodotus, and Mattathias, to make peace. When the terms had been fully considered, and the leader had informed the people, and it had appeared that they were of one mind, they agreed to the covenant. They appointed a day to meet together by themselves, and when the day came, and stools were set out for them, Judas stationed armed men in convenient places, in case some treachery should suddenly be undertaken by the enemies, however, they had a peaceful conference.

Nicanor stayed on in Jerusalem and did nothing out of the way, but dismissed the flocks of people that had gathered. He would not willingly have Judas thrown out of his sight, for he loved the man from his heart and he begged him also to take a wife and to father children, so he married, was peaceful, and experienced this life.

When Alcimus noticed their goodwill for one another, he took the covenant that had been made and went to Demetrius. He told him that Nicanor was disloyal to the government, for he had appointed that conspirator against the kingdom, Judas, to be his successor. The king became excited and, provoked by the false accusations of that depraved man, wrote to Nicanor, stating that he was displeased with the covenant and commanding him to send the Hammer to Antioch as a prisoner without delay.

When Nicanor heard this, he was very confused and was concerned that the articles which were agreed on would be nullified while the man was not at fault. Since it was not possible to oppose the king, he watched for an opportunity to accomplish this by a stratagem. When the Hammer saw that Nicanor was more austere in his dealings with him and was meeting him more rudely than had been his custom, concluded that this austerity did not spring from the best motives. So he gathered many of his men and went into hiding from Nicanor. When the latter became aware that he had been cleverly outwitted by the man, he went to the great and holy temple while the priests were offering the customary sacrifices, and commanded them to hand the man over.

When they swore that they could not tell where the man was, he stretched out his right hand towards the temple, and this oath, "If you will not deliver me Judas as a prisoner, I will level this temple of God to the ground, and I will rip down the altar, and erect a temple to Sabaoth."

After these words, he departed, and the priests lifted their hands towards Shamayim and implored he who was always a defender of their nation, saying "Lord of all, who needs nothing, you were pleased that there was a temple for your habitation among us, sacred Lord, protect the asbestos[4] that was recently cleansed and stop every unrighteous mouth."

Razis, one of the elders of Jerusalem was there and denounced by Nicanor as he was a lover of his countrymen, and a man of very good report, who for his kindness was called a father of the Judeans. In the earlier times, when they did not mix themselves with the Greeks, he had been accused of being Judahite, and boldly jeopardized his body and life vehemently for the religion of the Judahites.

Nicanor, wishing to exhibit the enmity which he had for the Judeans, sent more than 500 soldiers to arrest him, as he thought by capturing him, it would hurt the Judeans greatly. When the troops were about to capture the tower and were forcing the door of the courtyard, they ordered that fire be brought and the doors burned. Being surrounded, Razis fell upon his own sword, preferring to die nobly rather than to fall into the hands of sinners and suffer outrages unworthy of his noble birth. In the heat of the struggle, he did not hit exactly, and the crowd was now rushing in through the doors. He bravely ran up on the wall, and manfully threw himself down into the crowd. But as they quickly drew back, a space opened and he fell in the middle of the empty space.

Nevertheless, there was still breath within him, and being inflamed with anger, he rose up, and though his blood gushed out like spouts of water. His wounds were terrible, yet he ran through the middle of the group and standing on a steep rock when most of his blood was gone, he ripped out his bowels, and threw them with both hands onto the crowd, and call on the lord of life[5] and breath to restore him again.

This was how he died.

2nd Maccabees: Chapter 14 Notes

1 Codex Alexandrinus: Dêmêtrion (ΔΗΜΗΤΡΙΟΝ). Translation: Demetrius

Between 161 and 150 BC, Demetrius I Soter was the ruler of the Seleucid Empire based in Syria.

2 Year 151 of the Seleucid era was 161 BC.

3 Codex Alexandrinus: Asidaeoe (ΑϹΙΔΑΙΟΙ). General translation: Hasideans

The Hasideans were a Judahite sect that were mentioned in the various books of the Maccabees, but nowhere else. Some scholars have theorized that they may be the precursors to the Pharisees or the Essenes. In 1st Maccabees, Judas was not listed as a Hasidean, but they did join his group.

4 Codex Alexandrinus: amianton (ΑΜΙΑΝΤΟΝ). Translation: asbestos

Asbestos was commonly used in the fire temples of the Zoroastrians as materials made from asbestos could be cleaned by placing them in fire. This text indicates the Judahites were using asbestos as well in the Second Temple.

5 Codex Alexandrinus: despozonta tês zôês (ΔΕCΠΟΖΟΝΤΑΤΗCΖΩΗC). Translation: Lord of life

The Greeks translated the name of the god Lahem, the Canaanite and Israelite god of life, bread, and meat, as Zôn, (Zῶν), Zōē (Ζωή), or Zôês (Ζωῆς) depending on context. Some Greeks also called Zeus: Zen (Ζην), meaning 'life,' as he was believed to be the source of all life. As Razis was certainly not worshiping Zeus, the translation of 'lord of life' in used.

2nd Maccabees: Chapter 15

When Nicanor heard that Judas and his men were in the region of Samaria, he made plans to attack them on the sabbath day as it would not be dangerous. The Judahites that were forced to go with him said, "Don't destroy them so cruelly and barbarously, but honor the day, which he who sees all things, has honored with sacredness above all other days."

The triple-cursed wretch asked if there was even a King of the sky[1] who had commanded the keeping of the sabbath day. They replied, "It is the Lord of Life[2] himself, the King of the sky, who ordered us to observe the seventh day!"

Then he replied, "I am a lord also, on earth, and I command you to take up arms and finish the king's business," but they would not do it.

This Nicanor in his utter boastfulness and arrogance had determined to erect a public monument of victory over Judas and his men. The Hammer always had confidence that the Lord would help him, and encouraged his people to not fear the nations coming against them, but to remember the help that they had received in former times from Shamayim, and now to look for the victory which the omnipotent would give them. Comforting them from the law and the prophets, and reminding them of the battles that they won before, he made them more cheerful.

Once he had stirred up their emotions, he gave them their orders, reminding them of the lies of the heathens and their breaking of oaths. He armed each of them not so much with confidence in shields and spears as with the inspiration of brave words, and he cheered them all by relating a dream, a sort of vision, which was worthy of belief. This was his vision:

> Onias, who had been a high priest, a virtuous and a good man, of modest bearing and gentle manner, one who spoke fittingly and had been trained from childhood in all that belongs to excellence, was praying with outstretched hands for the whole body of the Judahites. After this, another man appeared with gray hairs, who was glorious, and who was wonderful and majestic. Then Onias said, "This is a lover of the brothers, who prays much for the people, and for the sacred city, Jeremiah the prophet of God."
>
> Jeremiah stretched out his right hand and gave to Judas a golden sword, and as he gave it he addressed him thus, "Take this holy sword, a gift from God, with which you will strike down your adversaries."

So being well comforted by the words of Judas, which were very good, and able to stir them up to valor, and to encourage the hearts of the young men, they determined not to set up camp, but courageously to attack them and bravely to decide the matter in battle, because the city and the sanctuary and the temple were in danger. They did not care for their wives, children, brothers, or parents, but cared only for the temple. Those that were in the city did not care in the least, being troubled by the conflict overseas.

When all was prepared, and the enemies were ready to advance, and the army was set in formation, and the beasts conveniently spaced, and the cavalry set at the wings, Maccabees saw the coming of the multitude, and the various preparations of armor, and the fierceness of the beasts, and stretched out his hands towards Shamayim, and called on the Lord that works wonders, knowing that victory comes not by arms, but even as it seems good to him, but gives it to those that are worthy.

He prayed, "Lord, you sent your messenger in the time of Hezekiah king of Judea, and killed 185,000 in the army of Sennacherib. Now, King Shamayim, send a great messenger in front of us to cause fear and horror to them. Through the might of your arm let those be stricken with terror, who come against your sacred people to blaspheme."

Then Nicanor and those who were with him came forward with trumpets and songs, but Judas and his company countered the enemies with mantras and prayer. So that fighting with their hands, and praying to God in their hearts, they killed no less than 35,000 men, for through the appearance of God they were greatly cheerful. When the battle was done, they returning with joy, as they knew that Nicanor lay dead in his harness. They made a great celebration and a noise, praising the omnipotent in their own language.

Judas, who was ever the chief defender of the citizens both in body and mind, and who continued his love towards his countrymen all his life, commanded to cut off Nicanor's head, and his hand with his arms, and bring them to Jerusalem. When he was there, and called those of his nation together, and set the priests before the altar, he sent for those who were of the tower, and showed them vile Nicanor's head, and the hand of that blasphemer, which proudly bragged he had stretched out against the holy temple of the omnipotent. When he had cut out the tongue of that ungodly Nicanor, he commanded that they should give pieces of it to the birds, and hung the reward of his madness before the temple.

Every man praised Shamayim, the glorious the Lord, saying, "Blessed is he that has kept his own temple undefiled."

He also hanged Nicanor's head on the tower, an obvious and manifest sign to all, of the aid of the Lord. They all decided with a common decree to in no case to let that day pass without remembering but to celebrate the thirtieth day of the twelfth month (which in the Syrian language is called Adar)[3] the day before Mordecai's day.

So it ended with Nicanor, and from that time on the Hebrews had the city in their control. Here I will end it. If I have done well, and as it is a fitting story, it is what I desired, and if it is short, that is what I meant as well. For as it is hurtful to drink wine or water alone, and as wine mingled with water is pleasant, and delights the taste, even so, finely framed speech delights the ears of those that read the story.

The end.

2nd Maccabees: Chapter 15 Notes

1 Codex Alexandrinus: ouranô dynastês (ΟΥΡΑΝΩ ΔΥΝΑСΤΗС). Translation: sky lord (or king)

Dynastês (Δυνάστης) was an epithet of Zeus and Poseidon by those that worshiped them as the supreme god of the Greeks. In this context, it was likely 'King of the sky' in the original Aramaic source text, as ouranô (οὐρανῷ) was singular for of 'sky' in Greek.

2 Codex Alexandrinus: cyrios zôn (ΚΥΡΙΟСΖΩΝ). Translation: Lord Life

The Greeks translated the name of the god Lahem, the Canaanite and Israelite god of life, as Zôn, (Ζῶν), Zōē (Ζωή), or Zôês (Ζωῆς) depending on context. Some Greeks also called Zeus Zen (Ζην), meaning 'life,' as he was believed to be the source of all life.

3 Codex Alexandrinus: Adar (ΑΔΑΡ). Translation: Adar

Adar is the twelfth month in the Hebrew calendar. The Hebrew Calendar is lunisolar, and so the months move somewhat in comparison to the Gregorian Calendar, and therefore the equivalent could be anywhere between February and April, depending on the year. However, Adar falls before the northern winter solstice, and therefore generally falls in March.

The fact that the scribal note refers to the name of the month in the Syrian language (Συριακη Φωνη), confirms that the Greek translation was made from Aramaic, not Hebrew, as the Greeks name for the Arameans was 'Syrians.'

3rd Maccabees: Chapter 1

When Philopator[1] learned from those who returned, that Antiochus[2] had re-exerted his dominance over the lands he ruled, he sent orders to all his infantry and cavalry, took his sister Arsinoe,[3] and marched all the way to Rafah,[4] where Antiochus and his armies were camped. Theodotus, who intended to carry out his plans, took with him the bravest of the soldiers who had previously been trusted to him by Ptolemy, and sneaked into the tent of Ptolemy at night, to kill him and end the war. But Dositheus, the son of Drimylus, a Judean by birth who rejected the laws and observances of his country, hid Ptolemy away and had another man sleep in his bed in the tent, who died in the place of the king.

A fierce battle then broke out. As the men of Antiochus were winning, Arsinoe went up and down the ranks constantly, crying with untidy hair, begging the soldiers to fight bravely for themselves, their children, and wives, and promised that if they were victorious, she would give them each two minas[5] of gold. In time, their enemies were defeated in combat and many of them were captured as prisoners. After winning the battle, the king then decided to travel to the neighboring cities, and encourage them. By doing this, and by making donations to their temples, he inspired his subjects with confidence.

The Judeans sent some of their council and their elders to him to take him gifts of greetings, and to congratulate him on what had happened, and he was all the more eager to visit them as soon as possible. After he had arrived in Jerusalem, he offered sacrifice to the Supreme God[6] and made thank-offerings and did what was fitting for the sacred place. Then, upon entering the place and being impressed by its excellence and its beauty, he wondered at the orderly arrangements of the temple, and he considered entering the sanctuary itself. When they told him that this was not allowed, not even members of their own nation were allowed to enter, nor even all of the priests, but only the high priest who was above all, and he only once a year, the king was by no means persuaded.

Even after the law had been read to him, he did not stop claiming that he should be allowed to enter, saying, "Even if other men are deprived of this honor, I shouldn't be!"

He asked why, when he entered every other temple, no one there had stopped him.

He was thoughtlessly answered by someone, "That he was wrong to brag of this."

"Well, since I have done this," he said, "Why shouldn't I at least enter, whether they wish it or not?"

The priests fell down in their sacred vestments imploring the Supreme God to come and help in time of need, and to avert the violence of the fierce aggressor, and when they filled the temple with crying and tears, then those who were outside in the city were scared and rushed out without knowing what was happening. Virgins, who had been locked up within their rooms, came out with their mothers, throwing dirt and ashes on their heads, and filling the streets with screaming. Women recently married, left their bridal rooms and the peace fitting them, and ran around in the city in a disorderly manner. New-born babes were abandoned by their mothers or the nurses who waited on them, some here, some there, in houses or in fields. These people swarmed to the supreme[7] temple in and fervor that could not be stopped.

Various prayers were offered up by those that assembled, because of what the king was profanely plotting. In addition, the bolder of the citizens would not tolerate the completion of his plans or the fulfillment of his intended purpose. They shouted to their fellows to take arms and die courageously for the ancestral law, and created a considerable disturbance in the sacred place, and being barely restrained by the old men and the elders, they resorted to the same posture of supplication as the others.

The elders who surrounded the king struggled in many ways to change his haughty mind from the plans he had made. But he, in his arrogance, listened to nothing, and began now to approach, determined to bring his plan to conclusion. When those who were around him observed this, they turned, together with our people, to call upon him who has all power to defend them in the present trouble and not to overlook this unlawful and haughty deed. The continuous, vehement, and concerted cry of the crowds resulted in an immense uproar, for it seemed that not only the men but also the walls and the whole earth around echoed, because indeed all at that time preferred death to the profanation of the place.

3rd Maccabees: Chapter 1 Notes

1 Codex Alexandrinus: Philopatôr (ΦΙΛΟΠΑΤΩΡ).
Translation: Philopator

There was only one Egyptian king known as Philopator, who was married to his sister named Arsinoe, and who fought a king named Antiochus: Ptolemy IV Philopator, who ruled the Ptolemy's empire between 221 and 204 BC. Ptolemy IV Philopator's sister and wife was Arsinoe III, and during their reign, Antiochus III of the Seleucid Empire invaded the Ptolemy's Empire and occupied Coele-Syria, which appears to be what the book is referring to, which would place the opening events of the book in the year 217 BC, around 50 years before Judas the Hammer's rebellion.

2 Codex Alexandrinus: Antiochou (ΑΝΤΙΟΧΟΥ).
Translation: Antiochus

In 221 BC, Antiochus III the Great launched an invasion of the Ptolemys' Empire and recaptured Coele-Syria from the Ptolemys. He also conquered most of Alexander's former Empire, including Thrace, most of Anatolia, the Armenian Highlands, and most of the territory of modern Iran, Afghanistan, Pakistan, Tajikistan, Turkmenistan, and Uzbekistan, and then around 200 BC, Judea.

3 Codex Alexandrinus: Arsinoên (ΑΡCΙΝΟΗΝ)

- LXX 381: Arsenoên (αρσενοην)

Arsinoe III Philopator was the Queen of Egypt and the dominions of the Ptolemys' Empire between 220 and 204 BC. She was married to her brother King Ptolemy IV Philopator.

4 Codex Alexandrinus: Raphian (ΡΑΦΙΑΝ)

- LXX 55: Rhaphian (ραφιαν)

Rafah is a town in the modern Palestinian Gaza Strip near the modern Egyptian border. At the time it was part of the Greek Kingdom of Egypt, as was Judea. The Battle of Rafah was fought on June, 22 to 27, 217 BC, between the armies of Ptolemy IV Philopator, king and pharaoh of Ptolemaic Egypt, and Antiochus III the Great of the Seleucid Empire. It was one of the largest battles fought in the Classical era, and the largest battle ever fought between the Greek Kingdoms. According to the Greek historian Polybius, Ptolemy had 70,000 infantry, 5,000 cavalry, and 73 war elephants, while Antiochus 62,000 infantry, 6,000 cavalry, and 102 war elephants. Ultimately Ptolemy was victorious, which secured Coele-Syria and Judea as provinces of the Ptolemy's Empire until the Battle of Panium in 200 BC.

5 Codex Alexandrinus: mnâs (ΜΝΑϹ). Translation: minas

A mina was 100 drachmas. The Greek name was derived from the Aramaic term mnh (מנה). The drachma was the equivalent of 4.3 grams.

6 Codex Alexandrinus: megistô theô (ΜΕΓΙϹΤΩΘΕΩ) Translation: biggest god

- LXX 52: megalô theô (μεγάλῳ θεῷ) Translation: big god

7 Codex Alexandrinus: panypertaton (ΠΑΝΥΠΕΡΤΑΤΟΝ) Translation: supreme, all-powerful

3rd Maccabees: Chapter 2

Now the high priest Simon bowed his knees near the sacred temple, spread out his hands in reverence, and made the following prayer:

"Lord Ba'al,[1] king of the skies[2] and master of all creation, sacred among the sacred, King, almighty, hear us who are oppressed by a wicked and profane one, who elates in his confidence and strength.

It is you, the creator of all, dominant power, who is a righteous governor, and judge all who act with pride and insolence. It was you who destroyed the former workers of unrighteousness, including the Gigantes,[3] who trusted in their strength and toughness, by covering them with a measureless flood.

It was you who made the Sodomites, those workers of exceeding iniquity, men notorious for their vices, an example to later generations when you covered them with fire and brimstone.

You made your power known when you caused the bold Pharaoh, the enslaver of Israel, to pass through many and diverse plagues. You rolled the depths of the sea over him when he pursued in chariots with a multitude of followers and gave safe passage to those who put their trust in you. I know your great state! These saw and felt the works of your hands, and praised you the omnipotent.

You, King,[4] when you created the illimitable and measureless earth, choose this city, and made this place sacred to your name, even though you need nothing. You glorified it with your illustrious presence, after constructing it to the glory of your great and honorable name. You promised, out of love to the people of Israel, that should we fall away from you, and become afflicted, and then come to this house and pray, you would hear our prayer. You are faithful and true. When you often aided our fathers who were hard-pressed, and in low estate, and delivered them out of great dangers, see now sacred king, how through our many and great sins we are made low, and made subject to our enemies, and have become weak and powerless.

We are in this low condition, and this bold and profane man seeks to dishonor this your sacred temple, consecrated out of the earth to the name of your majesty. Your living place, Shamayim of the skies,[5] is indeed unapproachable by men. But since it seemed good to you to exhibit your glory among your people Israel, you sanctified this place. Don't punish us because of the uncleanness of their men, or chastise us because of their profanity, in case the lawless ones should boast in their rage, and exult in great pride, saying, 'We have trampled through the sacred temple, as idolatrous temples are trampled through.'

Erase our iniquities, and do away with our errors, and show your compassion in this hour. Let your mercy quickly appear to us. Grant us peace, that the thrown down and brokenhearted may praise you with their voices."

At that time, the all-seeing God,[6] all-father, and sacred of sacred, listened to the prayer, and scourged the man greatly, who was puffed up with scorn and insolence. Shaking him to and fro like a reed in the wind, he threw him to the pavement, powerless, with paralyzed limb, and by a righteous judgment deprived him of the faculty of speech. His friends and bodyguards, observing the swift punishment which had suddenly befallen him, were struck with great terror, and afraid that he would die, and quickly removed him.

When, after some time, he had returned to being himself, this severe check caused no repentance within him, but he departed with bitter threats. He traveled to Egypt, and grew worse in wickedness with his drunken companions, who were lost to all goodness, and not satisfied with countless acts of impiety, his audacity also increased in that he made evil reports there, and many of his friends, watching his purpose closely, joined in furthering his desires. His purpose was to indict a public stigma on our race, and so he erected a column at the tower and engraved the following on it:

> Entrance to the temple is refused to all those who will not sacrifice, all the Judeans are to be registered like other people. Those who resist are to be forcibly seized and put to death. Those who are registered have to be marked on their persons by the ivy-leaf symbol of Dionysus,[7] and to be set apart with these limited rights.

In order that he was not seen as hating them all, he had it written underneath that if any of them should decide to join the community of those initiated in the rites, they should have equal rights with the Alexandrians. Some of those who were in the city, therefore, abhorring any approach to the city of piety, unhesitatingly gave in to the king and expected to gain some great honor from future connections with him. A nobler spirit, however, prompted the majority to cling to their religious observances and by paying taxes so they might live unmolested, these wanted to escape the registration, cheerfully looking forward to future aid, they abhorred their own apostates, considering them to be national enemies, and banning them from the normal social interactions.

3rd Maccabees: Chapter 2 Notes

1 Codex Alexandrinus: Cyrie Cyrie (ΚΥΡΙΕΚΥΡΙΕ).
Translation: Lord Lord

This term was also used in the Book of Ezekiel, and the quote of Nehemiah from the unknown source found in 2nd Maccabees, which suggests the term was in widespread use before the Hasmonean Dynasty. The term Lord Lord, could only have been translated from Adon Ba'al (𐡀𐡃𐡍 𐡁𐡏𐡋𐡀) in the Aramaic texts the Greeks translated Ezekiel from, as both adon and ba'al translate as 'lord.' As this letter has Aramaic loanwords, and the Judeans and Egyptian Israelites corresponded in Aramaic, it is logical to conclude the letter was written in Aramaic, and, therefore, it included the term Lord Ba'al.

2 Codex Alexandrinus: basileu tôn ouranô (ΒΑCΙΛΕΥ ΤΩΝ ΟΥΡΑΝΩΝ). Translation: king of the skies

- LXX 74: basileus tôn ouranôn (βασιλευσ τοον ουρανοον)

The term 'king of the skies' would have been translated from 'mlk hšmyn' (𐡌𐡋𐡊 𐡄𐡔𐡌𐡉𐡍), meaning king of Shamayim, the Israelite name for the vaulted sky above the flat earth, as well as a proper name or title for its ruling god.

3 Codex Alexandrinus: Gigantes (ΓΙΓΑΝΤΕC)

The Greeks translated the term as Gigantes, a tribe of demigods that fought the gods in the Gigantomachy, the war between the Gigantes and gods. In the earliest depictions, they were fully human, however, in the Classical Era, they started being depicted as having snakes for legs, like the Gnostic depictions of Iaw. The Romans conflated the Gigantes with the Titans, and so the Latin word Giant became synonymous with something that's very large, however, the Greek translators could not have intended that meaning.

The reference to the Gigantes being destroyed in a flood, is clearly a reference to the Gigantes in the Septuagint's Genesis chapter 6, who were destroyed in Noah's flood. In Masoretic Genesis, the term used for Gigantes was Nefilim (נְּפִלִ֖ים). While most Christian translations of both the Septuagint and the Masoretic Text translate this word as 'giant,' neither the Greek nor Hebrew terms mean 'giant.'

The Hebrew term is accepted as meaning 'fallen,' and, the term is likely related to the Aramaic name for the Orion constellation, Npylyȧ (𐡍𐡐𐡉𐡋𐡉𐡀). The term Nefilim (נְּפִלִ֖ים) likely originated as a description of the Orionid meteor shower that happens each year, between October 2 and November 7, as the Earth passes through the debris left by Halley's Comet. Peaks of 70 meteors a minute have been recorded, and these meteors fall from the region of the sky where Orion's upstretched arm is located.

The region of the sky where the constellations Orion and Lepus are located was known as the asterism Sȧh (𓋴𓂝𓅜𓎛𓇼) in the religion of the Egyptian Old Kingdom, which represented Sah, the father of the gods. The Akkadian version of Sah was Ān (𒀭), who was also the father of the gods, and represented by the stars of Orion. The name Orion (Ωριων) was derived from the Akkadian term úruān (𒌷𒊒𒀭), meaning 'Light of An,' as the early Greeks learned of the asterism from the Canaanites that had settled in Cyprus. The name Uranus (Οὐρανός) was likewise derived from the Akkadian term ùruanna (𒌨𒊒𒀭𒈾), meaning 'roof sky stone,' which was also the Greek interpretation of Uranus, as the ceiling above the flat Earth.

As the Greeks neither translated nor transliterated the term Nephilim in Genesis, it is unlikely it was in the Aramaic text they translated, suggesting whatever term they found in the text was either conceptually or phonetically similar to the Greek Gigas (Γίγας). A more detailed version of this story appears in the Books of Enoch, where the term was translated into Ge'ez as ôyryn (ዐየረየነ) meaning 'watchers' or 'guardians'. A similar term, egirô (εγείρω) meaning 'awaken,' appears to have been used in the Greek translation of Secrets of Enoch, which was later transliterated into Old Slavonic as Grigori (ⰃⰓⰋⰃⰑⰓⰋ). This indicates the original term was likely something that meant 'watcher' and sounded like Gigas, and given the connections to Mount Hermon, the Orion constellation, and thereby the god An, and his children the anAnuna (𒀭𒀀𒉣𒈾), which were also mentioned in the verse in Cosmic Genesis, the original term in the Cuneiform text was almost certainly Igigi (𒅆𒄀𒄀).

The Igigi were described as being a group of lesser gods that rebelled against the rule of the anAnuna, which translates as 'sons of the deitysky,' and their name was the homophone of the Akkadian word igigi (𒀭𒅆𒄀) meaning to 'observe and measure.'

4 Codex Alexandrinus: basileu (ΒΑCΙΛΕΥ). Translation: king

• LXX 19: basileus (uλσιλбυσ)

In this verse, Simon is using the term king, which in Aramaic was mlkå (𐡀𐡊𐡋𐡌) as a name, the same way the Moabites referred to their God mlk (𐤊𐤋𐤌), generally transliterated into English as Moloch. Mlk, the king of the gods, was commonly worshiped throughout Canaan, and based on the writing of Baruch, was believed to have been the god of Moses in the time of Jeremiah. As it was a title, King, it could have been applied to any god, in this verse, Simon appears to use it as a title for Lord Ba'al. Given the reaction of El to Simon's prayer, it seems likely the author meant that he was praying to Moloch, not El.

5 Codex Alexandrinus: ouranos tou ouranou (ΟΥΡΑΝΟC ΤΟΥΟΥΡΑΝΟΥ). Translation: sky of skies, Shamayim of Shamayim (Canaanite and Israelite sky god).

Shamayim was both the personification of the sky in the Israelite religion, and the vaulted sky where the god Shamayim was believed to live. In this verse, Simon is calling on Shamayim (the god) in Shamayim (the vaulted sky).

6 Codex Alexandrinus: theos (ΘΕΟC). Translation: god

In this verse, the Greek word theos (Θεὸς) is being used as a proper name, not a title, which suggests the original term used was El, the Canaanite, Israelite, and Aramean name of the creator god, who left the word to his children the Elohim to rule. The reference to his being the all-father (Προπάτωρ) in the sentence confirms that he is the progenitor of the gods.

7 Codex Alexandrinus: Dionysô (ΔΙΟΝΥCΩ)

- LXX 19: Dionysou (Διονύσου)

Dionysus was the Greek name of the Judean god Sabaoth (Σαβαώθ). Dionysus was also the Greek name of the Phrygian and Thracian god Sabazios (ΣΑΒΑΖΙΟΣ), explaining why Philip the Phrygian would have been appointed to rule Jerusalem decades late in 2nd Maccabees. The name Sabaoth (Σαβαώθ) was later translated into Hebrew as ṣbåwt (צבאות), meaning 'armies,' which is likely a direct translation of the Aramaic term. The fact that Dionysus was the Greek name of Sabaoth and Sabazios was recorded by the many Classical Era scholars, including Strabo, Diodorus Siculus, Tacitus, Lydus, Cornelius Labeo, and Plutarch.

3rd Maccabees: Chapter 3

When the impious king comprehended this situation, he became so infuriated that not only was he enraged angry that he no longer limited his rage to the Judahites in Alexandria. Persecuting more heavily on those who lived in the country, he gave orders that they should be quickly collected into one place, and cruelly tortured to death. While this was going on, a defamatory rumor was made abroad by men who had banded together to injure the tribe of Judah. They charged that the Judahites kept them from following the laws. Now, while the Judahites always maintained a feeling of complete loyalty towards the kings, as they worshiped God and observed his law, they made certain distinctions and avoided certain things. Some people held them in disgust, although they adorned their conversation with works of righteousness, they had established themselves in the good opinion of the world.

What all the rest of mankind said, was, however, not considered by the foreigners, who said much of the exclusiveness of the Judahites about their worship and foods and alleged that they were unsociable men, hostile to the king's interests, refusing to associate with him or his troops. In this way of speaking, they brought a great deal of hatred against them. This unexpected uproar and sudden convergence of people was noticed by the Greeks that lived in the city, concerning men who had never harmed them. It was not in their power to aid them, as oppression was all was around, but they encouraged those during their troubles and expected a favorable return in their affairs.

"He who knows all things, will not," they said, "disregard such a great people."

Some of the neighbors, friends, and acquaintances of the Judahites, even called them secretly to meetings, and pledged them their assistance, promising to do their very utmost for them. The king, elated with his prosperous fortune, and not regarding the superior power of God, but thinking to continue in his purpose, wrote the following letter to the prejudice of the Judahites:

> King Ptolemy Philopator, to the commanders and soldiers in Egypt, and in all places, health and happiness!
>
> I am quite well, as are my affairs.
>
> Since our Asiatic campaign, the particulars of which you know was not given lightly but which by the aid of the gods and by our own vigor, has been brought to a successful conclusion as we expected, we resolved, not with strength of spear, but with gentleness and much humanity, as it were to nurse the inhabitants of Coele-Syria and Phoenicia and to be their willing benefactors.
>
> Having given considerable sums of silver to the temples of the several cities, we proceeded even as far as Jerusalem and went up to honor the temple of these wretched beings

who never cease from their foolishness. To outward appearances, they received us willingly but lied by their actions. When we were eager to enter their temple, and to honor it with the most beautiful and exquisite gifts, they were so carried away by their old arrogance, as to forbid us the entrance, while we, out of our patience towards all men, refrained from exercising our power on them.

Thereby, exhibiting their enmity against us, they alone among the nations lift up their heads against kings and benefactors, as men unwilling to submit to anything reasonable. We then, having endeavored to make allowance for the madness of these people, and on our victorious return, treating all people in Egypt courteously, acted in a manner that was appropriate.

Accordingly, bearing no ill-will against their families in Jerusalem, but rather remembering our connection with them, and the numerous matters with sincere a heart trusted to them from an ancient time, we wished to venture a total alteration of their state, by giving them the rights of citizens of Alexandria, and to admit them to the everlasting rites of our solemnities.

All this, however, they have taken in a very different spirit. With their innate malice, they have spurned the fair offer, and constantly inclining to evil, have rejected the inestimable rights. Not only so, but by using speech, and by refraining from speech, they hate the few among them who are heartily disposed towards us, thinking that their foolish plans will force us to cancel our reforms.

Having then, received certain evidence that these Judeans carry us every sort of ill-will, we must look forward to the possibility of some sudden trouble among ourselves, when these disrespectful men may turn traitors and barbarous enemies.

Therefore as soon as the contents of this letter become known to you, in that same hour, we order that those Judahites who live among you, with their wives and children, are to be sent to us in iron chains, insulted and abused to be tortured to death, cruel and disgracefully, suitable for rebels. By the punishment of them as one group, we see that we have found the only means of establishing our affairs for the future on a firm and satisfactory basis.

Whoever will hide a Judahite, whether it is an old man, child, infant, will be tortured to death with his whole house. Whoever will inform against the Judahites, besides receiving the property of the person informed on, will be presented with two thousand drachmas from the royal treasury, will be set free, and will be crowned. Whatever place will shelter a Judahite, will, when he is hunted out, be burnt down, and be forever rendered useless to every living being for all time to come.

This was the king's letter.

3rd Maccabees: Chapter 4

Wherever this decree was received, the people celebrated joyously and shouting as if their long-pent-up, hardened hatred, were now to show itself openly. The Judahites experienced great pangs of sorrow, and wept greatly, while all things around them were depressing, their hearts were set on fire as they mourned the sudden slaughter which was ordered against them. What home, or city, or inhabited place at all, or what streets was there which they did not fill with wailing and lamentation?

They were expelled unanimously by the generals in several cities with such stern and pitiless feelings that the exceptional nature of the punishment even moved some of their enemies. These, influenced by sentiments of common humanity, and reflecting on the uncertain issue of life, shed tears at this their miserable expulsion. A crowd of long-haired old men was driven out, with crippled bent feet, urged onward by the impulse of a violent, shameless force to move quickly.

Girls who had entered the bridal chamber quite recently, to enjoy the partnership of marriage, exchanged pleasure for misery, and with dirt scattered on their myrrh-anointed heads, were rushed out unveiled, and, in the middle of terrible insults, set up with one voice a lamentable cry instead of the marriage hymn. Bound, and exposed to the public gaze, they were rushed violently aboard ships. The husbands of these, in the prime of their youthful vigor, instead of crowns wore collars around their necks. Instead of feasting and youthful happiness, they spent the rest of their nuptial days wailing, and saw only the grave at hand. They were dragged along by unyielding chains, like wild beasts. Some had their necks forced into the benches of the rowers, while the feet of others were trapped in shackles.

The planks of the deck above them blocked out the light and shut out the day on every side so that they might be treated like traitors during the whole voyage. They were transported in these vessels, and in the end, arrived at Canopus.[1] The king had ordered them to be thrown into the huge horse-track,[2] which was built outside of the city. This place was well suited by its location to expose them to the view of all visitors into the city, and those who traveled from the city into the country. They could not communicate with his armies, as they were deemed unworthy of any civilized accommodation.

When the king heard that their brothers in the city often went out and mourned the melancholy distress of these victims, he was full of rage, and commanded that they should be subjected to the exact same treatment.

The whole nation was now to be registered. Every individual was to be specified by name, not for hard service of labor which we have recently mentioned, but so he might expose them to the previously mentioned tortures, and finally, quickly in one day, might slaughter them through his cruelties. The registration of these men was carried on cruelly, zealously, and assiduously, from the rising of the sun until its going down, and did not end for 40 days.

The king was filled with great and constant joy and celebrated banquets before the temple idols. His erring heart, far from the truth, and his profane mouth, gave glory to idols, deaf and incapable of speaking or aiding, and made an unworthy speech against the greatest god. At the end of the above-mentioned interval of time, the registrars brought word to the king that the multitude of the Judeans was too great for registration, as there were many still left in the land, some were in inhabited houses, and others were scattered about in various places, so that all the commanders in Egypt were insufficient for the work. The king threatened them, and accused them of taking bribes to allow the Judahites to escape, but was then convinced of the truth of what had been said. They both said and proved, that paper and pens had failed them for the carrying out of their purpose. This was the active interference of the unconquerable providence which assisted the Judahites from the sky.[3]

3rd Maccabees: Chapter 4 Notes

1 Codex Alexandrinus: Schedian (ϲχεδιαν)

Schedia was another name for Canopus, a port-city near Alexandria, Egypt.

2 Codex Alexandrinus: ippodromô (ιπποδρομω)

- LXX 19: ippodromiô (ιπποδρομιω)

A hippodrome was a Greek horse-track.

3 Codex Alexandarinus: ouranou (ουρανου). Translation: vaulted sky, Uranus (Greek sky god)

Uranus was used as the Greek translation for Shamayim, the Israelite sky god, as well as the Judahite term for the vaulted sky, the giant metal sky above the flat Earth.

3rd Maccabees: Chapter 5

Then he called Hermon, who was in charge of the elephants. Full of rage, altogether fixed in his furious design, he commanded him, with a quantity of unmixed wine and handfuls of incense, infused to drug the elephants early on the following day. These 500 elephants, after being infuriated by the large drafts of frankincense, were to be led up to the execution of death on the Judahites. The king, after issuing these orders, went to his feast and gathered together all those of his friends and of the army who hated the Judahites the most.

The master of the elephants, Hermon, fulfilled his commission punctually. The underlings appointed for the purpose went out in the evening and bound the hands of the miserable victims, and took other precautions for their security at night, thinking that the whole race would perish together. The heathens believed the Judahites to be without any protection, for chains held them down. They invoked the Omnipotent Lord,[1] and ceaselessly implored with tears their merciful god to end the evil purpose which had gone out against them and to deliver them by extraordinary manifestation from that death which was in store for them. Their litany so earnest went up to Shamayim.

Hermon had drugged his pitiless elephants with large drafts of wine mixed with frankincense and presented himself at the courtyard early in the morning to report to the king that everything was ready. But, he who gives whatever he wishes, sent upon the king a portion of sleep, and so he slept both night and day. By this sweet and profound influence of the Lord, he was overcome by such a deep sleep that he failed in his unjust purpose and was completely frustrated in his inflexible plan. The Judahites, having survived the hour which had been chosen, praised their sacred god, and again prayed to him who is easily reconciled to display the strength of his powerful hand to the prideful Greeks.

The middle of the tenth hour had almost arrived, when the master of ceremonies saw the guests who had been invited, he came and shook the king. He gained his attention with difficulty, hinting that the mealtime was almost over, and talked the matter over with him. The king listened to this, and then returned to his alcohol, and ordered the guests to sit down before him. Then this was done, he asked them to enjoy themselves, and to indulge in joy at this somewhat late hour of the banquet. The conversation grew, and the king sent for Hermon, and inquired about him, with fierce denunciations about why the Judahites had been allowed to survive the day. Hermon explained that he had followed his orders at night, and this was confirmed by his friends. The king, then, with a barbarity exceeding that of Phalaris, said, "They might thank my sleep for this day. Don't lose time, go get the elephants ready for tomorrow, as you did before, for the destruction of these cursed Judahites."

When the king said this, the people present were happy and approved, and then each man went to his own home. They did not sleep that night, as much as make cruel jokes about those deemed miserable. The morning cock had just crowed when Hermon harnessed the beasts and stimulated them in the great colonnade. The city crowds were collected together to see the hideous spectacle and waited impatiently for the dawn. The Judahites, breathless with momentary suspense, stretched out their hands, and prayed to the greatest god in mournful strains, again to help them quickly. The sun's rays were not yet spread about, and the king was waiting for his friends, when Hermon came to him, calling out and saying that his desires would now be realized.

The king, receiving him, was astonished at his rudeness, and, overwhelmed with a terrible spirit about everything asked about the object of this earnest preparation. This was the working of that supreme god who had made him forget his purpose. Hermon, and all his friends, pointed out the preparation of the animals, saying, "They are ready, my king, according to your own strict orders."

The king was filled with fierce anger at these words, for, by the providence of God his mind had become entirely confused regarding these things. He looked hard at Hermon, and threatened him as follows, saying, "If your parents or your children were here, I would send them to these wild beasts, but not these innocent Judahites, who have loyally served me and my forefathers. Had it not been for our familiar friendship, and the claims of your office, your life would have gone for theirs."

Hermon, being threatened in this unexpected and alarming manner, was visibly troubled and depressed. His friends sneaked out one by one and dismissed the assembled multitudes to their respective occupations. The Judahites, having heard of these events, praised the glorious god and king of kings, because they had obtained this help, too, from him. Now the king arranged another banquet like the first and proclaimed an invitation to the celebration. He summoned Hermon to his presence, and said threateningly, "How often, wretch, must I repeat my orders to you about these same persons? Once more, arm the elephants for the morning for the extermination of the Judahites!"

His family, who were reclining with him, wondered at his instability, and so expressed themselves, "King, how long do you treat us as of men without reason? This is the third time that you have ordered their destruction. When the thing is to be done, you change your mind and cancel your instructions. This causes a feeling of expectation and causes problems in the city. It swarms with factions, and is continually on the point of riot."

The king, just like another Phalaris, a prey to thoughtlessness, made no account of the changes which his own mind had undergone, in issuing the deliverance of the Judahites. He swore a fruitless oath and determined immediately to send them to Hades,[2] crushed by the knees and feet of the elephants. He would also invade Judea, and level its towns with fire and the sword, and destroy that temple which the Greeks could not enter, and prevent sacrifices forever from being offered up there. Joyfully his friends left, together with his family, and, trusting in his determination, arranged their forces as a guard at the most convenient places throughout the city. The master of the elephants urged the beasts into an almost maniacal state, drenched them with incense and wine, and armored them with terrible weapons.

Early in the morning, when the city was now filled with an immense number of people at the horse-track, he entered the palace and called the king to the business in hand. The king's heart teemed with impious rage, and he rushed out with the mass, along with the elephants. With hard feelings and pitiless eyes, he longed to watch the hard and wretched doom of the Judahites. But the Judahites, when the elephants walked out at the gate, followed by the armed force, and when they saw the dirt raised by the throng and heard the loud cries of the crowd, thought that they had come to the last moment of their lives, to the end of what they had expected.

They began to cry and moan and kissed each other. They hugged their closest relatives, fathers with their sons, mothers with their daughters. Other women held their infants to their breasts, which drew what seemed to be their last milk. Nevertheless, when they thought of the safety previously granted them from Shamayim, they prostrated themselves together, and even removed the suckling children from the breasts, and sent up a very great cry begging the Omnipotent Lord to reveal himself and have mercy on those who now lay at the gates of Hades.

3rd Maccabees: Chapter 5 Notes

1 Codex Alexandrinus: pantocratora cyrion (ΠΑΝΤΟΚΡΑΤΟΡΑΚΥΡΙΟΝ). Translation: all-powerful (or omnipotent) lord

2 Codex Alexandrinus: aedou (ΑΙΔΟΥ). Translation: Hades

Hades was the fiery Greek underworld, which was adopted by Christians and Buddhists. The term Hades was generally used in the Septuagint as a translation for She'ol (שְׁאוֹל), the Israelite underworld, not Mot the Canaanite god of death and Israelite messenger of death, whose name was translated as Thanatos.

3rd Maccabees: Chapter 6

Eleazar, an illustrious priest of the country, who had lived a long length of days, and whose life had been lived in with virtue, caused the presbyters who were around him to cease to cry out to the Sacred God, and prayed:

"King ruling everything, Highest, supreme god, who regulates the whole creation with your tender mercy, look on the descendants of Abraham, on the children of the sanctified Jacob, your sanctified inheritance, Father, now being wrongfully destroyed as foreigners in a foreign land.

You destroyed Pharaoh, with his armies of chariots when that lord of this same Egypt was puffed up with lawless brutality and loud voice. Shedding the beams of your mercy on the tribes of Israel, you overwhelmed him with his proud army.

When Sennacherib, the terrible king of the Assyrians, prideful in his countless armies, had subdued the whole land with his spear and was lifting himself against your sacred city, with terrible boasting to be endured, you, Lord, demolished him and showed your might to many nations.

When the three friends in the land of Babylon of their own will expose their lives to the fire rather than serve vain things, you sent a dewy coolness through the fiery furnace, and turned the fire on all their adversaries.

It was you who, when Daniel was hurled, through slander and envy, as prey to lions, brought him back unharmed into the light.

When Jonah was trapped in the belly of Cetus,[1] you looked on him, Father, and returned him to the sight of his own people.

Now, you who hate insolence, you, who abound in mercy, you, who are the protector of all things, come quickly to those of the tribes of Israel, who are insulted and hated by lawless Greeks. If our life has been stained with iniquity during our exile, deliver us from the hand of the enemy, and destroy us Lord by the death which you prefer. Don't let the vain-minded congratulate vain idols at the destruction of your beloved, saying, 'Their god did not save them.'

You, who are supreme and almighty, Eternal One, look! Have mercy on us who are being withdrawn from life, like traitors, by the unreasoning insolence of lawless men. Let the heathens cower before your invincible might today, glorious one, who has all power to save the tribe of Jacob.

The whole band of infants and their parents with tears beg you. Let it be shown to all the nations that you are with us, Lord, and have not turned your face away from us, but as you said, that you would not forget them even in the land of their enemies, fulfill this saying Lord!"

When Eleazar had ended his prayer, the king came to the horse-track with the wild beasts, and with his great power. When the Judahites saw this, they cried out loudly to Shamayim, so that the surrounding valleys resounded, and caused irrepressible mourning throughout the army. Then the all-glorious, all-powerful, and true god, displayed his sacred countenance and opened the gates of the sky, from which two messengers, dreadful in form, came down and were visible to everyone except the Judahites. They stood opposite, and filled the enemies' army with confusion and fear, and trapped them with immovable shackles.

A cold shudder came over the body of the king, and fear paralyzed the vehemence of his spirit. They turned back the animals on the armed forces which followed them, and the animals trod them down and destroyed them. The king's anger was converted into compassion, and he wept at his own machinations. When he heard the cry, and saw them all on the verge of slaughter, with tears he angrily threatened his friends, saying, "You have governed badly, and have exceeded all tyrants in cruelty, and me, your benefactor, you have labored to deprive me at once of my dominion and my life by secretly devising measures damaging to the kingdom. Who is gathered here? Each unreasonably removed from his home? Those who, in loyalty to us, held the fortresses of the country? Who has consigned undeserved punishment to those who in goodwill towards us from the beginning have in all things surpassed all nations, and who often have engaged in the most dangerous undertakings? Loosen! Loosen the unjust shackles! Send them to their homes in peace, and undo what has been done. Release the sons of the omnipotent living god Shamayim, who from our ancestors' times until now has granted glorious and uninterrupted prosperity to our affairs."

These things he said, and they released them the same moment, and having now escaped death, praised God their sacred savior. The king then departed to the city, and called his financier to him, and commanded him to provide a seven days' quantity of wine and other materials for feasting for the Judahites. He decided that they should keep a joyous festival of deliverance in the very place in which they expected to meet with their destruction. Then they who were previously hated and close to Hades, even part-way into it, partook of the cup of salvation instead of a terrible and lamentable death.

Full of exultation, they left the place intended for their death and burial, to banqueting halls. Ending their miserable crying, they took up the subject of their fatherland, hymning their praise of god their wonder-working savior. All groans and wailing were laid aside. They danced in token of serene joy.

Also, the king collected a number of guests for the occasion and returned unending thanks with much magnificence for the unexpected deliverance afforded him. Those who had marked them out as for death and carrion-eaters, and had registered them with joy, howled aloud, and were clothed with shame, and had the fire of their rage ingloriously put out. But the Judahites, as we just said, danced and then feasted, giving glad thanksgivings and songs. They made a public ordinance to commemorate these things for generations to come, as long as they should be foreigners. They established these days as days of celebration, not for drinking or luxury, but because God had saved them.

They requested the king to send them back to their homes. They were being registered from the twenty-fifth of Pashons[2] to the fourth day of Epip,[3] a period of forty days. The measures taken for their destruction lasted from the fifth of Epip until the seventh, that is, three days. The Ruler over all did during this time manifest his mercy gloriously and delivered them all unharmed. They feasted on the king's provisions up to the fourteenth day and then asked to be sent away. The king praised them, and wrote the following letter, of magnanimous importance to them, to the commanders of every city.

3rd Maccabees: Chapter 6 Notes

1 Codex Alexandrinus: cêtous (ΚΗΤΟΥϹ). Translation: Cetus (sea-monster in Greek mythology), whale, sea-monster, Cetus (constellation)

2 Codex Alexandrinus: Pachon (ΠΑΧΩΝ)

- LXX 58: Pachôn mênos (πἀχοον μῆνος). Translation:

Pachon month

- LXX 542: pachnôn (πἀχνοον)

Pashons (Παϣονс / بشنس) was the ninth month of the later ancient Egyptian civil calendar and Coptic calendar. Since 25 BC, when leap days were added, it has been in approximately May of the Julian calendar.

3 Codex Alexandrinus: Epiphi (ΕΠΙΦΙ)

Epip (Ⲉⲡⲓⲡ / أبيب) was the eleventh month of the later ancient Egyptian civil calendar and Coptic calendar. Since 25 BC, when leap days were added, it has been in approximately July of the Julian calendar.

3rd Maccabees: Chapter 7

"King Ptolemy Philopator to the commanders throughout Egypt, and to all who are set over affairs, joy, and strength.

We, too, and our children are well, and the greatest god has directed our affairs as we wish. Some of our malicious friends vehemently urged us to punish the Judahites of our realm in one group, with the infliction of a monstrous punishment. They pretended that our affairs would never be in a good state until this took place. 'Such,' they said, 'was the hatred borne by the Judahites to all other people.' They brought them shackled in terrible chains like slaves, no, like traitors. Without investigation or trial, they tried to slaughter them. They buckled themselves with savage cruelty, worse than Scythian customs.

For this reason, we severely threatened them, yet, with the mercy which we extend to all men we ultimately permitted them to live. Finding that the God in the skies[1] placed a shield of protection over the Judahites to preserve them and that he fought for them as a father always fights for his sons, and taking into consideration their constant loyalty towards us and towards our ancestors, we have, as we should, acquitted them of every sort of charge. We have dismissed them to their various homes, bidding all men everywhere to do them no wrong, or unfairly hate them about their past.

For you know that should we conceive any evil plan, or in any way aggrieve them, we will ever have as our opposite, not man, but the dominant force of the highest god. From him, there will be no escape, as the avenger of such deeds.

Farewell."

When they had received this letter, they were not quick to leave immediately. They petitioned the king to be allowed to inflict fitting punishment on those of their race who had willingly transgressed the sacred god, and the law of God. They alleged that men who had for their bellies' sake transgressed the ordinances of God, would never be faithful to the interests of the king. The king admitted the truth of this reasoning and commended them. Full power was given to them, without a warrant or special commission, to slaughter those who had transgressed the law of God boldly in every part of the king's dominions. Their priests, then, as it was decided, saluted him with good wishes, and all the people echoed with "Alleluia."[2]

They then joyfully departed. Then they punished and murdered with ignominy every polluted Judahite that fell in their way, slaughtering in that day more than 300 men, and celebrating the destruction of the wicked as a time of joy. They themselves having held tight to their God even to death and having enjoyed a full deliverance, departed from the city garlanded with sweet-flowered wreaths of every kind. Shouting in joy, with songs of praise, and melodious hymns they thanked the god of their forefathers, the eternal savior of Israel. Having been saved from Ptolemy, and in that freight-exporting district, where the fleet waited for them for seven days as per the general wishes, they partook in a banquet of deliverance, for the king generously granted them the means of returning home.

They were accordingly taken back in peace, while they gave thanks, and decided to keep these days during their stay as days of celebration. These they recorded as sacred on a pillar, once they had dedicated the place of their celebration to be one of prayer. They departed unharmed, free, abundant in joy, preserved by the king's command, by land, sea, and river, each to his own home. They had more weight than before among their enemies, and were honored and were feared, and no one in any way robbed them of their goods. Every man received back his own, according to inventory, and those who had taken their goods gave them back in the greatest terror. For the greatest god worked with perfectness wonders for their salvation. Blessed is the redeemer of Israel forever, Amen.[3]

3rd Maccabees: Chapter 7 Notes

1 Codex Alexandrinus: epouranion theon (ΕΠΟΥΡΑΝΙΟΝ ΘΕΟΝ). Translation: in-heaven god

2 Codex Alexandrinus: Alleluia (ΑΛΛΗΛΟΥΙΑ)

Hallelujah is the more common Hebrew transliteration of hllwyh (הללויה) which translates in English as 'Praise Yah.' The term was used since at least the late bronze age, although originally meant 'Praise quickly' in Canaanite. The Greek variant of Alleluia, is accepted as being derived from the Aramaic variant hållwyå (𐡄𐡋𐡋𐡅𐡉𐡀), indicating that this text was likely written in Aramaic.

3 Codex Alexandrinus: Amên (ΑΜΗΝ)

4th Maccabees: Chapter 1

I am going to demonstrate a most philosophical proposition, namely, that religious reasoning is the absolute master of the emotions. I would willingly advise you to give the utmost thought to philosophy. Reason is necessary to everyone as a step to science, and more especially does it embrace the praise of prudence, the highest virtue. If, then, reasoning appears to hold the mastery over the emotions which stand in the way of temperance, such as gluttony and lust, it certainly also and manifestly has the rule over the affections which are contrary to justice, such as malice, and of those which are hindrances to bravery, such as anger, pain, and fear.

How, then, is it, perhaps some may say, that reasoning, if it rules the affections is not also master of forgetfulness and ignorance? They attempt a ridiculous argument. For reasoning does not rule over its own affections, but over those that are contrary to justice, bravery, temperance, and prudence, and yet over these, to withstand, without destroying them. I might prove to you, from many other considerations, that religious reasoning is the sole master of the emotions, but I will prove it with the greatest force from the fortitude of Eleazar, and seven brothers, and their mother, who suffered death in defense of virtue.

For all these, commanded to torture and even to death, by this contempt, demonstrated that reasoning has command over the emotions. For their virtues, then, it is right that I should commend those men who died with their mother at this time on behalf of righteousness, and for their honors, I may count them as happy. For they, winning admiration not only from men in general but even from the persecutors, for their bravery and endurance, became the means of the destruction of the tyranny against their nation, having conquered the tyrant by their endurance, so that through them their country was purified.

We may now consider the question, having commenced, as is our used, with laying down the doctrine, and so proceed to the account of these persons, giving glory to the all-knowing god. The question is, therefore, whether reasoning is an absolute master of the emotions. Let us determine, then, What is reasoning? And what emotion? And how many kinds of emotions? And whether reasoning bears sway over all of these? Reasoning is, then, intellect accompanied by a life of righteousness, putting first the consideration of wisdom.

Wisdom is a knowledge of divine and human things, and of their causes. This is contained in the education of the law, by which we learn divine things reverently, and human things profitably. The forms of wisdom are prudence, justice, bravery, and temperance. The leading one of these is prudence, by whose means it is, that reasoning rules over the emotions. Of the emotions, pleasure and pain are the two most comprehensive, and they also by nature refer to the mind. There are many attendant affections surrounding pleasure and pain. Before pleasure is lust, and after pleasure is a joy. Before pain is fear, and after the pain is sorrow.

Anger is an affection, common to both pleasure and to pain if anyone is paying attention when it comes to him. There exists in pleasure a malicious disposition, which is the most multifaceted of all the affections. In the mind, it is arrogance, love of silver, vanity, contention, faithlessness, and the evil eye. In the body, it is greediness, gluttony, and solitary gluttony. As pleasure and pain are, therefore, two growths of the body and the mind, so there are many offshoots of these emotions. Reasoning, the universal husbandman, purging and pruning these severally, and binding round, and watering, and transplanting, in every way improves the materials of the morals and affections.

Reasoning is the leader of the virtues, but it is the sole ruler of the emotions. Observe then first, through the very things which stand in the way of temperance, that reasoning is the absolute ruler of the emotions. Temperance consists of a command over the lusts, but of the lusts, some belong to the mind, others to the body, and over each of these classes the reasoning appears to carry sway.

From where is it, otherwise, that when urged on to forbidden meats, we reject the gratification which would ensue from them? Is it not because reasoning is able to command the appetites? I believe so.

Here it is, then, that when lusting after water-creatures and birds, and four-footed beasts, and all kinds of food which are forbidden us by the law, we hold ourselves back through the mastery of reasoning. For the affections of our appetites are resisted by the temperate understanding, and bent back again, and all the impulses of the body are reined in by reasoning.

4th Maccabees: Chapter 2

What wonder, that the lusts of the mind, after participation with what is beautiful, are frustrated, on this ground, therefore, the temperate Joseph is praised in that by reasoning, he subdued, on reflection, the indulgence of sense. For, although young and ripe for sexual intercourse, he held back by thinking about the stimulus of his emotions. It is not merely the stimulus of sensual indulgence, but that of every desire, that reasoning is able to master. For instance, the law says, 'You will not covet your neighbor's wife or anything that belongs to your neighbor.'

Now, then, since it is the law which has forbidden us to desire, I will much more easily persuade you, that reasoning is able to govern our lusts, just as it does the affections which are impediments to justice. How is a solitary eater, a glutton, and a drunkard reclaimed, unless it is clear that reasoning is master of the emotions? A man, therefore, who regulates his life by the law, even if he is a lover of silver, immediately puts force on his own disposition, lending to the needy without interest, and canceling the debt on the upcoming sabbath.

Should a man be stingy, he is ruled by the law acting through reasoning, so that he does not glean his harvest crops or vintage, and in reference to other points, we may perceive that it is reasoning that conquers his emotions. For the law conquers even affection towards parents, not surrendering virtue on their account. It prevails over marriage love, condemning it when transgressing law. It masters over the love of parents towards their children, for they punish them for vice, and it domineers over the intimacy of friends, reproving them when wicked.

Think it not a strange assertion that reasoning can on behalf of the law conquer even enmity. It doesn't allow the cutting down of the cultivated plants of an enemy, but saves it from the destroyers, and collects their fallen ruins. Reason appears to be master of the more violent emotions, as the love of empire and empty boasting, and slander. For the temperate understanding repels all these malignant emotions, as it does anger, for it masters even this. Moses, when angered against Dathan and Abiram, did nothing to them in anger, but regulated his anger by thinking.

For the temperate mind is able, as I said, to be superior to the emotions, and to transfer some, and destroy others. Why else does our most wise father Jacob blame Simeon and Levi for having irrationally slaughtered the whole tribe of the Shechemites, saying, "Cursed is their anger." If reasoning didn't possess the power of subduing angry affections, he wouldn't have said this.

At the time when God created man, he implanted within him his emotions and moral nature. At that time he enthroned above all the sacred leader mind, through the medium of the senses. He gave a law to this mind, by living according to which it will maintain a temperate, and just, and good, and manly reign. How, then, a man may say, if reasoning is master of the emotions, has it no control over forgetfulness and ignorance?

4th Maccabees: Chapter 3

The argument is exceedingly ridiculous, for reasoning does not appear to carry sway over its affections, but over those of the body, in such a way as that anyone of you may not be able to root out desire, but reasoning will enable you to avoid being enslaved to it. One may not be able to root out anger from the mind, but it is possible to withstand anger. Anyone of you may not be able to eradicate malice, but reasoning has the force to work with you to prevent you from yielding to malice.

Reasoning is not an eradicator, but an antagonist of the emotions. This may be more clearly understood from the thirst of King David. After David had been attacking the foreigners for the whole day, and he and his nation's soldiers had killed many of them, then when evening came, sweating and very weary, he went to the royal tent, around which the entire army of our ancestors was camped. Now all the rest of them were at supper, but the king was very thirsty, and although he had many wells, he could not by their means quench his thirst. but a certain irrational longing for the water in the enemy's camp grew stronger and fiercer on him and consumed him with languish. Therefore his body-guards were troubled at this longing of the king, and two valiant young soldiers, reverencing the desire of the king, put on their armor, and taking a pitcher, got over the ramparts of the enemies, and unseen by the guardians of the gate, they went throughout the whole camp of the enemy on a mission. Having boldly discovered the fountain, they filled out of it the draft for the king. But he, though parched with thirst, reasoned that a draft reputed of equal value to blood would be dangerous to his mind. Therefore, setting up reasoning in opposition to his desire, he poured out the draft to God.

The temperate mind has power to conquer the pressure of the emotions, and to quench the fires of excitement, and to wrestle down the pains of the body, however excessive, and, through the excellency of reasoning, to detest all the assaults of the emotions. The occasion now invites us to give an illustration of temperate reasoning from history. At a time when our fathers were in possession of undisturbed peace through obedience to the law and were prosperous, Seleucus I Nicanor[1] the king of Asia,[2] both provided them silver for divine service and accepted their form of government, then certain persons, bringing in new things contrary to the general agreement, in various ways fell into calamities.

4th Maccabees: Chapter 3 Notes

1 Codex Sinaiticus: Seleucon ton Nicanora (ϹΕΛΕΥΚΟΝ ΤΟΝΝΙΚΑΝΟΡΑ)

Seleucus I Nicator founded the Seleucid Empire when Alexander the Great died, and subjugated the eastern regions of Alexander's Empire. He ruled between 305 and 281 BC, initially just over the Persian and Median regions, and by 302 BC his empire extended into modern Syria and Turkey.

2 Codex Sinaiticus: Asias (ΑϹΙΑϹ). Translation: Asia (or Anatolia)

The Seleucid Empire spanned Southwest Asia from the Mediterranean coast of Syria to the Indus River in Pakistan, at the time the story takes place.

4th Maccabees: Chapter 4

A certain man named Simon, who was in opposition to Onias, who once held the high priesthood for life and was an honorable and good man, by slandering him in every way, could not damage him in the eyes of the people and left as an exile with the intent of betraying his country. After traveling to Apollonius, the military governor of Syria, Phoenicia, and Cilicia, he said, "Having goodwill towards the king's affairs, I have come to inform you that infinite private wealth is stored in the treasuries of Jerusalem which does not belong to the temple, but belongs to King Seleucus."

When Apollonius learned of this he praised Simon for his care towards the king's interests, and went to Seleucus and informed him of the treasure. Receiving authority over it, he quickly advanced into our country with the cursed Simon and a very large force. He said that he came with the commands of the king that he should take the private silver from the treasury. The nation, indignant at this proclamation, and replying to the effect that it was extremely unfair that those who had committed deposits to the sacred treasury should be deprived of them, resisted as well as they could. But Apollonius went with threats into the temple.

The priests, with the women and children, prayed to God to throw his shield over the sacred place, and before

Apollonius, while he was going up with his armed force to the seizure of the treasury, there appeared from the sky messengers riding on horseback, all radiant in armor, filling them with terror and trembling. Apollonius fell half-dead on the court which is open to all nations, and extended his hands to the sky, and implored the Hebrews, with tears, to pray for him, and begged the heavenly army. He said that he had sinned, and was consequently worthy of death, but that if he were saved, he would tell all men the blessedness of the sacred place.

Onias the high priest, influenced by these words, and also for the other reason, being anxious that King Seleucus should think that Apollonius was slain by human device and not by divine punishment, prayed for him, and he was therefore unexpectedly saved and departed to tell the king what had happened to him. But on the death of King Seleucus, his son Antiochus Epiphanes succeeded to the kingdom, a terrible man with haughty pride, who deposed Onias from the high priesthood and appointed his brother Jason to be high priest, who had agreed that if he would give him this authority he would pay 3,660 talents annually.

He committed to him the high priesthood and rule over the nation, and he both changed the customs of the people living there and perverted their civil customs into all lawlessness. Not only did he erect a gymnasium on the very citadel of our country, but he neglected the guardianship of the temple. Which through divine vengeance instigated Antiochus himself against them, for while being at war with Ptolemy in Egypt, he heard that when a report of his death was spread abroad, the inhabitants of Jerusalem had greatly rejoiced, and he quickly marched against them. Having subdued them, he established a decree that if any of them lived according to the laws of his country he would die.

When he could not destroy the obedience to the law of the nation through his decrees, but saw all his threats and punishments without impact, as even women who knew beforehand the punishment, continued to circumcise their children, and were thrown down a cliff along with there children. When, therefore, his decrees were ignored by the people, he compelled through torture, every one of this race to taste forbidden meats and reject the Jewish religion.

4th Maccabees: Chapter 5

The tyrant Antiochus, therefore, sitting in public state with his assessors on a certain lofty place, with his armed troops standing in a circle around him, commanded his lancers to seize every one of the Hebrews and to compel them to taste the pork and things offered to idols. Should any of them be unwilling to eat the cursed food, they were to be tortured on the wheel until death. When many had been seized, a foremost man of the assembly, a Hebrew, by name Eleazar, a priest by family, by profession a lawyer, and advanced in years, and for this reason known to many of the king's followers, was brought near to him.

Antiochus seeing him, said, "I would counsel you, old man, before your tortures begin, to taste the pork, and save your life, for I feel respect for your age and gray hair, which since you have had so long, you appear to me to be no philosopher in retaining the superstition of the Jews. Why, therefore, since nature has conferred on you the most excellent flesh of this animal, do you hate it? It seems senseless not to enjoy what is pleasant, but not disgraceful. Yet from notions of sinfulness, you reject the gift of nature. You will be acting, I think, still more senselessly, if you follow vain conceits about the truth. You will, moreover, be despising me to your own punishment. Will you not awake from your trivial philosophy? Give up the folly of your notions, and regain understanding worthy of your age. Search into the truth for an expedient course? Consider my kindly admonition, and have pity on your own years. Keep in mind that if there is any power which watches over this religion of yours, it will pardon you for all transgressions of the law which you commit through compulsion."

While the tyrant incited him in this manner to the unlawful eating of meat, Eleazar begged permission to speak. Having received permission to speak, he began said, "We, Antiochus, who believe that we live under divine law, consider no compulsion to be so forcible as obedience to that law, therefore we consider that we shouldn't in any point transgress the law. Indeed, if our law was (as you suppose) not truly divine, and if we wrongly think it divine, we should have no right even in that case to destroy our sense of religion. Don't think eating the unclean is a minor offense. Transgression of the law, whether in small or great matters, is of equal importance, for in either case the law is equally slighted."

"You deride our philosophy, as though we lived irrationally in it. Yet it instructs us in temperance so that we are superior to all pleasures and lusts, and it exercises us in bravery so that we cheerfully undergo every grievance. It instructs us in justice so that in all our dealings we render what is due, and it teaches us piety so that we worship correctly the one and only god. Therefore we don't eat the unclean, as we believe that the law was established by God, and we are convinced that the creator of the world, in giving his laws, sympathizes with our nature. Those things which are convenient to our souls, he has directed us to eat, but those which are repugnant to them, he has banned. But, tyrant, you not only force us to break the law, but also to eat, so that you may ridicule us as we eat profanely. You will not have this reason to laugh at me, nor will I transgress the sacred oaths of my forefathers to keep the law. No, not if you pluck out my eyes, and eat my guts. I am not so old and void of bravery. My rational powers are youthful in defense of my religion."

"Now then, prepare your wheels, and light a fierce flame. I will not in my old age break the law of my country. I will not betray you, law, my instructor! Or forsake you, beloved self-control! I will not put you to shame, philosopher reason. Or deny you, honored priesthood and science of the law. Mouth! You will not pollute my old age or the full stature of a perfect life. My fathers will receive me pure, not having failed before your compulsion, even to death. For over the ungodly you will tyrannize, but you will not lord it over my thoughts about religion, either by your arguments or through deeds."

4th Maccabees: Chapter 6

When Eleazar had answered the exhortations of the tyrant in this manner, the lancers came up and rudely hauled Eleazar to the instruments of torture. First, they stripped the old man, adorned as he was with beautiful clothes. Then tying back his arms and hands, they disdainfully whipped him with stripes, as a herald shouted, "Obey the commands of the king!"

But Eleazar, the high-minded and truly noble, like one tortured in a dream, did not feel it at all. He raised his eyes to the sky, and the old man's flesh was stripped off by the scourges, and his blood streamed down, and his sides were pierced through. Falling to the ground, his body had no strength to support the pains, yet he kept his reason upright and unbending. Then one of the harsh lancers leaped on his belly as he was falling, to force him upright. He endured the pains, and despised the cruelty, and persevered through the indignities, and like a noble athlete, the old man, when struck, ignored his torturers. He was sweating and panting for breath, and was admired by the very torturers for his courage. Therefore, partly in pity for his old age and partly from the sympathy of acquaintance, and partly in admiration of his endurance, some of the attendants of the king asked, "Why do you unreasonably destroy yourself, Eleazar, with these miseries? We will bring you some meat cooked by yourself, and you can save yourself by pretending that you have eaten pork."

Eleazar, as though the advice more painfully tortured him, cried out, "Don't let us who are children of Abraham be so evil advised as by giving way to make use of an unbecoming pretense, for it is irrational, if having lived up to old age in all truth, and having scrupulously guarded our character for it, we should now turn back, and ourselves should become a pattern of impiety to the young, as being an example of unclean-eating. It would be disgraceful if we should live on for some short time, and be scorned by all men for cowardice, and be condemned by the tyrant for cowardliness, by not contending to the death for our divine law. Therefore you, children of Abraham, die nobly for your religion! You lancers of the tyrant, why do you delay?"

Seeing him so high-minded against misery, and not changing by their pity, they led him to the fire, and then with their wickedly contrived instruments, they burnt him on the fire and poured stinking fluids down into his nostrils. Over time, he was burnt down to the bones, and about to die, when he raised his eyes toward the sky, and said, "You know, God, that when I might have been saved, I am murdered for the sake of the law by tortures of fire. Be merciful to your people, and be satisfied with the punishment of me on their account.

Let my blood be a purification for them, and take my life in repayment for theirs."

While still speaking the sacred man died, noble in his torments, and even to the agonies of death he resisted in his reasoning for the sake of the law. Therefore, religious reasoning is master of the emotions. For had the emotions been superior to reasoning, I would have given them the witness of this mastery. But now, since reasoning conquered the emotions, we befittingly awarded it the authority of first place. It is but fair that we should suffer, that the power belongs to reasoning since it masters external miseries. It would be ridiculous if it were not so, and I proved that reasoning has not only mastered pains, but that it is also superior to the pleasures, and withstands them.

4th Maccabees: Chapter 7

The reasoning of our father Eleazar, like a first-rate pilot, steered the ship of piety in the sea of emotions, and flouted the threats of the tyrant, and overwhelmed with the torturers, in no way shifted the rudder of piety until it sailed into the harbor of victory over death. No besieged city has ever held out against many and various war-machines, as that sacred man did when his pious mind was tried with the fiery trial of tortures and racking, and he moved his torturers through the religious reasoning that shielded him.

Father Eleazar, projecting his disposition, broke the raging waves of the emotions as with a jutting promontory. Priest worthy of the priesthood! You did not pollute your sacred teeth, or make your appetite, which had always embraced the clean and lawful, a partaker of profanity. Follower of the law and sage devoted to a divine life! Of such a character should those be, who perform the duties of the law at the risk of their own blood and defend it with generous sweat by suffering even to death! You, father, have gloriously established our right government by your endurance, and the making of much account our past service, prevented its destruction, and, by your deeds, have made credible the words of philosophy. Aged man of more power than tortures, elder more vigorous than fire, greatest king over the emotions, Eleazar!

Like father Aaron, armed with a censer rushed through the consuming fire and vanquished the flame-bearing messenger, so, Eleazar, the descendant of Aaron, burnt away in the fire, did not give up his reasoning. What is most wonderful though, an old man, though the strength of his body was now spent, and his muscles were relaxed, and his sinews worn out, he recovered his youth. With the spirit of reasoning, and the reasoning of Isaac, he reasoned with the multiple heads of the cunning Korahites[1] in blessed old age, with reverend gray head, after a life obedient to the law, which the faithful seal of death perfected.

If an old man, through religion, defied torture even to death, clearly religious reasoning is the ruler of the emotions. Some might say it is not all who conquer emotions as all do not possess wise reasoning. But they who have meditated on religion with their whole heart, these alone can master the emotions of the flesh. They who believe in God don't die, for, like our forefathers, Abraham, Isaac, and Jacob, they live for God. This circumstance, then, is by no means an objection, that some who have weak reasoning, are governed by their emotions, since what person, walking religiously by the rule of philosophy, and believing in God, and knowing that it is a blessed thing to endure all kinds of hardships for virtue, would not, for the sake of religion, master his emotion?

For only the wise and brave man is lord over his emotions. Why is it, that even boys taught the philosophy of religious reasoning, have conquered even more terrible tortures, when the tyrant was manifestly vanquished in his first attempt, in being unable to force the old man to eat the unclean thing.

4th Maccabees: Chapter 7 Notes

1 Codex Sinaiticus: logismô tên polycephalon streblan enicêsen (λογισμω την πολυκεφαλον στρεβλαν ενικησεν). Translation: calculation (or reasoning, reflection, wisdom, argument) the many-headed (or multiple hears) distorted (or twisted) enicêsen (possibly 'annulment,' of 'the Korahites' via Samaritan)

• Codex Alexandrinus: logismô tên polycephalon streblan êcyrôsen (λογισμω την πολυκεφαλον στρεβλαν ηκυρωσεν). Translation: calculation (or reasoning, reflection, wisdom, argument) the many-headed (or multiple hears) distorted (or twisted) êcyrôsen (possibly 'annulment,' of 'the Korahites' via Samaritan)

The final word in the sentence is not proper Greek, but is similar to the Greek word acyrôsê (ακύρωση), meaning 'annulment,' or 'invalidate' in modern Greek, but is not documented in ancient Greek. The word and story suggest the Greek term was a corrupted transliteration of 'the Korahites' (ࠄࠒࠓࠇࠉࠌ), with the Y (ࠉ) mistaken for an S (ࠎ). This would probably only have been possible in the Classical era Samaritan version of the Canaanite script, indicating that the dispute between Aaron and the Korahites that the author is referring to was in a Samaritan work, which would explain why there are repeated references to the sons of Abraham in the book.

4th Maccabees: Chapter 8

For this is why even the very young, by following a philosophy in accordance with devout reason, have prevailed over the most painful instruments of torture. For when the tyrant was conspicuously defeated in his first attempt, being unable to compel an aged man to eat defiling foods, then in a violent rage, he commanded that others of the Hebrew captives be brought and that any who ate defiling food would be freed after eating, but if any were to refuse, they would be tortured even more cruelly.

When the tyrant had given these orders, seven brothers, all handsome, modest, noble, and accomplished in every way, were brought before him along with their aged mother. When the tyrant saw them, grouped about their mother as though a chorus, he was pleased with them. Struck by their appearance and nobility, he smiled at them, and summoned them nearer and said, "Young men, with favorable feelings I admire each and every one of you, and greatly respect the beauty and the number of such brothers. Not only do I advise you not to display the same madness as that of the old man who has just been tortured, but I also exhort you to yield to me and enjoy my friendship. Just as I am able to punish those who disobey my orders, so I can be a benefactor to those who obey me. Trust me, then, and you have positions of authority in my government if you will renounce the ancestral tradition of your national life. Enjoy your youth by adopting the Greek way of life and by changing your manner of living. But if by disobedience you rouse my anger, you will compel me to destroy each and every one of you with dreadful punishments through tortures. Therefore take pity on yourselves. Even I, your enemy, have compassion for your youth and handsome appearance. Won't you consider this, that if you disobey, nothing remains for you but to die on the rack?"

When he had said these things, he ordered the instruments of torture to be brought forward to persuade them out of fear to eat the defiling food. When the lancers had placed before them wheels and joint-dislocators, rack and hooks and catapults and cauldrons, braziers and thumbscrews and iron claws and wedges and bellows, the tyrant resumed saying, "Be afraid, young men. Whatever justice you revere will be merciful to you when you transgress under compulsion."

But when they had heard the inducements and saw the dreadful devices, not only were they not afraid, but they also opposed the tyrant with their own philosophy, and by their right reasoning nullified his tyranny. Let us consider, on the other hand, what arguments might have been used if some of them had been cowardly and unmanly. Would they not have been the following?

"Wretches that we are, and so senseless! Since the king has summoned and exhorted us to accept kind treatment if we obey him, why do we take pleasure in vain resolves and venture in disobedience that brings death? Men and brothers, should we not fear the instruments of torture and consider the threats of torments, and give up this vain opinion and this arrogance that threatens to destroy us? Let us take pity on our youth and have compassion for our mother's age, and let us seriously consider that if we disobey we are dead! Also, divine justice will excuse us for fearing the king when we are under compulsion. Why do we banish ourselves from this most pleasant life and deprive ourselves of this delightful world? Let us not struggle against compulsion or take hollow pride in being put to the rack. Not even the law itself would arbitrarily put us to death for fearing the instruments of torture. Why does such contentiousness excite us and such a fatal stubbornness please us when we can live in peace if we obey the king?"

The youths though about to be tortured, neither said any of these things nor even seriously considered them. For they were contemptuous of the emotions and sovereign over agonies, so that as soon as the tyrant had ceased counseling them to eat defiling food, all with one voice together, as from one mind, said:

4th Maccabees: Chapter 9

"Why do you delay, tyrant? We are ready to die rather than transgress our ancestral commandments. We are obviously putting our forefathers to shame unless we should practice ready obedience to the law and to Moses our counselor. Tyrant and counselor of lawlessness, in your hatred for us do not pity us more than we pity ourselves. For we consider this pity of yours which insures our safety through transgression of the law to be more grievous than death itself. You are trying to terrify us by threatening us with death by torture, as though a short time ago you learned nothing from Eleazar. And if the aged men of the Hebrews because of their religion lived piously while enduring torture, it would be even more fitting that we young men should die despising your coercive tortures, which our aged instructor also overcame."

"Therefore, tyrant, put us to the test, and if you take our lives because of our religion, do not suppose that you can injure us by torturing us. For we, through this severe suffering and endurance, shall have the prize of virtue and shall be with God, for whom we suffer, but you, because of your bloodthirstiness toward us, will deservedly undergo from the divine justice eternal torment by fire."

When they had said these things the tyrant not only was angry, as he was at those who are disobedient, but also was enraged, as he was at those who are ungrateful. Then at his command the lancers brought forward the eldest, and having torn off his tunic, they bound his hands and arms with thongs on each side. When they had worn themselves out beating him with scourges, without accomplishing anything, they placed him on the wheel. When the noble youth was stretched out around this, his limbs were dislocated, and with every member disjointed he denounced the tyrant, saying, "Most abominable tyrant, enemy of heavenly justice, savage of mind, you are mangling me in this manner, not because I am a murderer, or as one who acts impiously, but because I protect the divine law."

When the lancers said, "Agree to eat so that you may be released from the tortures."

He replied, "You abominable lackeys, your wheel is not so powerful as to strangle my reason. Cut my limbs, burn my flesh, and twist my joints, through all these tortures I will convince you that children of the Hebrews alone are invincible where virtue is concerned."

While he was saying these things, they spread fire under him, and while fanning the flames they tightened the wheel further. The wheel was completely smeared with blood, and the heap of coals was being quenched by the drippings of gore, and pieces of flesh were falling off the axles of the machine. Although the ligaments joining his bones were already severed, the courageous youth, worthy of Abraham, did not groan, but as though transformed by fire into immortality, he nobly endured the racking.

"Imitate me, brothers," he said. "Do not leave your post in my struggle or renounce our courageous family ties. Fight the sacred and noble battle for religion. Thereby the just Providence of our ancestors may become merciful to our nation and take vengeance on the cursed tyrant."

When he had said this, the saintly youth broke the thread of life. While all were marveling at his courageous spirit, the lancers brought in the next eldest, and after fitting themselves with iron gauntlets having sharp hooks, they bound him to the torture machine and catapult.

Before torturing him, they inquired if he were willing to eat, and they heard his noble decision. These leopard-like beasts tore out his sinews with the iron hands, flayed all his flesh up to his chin, and tore away his scalp. But he steadfastly endured this agony and said,

"How sweet is any kind of death for the religion of our ancestors!"

He said to the tyrant, "Do you not think, you most savage tyrant, that you are being tortured more than I, as you see the arrogant design of your tyranny being defeated by our endurance for the sake of religion? I lighten my pain by the joys that come from virtue, but you allow torture by the threats that come from impiety. You will not escape, you most abominable tyrant, the judgments of the divine anger."

4th Maccabees: Chapter 10

When he too had endured a glorious death, the third was led in, and many repeatedly urged him to save himself by tasting the meat, but he shouted, "Do you not know that the same father fathered me as well as those who died, and the same mother carried me and that I was raised on the same teachings? I do not renounce the noble kinship that binds me to my brothers."

Enraged by the man's boldness, they disjointed his hands and feet with their instruments, dismembering him by prying his limbs from their sockets, and breaking his fingers and arms and legs and elbows. Since they were not able in any way to break his spirit, they abandoned the instruments and scalped him with their fingernails in a Scythian way. They immediately brought him to the wheel, and while his vertebrae were being dislocated by this, he saw his own flesh torn all around and drops of blood flowing from his entrails. When he was about to die, he said, "We, most abominable tyrant, are suffering because of our godly training and virtue, but you, because of your impiety and bloodthirstiness, will undergo unending torments."

When he too had died in a manner worthy of his brothers, they dragged in the fourth, saying, "As for you, do not give way to the same insanity as your brothers, but obey the king and save yourself."

But he said to them, "You do not have a fire hot enough to make me play the coward. No! By the blessed death of my brothers, by the eternal destruction of the tyrant, and by the everlasting life of the pious, I will not renounce our noble family ties. Contrive tortures, tyrant, so that you may learn from those who I am a brother to those who have just now been tortured."

When he heard this, the bloodthirsty, murderous, and completely abominable Antiochus gave orders to cut out his tongue. But he said, "Even if you remove my organ of speech, God hears also those who are mute. See, here is my tongue, cut it off, for in spite of this you will not make our reason speechless. Gladly, for the sake of God, we let our bodily members be mutilated. God will visit you swiftly, for you are cutting out a tongue that has been melodious with divine hymns."

4th Maccabees: Chapter 11

When he too died, after being cruelly tortured, the fifth leaped up, saying, 'I will not refuse, tyrant, to be tortured for the sake of virtue. I have come of my own accord so that by murdering me you will incur punishment from the heavenly justice for even more crimes. Hater of virtue, hater of humankind, for what act of ours are you destroying us in this way? Is it because we revere the creator of all things and live according to his virtuous law? But these deeds deserve honors, not tortures.' While he was saying these things, the lancers bound him and dragged him to the catapult; they tied him to it on his knees, and fitting iron clamps on them, they twisted his back around the wedge on the wheel, so that he was completely curled back like a scorpion, and all his members were disjointed. In this condition, gasping for breath and in the anguish of body, he said, "Tyrant, they are splendid favors that you grant us against your will, because through these noble sufferings you give us an opportunity to show our endurance for the law."

When he too had died, the sixth, a mere boy, was led in. When the tyrant inquired whether he was willing to eat and be released, he said, "I am younger in age than my brothers, but I am their equal in mind. Since to this end, we were born and bred, we should likewise die for the same principles. So if you intend to torture me for not eating defiling foods, go on torturing!" When he had said this, they led him to the wheel. He was carefully stretched tight on it, his back was broken, and he was roasted from underneath. To his back, they applied sharp spits that had been heated in the fire and pierced his ribs so that his entrails were burned through.

While being tortured he said, "Contest befitting holiness, in which so many of us brothers have been summoned to an arena of suffering for religion, and in which we have not been defeated! For religious knowledge, tyrant, is invincible. I also, equipped with nobility, will die with my brothers, and I myself will bring a great avenger on you, you inventor of tortures and enemy of those who are truly devout. We, six boys, have paralyzed your tyranny. Since you have not been able to persuade us to change our minds or to force us to eat defiling foods, is not this your downfall? Your fire is cold to us, and the catapults painless, and your violence powerless. For it is not the lancers of the tyrant but those of the divine law that are set over us, therefore, unconquered, we hold fast to reason."

4th Maccabees: Chapter 12

When he too, thrown into the cauldron, had died a blessed death, the seventh and youngest of all came forward. Even though the tyrant had been vehemently insulted by the brothers, he felt strong compassion for this child when he saw that he was already in shackles. He summoned him to come nearer and tried to persuade him, saying, "You see the result of your brothers' stupidity, for they died in torment because of their disobedience. You too, if you do not obey, will be miserably tortured and die before your time, but if you yield to persuasion you will be my friend and a leader in the government of the kingdom."

When he had appealed to him, he sent for the boy's mother to show compassion on her who had been bereaved of so many sons and to influence her to persuade the surviving son to obey and save himself. But when his mother had exhorted him in the Hebrew language, as we will tell a little later, he said, "Let me loose, let me speak to the king and to all his friends that are with him."

Pleased by the boy's statement, they freed him at once, as he ran to the nearest brazier, he shouted, "You terrible tyrant, most impious of all the wicked, since you have received good things and also your kingdom from God, were you not ashamed to murder his servants and torture on the wheel those who practice religion? Because of this, justice has laid up for you intense and eternal fire and tortures, and these throughout all time will never let you go. As a man, were you not ashamed, you most savage beast, to cut out the tongues of men who have feelings like yours and are made of the same elements as you, and to maltreat and torture them in this way? Certainly, by dying nobly, they have fulfilled their service to God, but you will wail bitterly for having killed without cause the contestants for virtue."

Then because he too was about to die, he said, "I do not desert the excellent example of my brothers, and I call on the God of our ancestors to be merciful to our nation, but on you, he will take vengeance both in this present life and when you are dead." After he had said this, he threw himself into the braziers and so ended his life.

4th Maccabees: Chapter 13

Since, then, the seven brothers despised suffering even to death, everyone must concede that devout reason is sovereign over the emotions. For if they had been slaves to their emotions and had eaten defiling food, we would say that they had been conquered by these emotions. But it was not so. Instead, by reason, which is praised before God, they prevailed over their emotions. The supremacy of the mind over these cannot be overlooked, for the brothers mastered both emotions and pains. How then can one fail to confess the sovereignty of right reason over emotion in those who were not turned back by fiery agonies? For just as towers jutting out over harbors hold back the threatening waves and make it calm for those who sail into the inner basin, so the seven-towered right reason of the youths, by fortifying the harbor of religion, conquered the tempest of the emotions. For they constituted a sacred chorus of religion and encouraged one another, saying, "Brothers, let us die like brothers for the sake of the law, let us imitate the three youths in Assyria[1] who despised the same ordeal of the furnace. Let us not be cowardly in the demonstration of our piety."

While one said, "Courage, brother," another said, "Carry up nobly," and another reminded them, "Remember where you came from, and the father by whose hand Isaac would have submitted to being slain for the sake of religion."

Each of them and all of them together looking at one another, cheerful and undaunted, said, "Let us with all our hearts consecrate ourselves to God, who gave us our lives and let us use our bodies as a bulwark for the law. Let us not fear him who thinks he is killing us, for great is the struggle of the mind and the danger of eternal torment lying before those who transgress the commandment of God. Therefore let us put on the full armor of self-control, which is the divine reason. For if we so die, Abraham and Isaac and Jacob will welcome us, and all the fathers will praise us."

Those who were left behind said to each of the brothers who were being dragged away, "Do not put us to shame, brother, or betray the brothers who have died before us."

You are not ignorant of the affection of family ties, which the divine and all-wise Providentia[2] has given through the fathers to their descendants and which was implanted in the mother's womb. There each of the brothers spent the same length of time and was shaped during the same period of time, and growing from the same blood and through the same life, they were brought to the light of day. When they were born after an equal time of gestation, they drank milk from the same fountains. From such embraces, brotherly-loving souls are nourished, and they grow stronger from this common nurture and daily companionship, and from both general education and our discipline in the law of God.

Therefore, when sympathy and brotherly affection had been so established, the brothers were more sympathetic to one another. Since they had been educated by the same law and trained in the same virtues and brought up in the right living, they loved one another all the more. A common zeal for nobility strengthened their goodwill towards one another, and their concord, because they could make their brotherly love more fervent with the aid of their religion. But although nature and companionship and virtuous habits had augmented the affection of family ties, those who were left endured for the sake of religion, while watching their brothers being maltreated and tortured to death.

4th Maccabees: Chapter 13 Notes

1 Codex Sinaiticus: Assyrias (ⲁⲥⲥⲩⲣⲓⲁⲥ). Translation: Assyria

The reference is to the three boys from the Book of Daniel, Hananiah, Azariah, and Mishael, who were thrown into the furnace, and whom the angel protected from the fire. They are mentioned later along with Daniel not being eaten by the lions, however, the Book of Daniel is set in the Babylonian Empire, not the Assyrian Empire.

It is theorized that the story of Hananiah, Azariah, and Mishael was originally independent from the book of Daniel, as he is not mentioned with them, other than a passing reference to the four of them being taken to Babylonia and forced to learn the Chaldean language, found in the Masoretic chapter 1.

The Septuagint includes two versions of Daniel, the common version was a translation made by Theodotion around 200 AD, which replaced the original Greek translation in the Septuagint. A few copies of the Old Greek translation survive, the most commonly sourced one being the version found in the Septuagint's Codex Chisianus. The Old Greek translation appears to have been made by High Priest Jaddua as the armies of Alexander the Great were approaching Jerusalem in 332 BC, meaning the story of the thee youths had already been added to the book of Daniel by the end of the Persian era, or he added it himself. While over a dozen variants of Daniel are known to exist, none of the Greek, Hebrew, Syriac, Latin, or Arabic versions place the events involving the three youths in Assyria, however, there must have been an accepted version of the story set in Assyria in the 1st century AD in order for this variant to have been accepted into the Septuagint. None of the known copies of 4th Maccabees place the event in Babylon.

One potential explanation was that event was once recorded as happening in the region of Assyria that had fallen under Babylonian control, however, there is no literary support for this. Another explanation is that the story of the three youths originally set in Assyria, but moved to Babylon by Jaddua as a warning to Alexander, as fire had been used extensively as a weapon in the seige of Tyre

2 Codex Sinaiticus: pronoia (ΠΡΟΝΟΙΑ). Translation: Providentia, and later divine providence

Providentia was the Roman deity of foresight.

4th Maccabees: Chapter 14

Furthermore, they encouraged them to face the torture, so that they not only despised their agonies but also mastered the emotions of brotherly love.

Reason, more royal than kings and freer than the free! Sacred and harmonious concord of the seven brothers on behalf of religion! None of the seven youths proved coward or shrank from death, but all of them, as though running the course towards immortality, rushed to death by torture. Just as the hands and feet are moved in harmony with the guidance of the mind, so those sacred youths, as though moved by an immortal spirit of devotion, agreed to go to death for its sake. Most sacred seven, brothers in harmony! For just as the seven days of creation move in a choral dance around religion, so these youths, forming a chorus, encircled the seven-times fear of tortures and dissolved it. Even now, we ourselves shudder as we hear of the suffering of these young men, and they not only saw what was happening, not only heard the direct word of threat, but also carried the suffering patiently, and in agonies of fire at that. What could be more excruciatingly painful than this? The power of fire is intense and swift, and it consumed their bodies quickly.

Do not consider it amazing that reason had full command over these men in their tortures, since the mind of woman despised even more diverse agonies, for the mother of the seven young men beared up under the racking of each one of her children.

Observe how complex is a mother's love for her children, which draws everything towards an emotion felt in her inmost parts. Even unreasoning animals, as well as human beings, have sympathy and parental love for their offspring. For example, among birds, the ones that are tame protect their young by building on the housetops, and the others, by building at the tops of mountains and the depths of chasms, in holes of trees, and on treetops, hatch the nestlings and ward off the intruder. If they are not able to keep the intruder away, they do what they can to help their young by flying in circles around them in the anguish of love, warning them with their own calls. Why is it necessary to demonstrate sympathy for children by the example of unreasoning animals, since even bees at the time for making honeycombs defend themselves against intruders and, as though with an iron dart, sting those who approach their hive and defend it even to the death? But sympathy for her children did not sway the mother of the young men, she was of the same mind as Abraham.

4th Maccabees: Chapter 15

The reason of the children, a tyrant over the emotions! Religion, more desirable to the mother than her children! Two courses were open to this mother, that of religion, and that of preserving her seven sons for a time, as the tyrant had promised. She loved religion more, the religion that preserves them for eternal life according to God's promise. In what manner might I express the emotions of parents who love their children? We impress on the character of a small child a wondrous likeness both of mind and of form. Especially is this true of mothers, who because of their birth pangs have a deeper sympathy towards their offspring than do the fathers.

Considering that mothers are the weaker sex and give birth to many, they are more devoted to their children. The mother of the seven boys, more than any other mother, loved her children. In seven pregnancies she had implanted in herself tender love towards them, and because of the many pains she suffered with each of them she had sympathy for them, yet because of the fear of God, she disdained the temporary safety of her children. Not only so, but also because of the nobility of her sons and their ready obedience to the law, she felt a greater tenderness towards them. For they were righteous and self-controlled and brave and magnanimous and loved their brothers and their mother so that they obeyed her even to death in keeping the ordinances.

Nevertheless, though so many factors influenced the mother to suffer with them out of love for her children, in the case of none of them were the various tortures strong enough to pervert her reason. But each child separately and all of them together the mother urged on to death for religion's sake. Sacred nature and affection of parental love, the yearning of parents towards offspring, nurture and indomitable suffering by mothers! This mother, who saw them tortured and burned one by one, because of religion did not change her attitude. She watched the flesh of her children being consumed by fire, their toes and fingers scattered on the ground, and the flesh of the head to the chin exposed like masks.

Mother tried now by more bitter pains than even the birth-pangs you suffered for them! Woman, who alone gave birth to such complete devotion! When the first-born breathed his last, it did not turn you aside, nor when the second in torments looked at you piteously nor when the third expired, nor did you cry when you looked at the eyes of each one in his tortures gazing boldly at the same agonies and saw in their nostrils the signs of the approach of death. When you saw the flesh of children burned on the flesh of other children, severed hands on hands, scalped heads on heads, and corpses fallen on other corpses, and when you saw the place filled with many spectators of the torturing, you did not shed tears. Neither the melodies of sirens nor the songs of swans attract the attention of their hearers as did the voices of the children in torture calling to their mother. How great and how many torments the mother then suffered as her sons were tortured on the wheel and with the hot irons! But devout reason, giving her heart a man's courage in the very middle of her emotions, strengthened her to disregard, for the time, her parental love.

Although she witnessed the destruction of seven children and the ingenious and various rackings, this noble mother disregarded all these because of faith in God. For as in the council chamber of her own mind she saw mighty advocates, nature, family, parental love, and the racking of her children, this mother held two ballots, one bearing death and the other deliverance for her children. She did not approve the deliverance that would preserve the seven sons for a short time, but as the daughter of God-fearing Abraham, she remembered his fortitude.

Mother of the nation, vindicator of the law and champion of religion, who carried away the prize of the contest in your heart! Nobler than males in steadfastness, and more courageous than men in endurance! Just as Noah's box, carrying the world in the universal flood, stoutly endured the waves, so you, Guardian of the law, overwhelmed from every side by the flood of your emotions and the violent winds, the torture of your sons, endured nobly and withstood the wintry storms that assail religion.

4th Maccabees: Chapter 16

If then, a woman, advanced in years and mother of seven sons, endured seeing her children tortured to death, it must be admitted that devout reason is sovereign over the emotions. Thus I have demonstrated not only that men have ruled over the emotions, but also that a woman has despised the fiercest tortures. The lions surrounding Daniel were not so savage, nor was the raging fiery furnace of Mishael so intensely hot, as was her innate parental love, inflamed as she saw her seven sons tortured in such varied ways. But the mother quenched so many and such great emotions by devout reason.

Consider this also: If this woman, though a mother, had been fainthearted, she would have mourned over them and perhaps said, "How wretched I am, and deeply unhappy! After bearing seven children, I am now the mother of none! Seven childbirths all in vain, seven profitless pregnancies, fruitless nurturing, and wretched nursing! In vain, my sons, I endured many birth-pangs for you and the more terrible anxieties of your upbringing. Alas for my children, some unmarried, others married and without offspring. I will not see your children or have the happiness of being called grandmother. Alas, I who had so many and beautiful children am a widow and alone, with many sorrows. When I die, I will have none of my sons to bury me."

Yet that sacred and God-fearing mother did not wail with such a lament for any of them, nor did she dissuade any of them from dying, nor did she grieve as they were dying. On the contrary, as though having a mind like adamant and giving rebirth for immortality to the whole number of her sons, she implored them and urged them on to death for the sake of religion. Mother, a soldier of God in the cause of religion, elder and woman! By steadfastness, you have conquered even a tyrant, and in word and deed, you have proved more powerful than a man.

When you and your sons were arrested together, you stood and watched Eleazar being tortured, and said to your sons in the Hebrew language, "My sons, noble is the contest to which you are called to carry witness for the nation. Fight zealously for our ancestral law. For it would be shameful if, while an aged man endures such agonies for the sake of religion, you young men were to be terrified by tortures. Remember that it is through God that you have had a share in the world and have enjoyed life, and therefore you should endure any suffering for the sake of God. For his sake also our father Abraham was zealous to sacrifice his son Isaac, the ancestor of our nation; and when Isaac saw his father's hand wielding a knife and descending on him, he did not cower. Daniel the righteous was thrown to the lions, and Hananiah, Azariah, and Mishael were hurled into the fiery furnace and endured it for the sake of God. You too must have the same faith in God and not be grieved. It is unreasonable for people who have religious knowledge not to withstand pain."

By these words, the mother of the seven encouraged and persuaded each of her sons to die rather than violate God's commandment. They knew also that those who die for the sake of God live with God, as do Abraham and Isaac and Jacob and all the patriarchs.

4th Maccabees: Chapter 17

Some of the lancers said that when she also was about to be seized and put to death she threw herself into the flames so that no one might touch her body.

Mother, who with your seven sons nullified the violence of the tyrant, frustrated his evil designs, and showed the courage of your faith! Nobly set like a roof on the pillars of your sons, you held firm and unswerving against the earthquake of the tortures. Take courage, therefore, sacred-minded mother, maintaining firm an enduring hope in God. The moon in the sky, with the stars, does not stand so august as you, who, after lighting the way of your star-like seven sons to piety, stand in honor before God and are firmly set in the sky with them. For your children were true descendants of father Abraham.

If it were possible for us to paint the history of your religion as an artist might, would not those who first saw it have shuddered as they saw the mother of the seven children enduring their varied tortures to death for the sake of religion? Indeed it would be proper to inscribe on their tomb these words as a reminder to the people of our nation, "Here lie buried an aged priest and an aged woman and seven sons, because of the violence of the tyrant who wished to destroy the way of life of the

Hebrews. They vindicated their nation, looking to God and enduring torture even to death."

Truly the contest in which they were engaged was divine, for on that day virtue gave the awards and tested them for their endurance. The prize was immortality in endless life. Eleazar was the first contestant, the mother of the seven sons entered the competition, and the brothers contended. The tyrant was the antagonist, and the world and the human race were the spectators. Reverence for God was the victor and gave the crown to its own athletes. Who did not admire the athletes of the divine legislation? Who was not amazed?

The tyrant himself and all his council marveled at their endurance, because of which they now stand before the divine throne and live the life of eternal blessedness. For Moses said, "All who are consecrated are under your hands."

These, then, who have been consecrated for the sake of God, are honored, not only with this honor, but also by the fact that because of them our enemies did not rule over our nation, the tyrant was punished, and the homeland purified, they have become, as it were, a ransom for the sin of our nation. Through the blood of those devout ones and their death as an atoning sacrifice, divine Providence preserved Israel that previously had been mistreated.

For the tyrant Antiochus, when he saw the courage of their virtue and their endurance under the tortures, proclaimed them to his soldiers as an example for their own endurance, and this made them brave and courageous for infantry battle and siege, and he ravaged and conquered all his enemies.

4th Maccabees: Chapter 18

Children of Israel, offspring of the descendant of Abraham, obey this law and exercise piety in every way, knowing that devout reason is master of all emotions, not only of suffering from within but also of those from without.

Therefore those who gave over their bodies in suffering for the sake of religion were not only admired by mortals but also were deemed worthy to share in a divine inheritance. Because of them, the nation gained peace, and by reviving observance of the law in the homeland they ravaged the enemy. The tyrant Antiochus was both punished on earth and is being chastised after his death. Since in no way whatever was he able to compel the Israelites to become pagans and to abandon their ancestral customs, he left Jerusalem and marched against the Persians.

The mother of the seven sons expressed also these principles to her children, "I was a pure virgin and did not go outside my father's house, but I guarded from the rib by which woman was made. No seducer corrupted me on a desert plain, nor did the destroyer, the deceitful serpent, defile the purity of my virginity. In the time of my maturity, I remained with my husband, and when these sons had grown up their father died. A happy man was he, who lived out his life with good children and did not have the grief of bereavement. While he was still with you, he taught you the law and the prophets. He read to you about Abel slain by Cain, and Isaac who was offered as a burnt-offering, and about Joseph in prison. He told you of the zeal of Phinehas, and he taught you about Hananiah, Azariah, and Mishael in the fire. He praised Daniel in the den of the lions and blessed him. He reminded you of the scripture of Isaiah, which says, 'Even though you go through the fire, the flame will not consume you.' He sang to you songs of the psalmist David, who said, 'Many are the plagues of the righteous.' He recounted to you Solomon's proverb, 'There is a tree of life for those who do his will.' He confirmed the query of Ezekiel, 'Will these dry bones live?' For he did not forget to teach you the song that Moses taught, which says, 'I kill and I make alive, this is your life and the length of your days.'"

Bitter was that day, and yet not bitter when that bitter tyrant of the Greeks quenched fire with fire in his cruel cauldrons, and in his burning rage brought those seven sons of the daughter of Abraham to the catapult and back again to more tortures, pierced the pupils of their eyes and cut out their tongues, and put them to death with various tortures. For these crimes, divine justice pursued and will pursue the cursed tyrant. But the sons of Abraham with their victorious mother are gathered together into the chorus of the fathers and have received pure and immortal minds from God, to whom is glory forever and ever, Amen.[1]

4th Maccabees: Chapter 18 Notes

1 Codex Sinaiticus: Amên (ΑΜΗΝ)

Septuagint Manuscripts

The following is a list of the Septuagint manuscripts referenced in the notes for this book.

LXX ℵ (Codex Sinaiticus) is dated to the 4th century. Sections are currently located at the British Library (Add. 43725) in London, Leipzig University (Gr. 1) in Leipzig, the National Library of Russia (Gr. 2; Gr. 259; Gr. 843; Fonds. d. Ges. f. alte Lit., Oct 156) in St. Petersburg, and Saint Catherine's Monastery (Neus Slg. MΓ 1) on Mount Sinai.

LXX A (Codex Alexandrinus) is dated to the 5th century. It is currently located at the British Library (Royal 1 D. VIII) in London.

LXX B (Codex Vaticanus) is dated to the 4th century. It is currently located at the Vatican Library (Gr. 1209) in Vatican City.

LXX V (Codex Venetus) is dated to the 8th century. It is currently located at the Marciana Library (Gr. 1) in Venice.

LXX 19 is dated to the 12th century. It is currently located at the Chigi Palace (R. VI. 38) in Rome.

LXX 29 is dated to the 14th century. It is currently located at the Marciana Library (Gr. 2) in Venice.

LXX 46 is dated to the 15th century. It is currently located at the National Library of France (Coisl. Gr. 4) in Paris.

LXX 52 is dated to the 14th century. It is currently located at the Laurentian Library (Acquisti 44) in Florence.

LXX 55 is dated to the 10th century. It is currently located at the Vatican Library (Regin. gr. 1) in Vatican City.

LXX 56 is dated to 1093. It is currently located at the National Library of France (Gr. 3) in Paris.

LXX 58 is dated to the 11th century. It is currently located at the Vatican Library (Regin. Gr. 10) in Vatican City.

LXX 62 is dated to the 11th century. It is currently located at the New College (44) in Oxford.

LXX 64 is dated to the 10th century. It is currently located at the

National Library of France (Gr. 2) in Paris.

LXX 71 is dated to the 13th century. It is currently located at the National Library of France (Gr. 1) in Paris.

LXX 74 is dated to the 13th century. It is currently located at the Laurentian Library (S. Marco 700) in Florence.

LXX 93 is dated to the 13th century. It is currently located at the British Library (Royal 1 D. II) in London.

LXX 98 is dated to the 13th century. It is currently located at the Royal Library (Σ-II-19) in El Escorial.

LXX 106 is dated to the 14th century. It is currently located at the Biblioteca Comunale Ariostea (187 I-III) in Ferrara.

LXX 107 is dated to 1334. It is currently located at the Biblioteca Comunale Ariostea (188 I) in Ferrara.

LXX 130 is dated to the 12th to 13th centuries. It is currently located at the Austrian National Library (Theol. Gr. 23) in Vienna.

LXX 311 is dated to the 12th century. It is currently located at the State Historical Museum of Russia (Syn. gr. 354) in Moscow.

LXX 340 is dated to the 11th century. It is currently located at the Vatopedi (39) on Mount Athos.

LXX 381 is dated to the 11th century. It is currently located at the Royal Library (Ω-1-13) in El Escorial.

LXX 534 is dated to the 11th century. It is currently located at the National Library of France (Coisl. Gr. 18) in Paris.

LXX 542 is dated to the 9th century. It is currently located at the National Library of France (Gr. 10) in Paris.

LXX 671 is dated to the 15th century. It is currently located at the Vatican Library (Vat. Gr. 348) in Vatican City.

LXX 728 is dated to the 14th or 5th century. It is currently located at the Biblioteca Marciana (Append I 13) in Venice.

LXX 771 is dated to the 10th century. Sections are currently located at Vatopedi Monastery (290 + 1213 Bl. 13-51) on the Mount Athos, and the National Library of Russia (Gr. 260) in St. Petersburg.

Alternative Translations

The following is a list of alternative translations that were used for comparative analysis.

The Peshitta is the Syriac translation of the Christian bible. The Old Testament was translated from older Aramaic and Hebrew sources during the late 2nd century AD. It is unclear if the books of Maccabees were translated from Greek or an Aramaic source, however, the Greek source seems more likely.

The Vetus Latina manuscripts are the old Latin translations of the Septuagint and other Israelite texts that predate Jerome's Latin Orthodox Bible in the 5th century.

The Codex Bobbiensis (VL 135) is an old Latin translation of Tobit, 2nd Maccabees, and the first two chapters of Esther dated to 875 BC. It is currently at the Ambrosia Library (E.26) in Milan. Based on some of the transliterations of names, is could not have been made from a known Greek translation, and therefore was either translated from Aramaic or Judahite.

Also Available

SEPTUAGINT SERIES:

- Septuagint: Cosmic Genesis
- Septuagint: Exodus
- Septuagint: Leviticus
- Septuagint: Numbers
- Septuagint: Deuteronomy
- Septuagint: Joshua
- Septuagint: Judges and Ruth
- Septuagint: Kingdoms
- Septuagint: Paralipomena
- Septuagint: Ezra
- Septuagint: Tobit
- Septuagint: Judith
- Septuagint: Esther
- Septuagint: Maccabees
- Septuagint: Psalms and the Prayer of Manasseh
- Septuagint: Job
- Septuagint: Solomon
- Septuagint: Wisdom of Joshua ben Sira and Odes
- Septuagint: Torah
- Septuagint: History, Volume 1
- Septuagint: History, Volume 2

Also Available

- Octateuch: The Original Orit

Enoch and Metatron Series:

- Books of Enoch Collection
- Books of Enoch and Metatron Collection
- Books of Metatron Collection
- Secrets of Enoch

Other Translations:

- Apocalypses of Ezra
- Arabic Maccabees
- Hebrew Maccabees
- Life of Adam and Eve
- Memories of the New Kingdom
- Septuagint's Esther and the Vetus Latina Esther
- Septuagint's Ezekiel and the Ba'al Cycle
- Septuagint's Job and the Testament of Job
- Septuagint's Proverbs and the Wisdom of Amenemope
- The Amarna Letters
- Testaments of the Patriarchs Collection
- Tobit and Ahikar
- Ugaritic Texts: Ba'al Cycle
- Wisdom of Ahikar

www.ingramcontent.com/pod-product-compliance
Lightning Source LLC
Chambersburg PA
CBHW061132120626
46546CB00005B/1753
* 9 7 8 1 9 9 8 2 8 8 6 4 9 *